Working Women in Jordan

Working Women in Jordan

Education, Migration, and Aspiration

FIDA J. ADELY

The University of Chicago Press
Chicago and London

The University of Chicago Press, Chicago 60637
The University of Chicago Press, Ltd., London
© 2024 by The University of Chicago
All rights reserved. No part of this book may be used or reproduced in any manner
whatsoever without written permission, except in the case of brief quotations in
critical articles and reviews. For more information, contact the University of Chicago Press,
1427 E. 60th St., Chicago, IL 60637.
Published 2024
Printed in the United States of America

33 32 31 30 29 28 27 26 25 24   1 2 3 4 5

ISBN-13: 978-0-226-83392-7 (cloth)
ISBN-13: 978-0-226-83394-1 (paper)
ISBN-13: 978-0-226-83393-4 (e-book)
DOI: https://doi.org/10.7208/chicago/9780226833934.001.0001

Library of Congress Cataloging-in-Publication Data

Names: Adely, Fida J., 1971– author.
Title: Working women in Jordan : education, migration, and aspiration / Fida J. Adely.
Description: Chicago : The University of Chicago Press, 2024. |
    Includes bibliographical references and index.
Identifiers: LCCN 2023043786 | ISBN 9780226833927 (cloth) |
    ISBN 9780226833941 (paperback) | ISBN 9780226833934 (ebook)
Subjects: LCSH: Women—Employment—Jordan. | Women—Education—Jordan. |
    Women—Jordan—Economic conditions.
Classification: LCC HQ1729 .A33 2024 | DDC 305.4095695—dc23/eng/20231011
LC record available at https://lccn.loc.gov/2023043786

♾ This paper meets the requirements of ANSI/NISO Z39.48-1992 (Permanence of Paper).

Contents

Introduction

Prelude: Three Stories of Migration

Jihan and I were sitting in the food court of Mecca Mall, one of many new spaces of consumption and middle-class socialization built in Amman in the last two decades. While most of my meetups with friends and research interlocutors occurred in cafés or people's homes, Jihan worked and lived near the mall. To accommodate her busy schedule, I met her at the mall, which was abuzz with activity. While clothing stores, perfumeries, and other shops line each floor, the mall is not only a place for commerce but also a site for leisure. Groups of young women, or women and children, wandered around "window shopping," chatting and laughing among themselves. The sounds from the children's indoor play area also rang through the air, giving an amusement park feel to parts of the mall.

I had first met Jihan in 2005 while conducting ethnographic research in a high school in a city in the north that her younger sister Nida attended. Though I knew her family well, Jihan resided in Amman away from them, so I had only met her briefly on previous visits. It was now the spring of 2011, and I asked Jihan to talk with me about her move to Amman several years earlier and what precipitated it. We talked for nearly three hours about work, marriage, and living on your own in Amman. She told me:

> I came to Amman to study nursing when I was eighteen. I did well on the *tawjihi* exams and I got a scholarship from the army. Without the scholarship, it would have been difficult for me to complete university education. You might say I had a choice in the matter, but given my family's financial situation and my father's illness, I didn't really have a choice. If I wanted a university education, I needed to take this scholarship and so I did, and here I

am almost ten years later. Since I graduated, I have been here in Amman, and I have helped my family, especially after my father's death. God bless his soul.

Jihan worked as a nurse and helped to support her family. She paid the university tuition costs of younger siblings and contributed to basic family expenses. Resources were stretched thin, and two siblings were still in high school when she started working. Once her sister Nida finished high school and secured admission to a local public university, Nida had to manage her tuition on her own. Jihan helped Nida when she could but was already overstretched. Nida had to take some time off from her university studies, but ultimately, with a loan and some part-time work as a tutor, Nida was able to complete her degree as well. Eventually, Nida also contributed to the education of her younger siblings, though she initially struggled to find a job. She was able to find employment by migrating for work as a teacher in an Arab Gulf country for a couple of years, after which she returned, seeking other opportunities in Jordan and eventually finding work in the humanitarian aid sector.

Lacking the grades in high school to be admitted, neither of Jihan's two older brothers had gone to university. As is often the case in Jordan, their sisters were more successful in pursuing education. Each of these brothers began working shortly after high school; however, without a university degree their options were limited. Furthermore, after a certain age they were expected to save their money for future marriage, leaving them little to invest in their younger siblings—a role that Jihan, and eventually Nida, took on. A younger brother initially struggled to pass the *tawjihi* exams required for university placement. He failed twice, and Jihan helped pay for private tutoring that many students have come to rely on to pass the high school examinations. For decades girls have been outperforming boys on this life-changing exam.

Jihan's decision at the age of eighteen to move to Amman to study nursing and to commit to a career as a military nurse, far from her family, had far-reaching implications for her, Nida, their other siblings, and their mother. Jihan took great pride in her career. She was an excellent nurse and received multiple promotions. She was also proud of the opportunities she had been able to give her siblings. In late 2015, after twelve years of living on her own, she moved back to her hometown with her mother and unmarried adult siblings. She returned because she was promoted and asked to manage a nursing unit at a new hospital in her hometown—a town that had grown rapidly in recent years due to its proximity to the Syrian border and the proliferation of international humanitarian and development organizations. However, her decisions had entailed sacrifices on her part, and as she entered her thirties, she reflected on her choices and the prospects of starting her own family.

Jihan's experience tells one particularly compelling story, and one that is perhaps more in keeping with experiences that have been documented elsewhere, namely that of single sisters supporting other siblings or elderly parents at the risk of not making the time to start their own family.[1] Nevertheless, Jihan's story is unique, and the narratives of migration that constitute the subject of this book are quite varied. As we shall see in the following chapters, there is no one typical story. Let us briefly consider the experiences of two other women: Maysoon and Rania. Unlike Jihan, Maysoon comes from a middle-class professional family. She is the youngest sibling and, when we met, the only one not yet married. She studied computer science and came to Amman to seek the independence she believed living and working in the capital would provide. However, she was surprised at how difficult it was to cover her expenses with her salary at an international tech corporation, and she resented that she had little money left over for leisure, exploration, and independent living. She ended up having to borrow money from her family and at times from friends, which she was embarrassed about. Even more disappointing was the class-based bias she experienced in the workplace as a woman from the provinces. Though her family's economic stability meant they could subsidize her life in Amman, she struggled to establish her independence and eventually found a job where she felt more respected. Although her professional situation improved, she grew increasingly frustrated with how society viewed her, as a single woman nearing thirty, even as she moved to establish an independent life for herself in Amman—the place she now considered home.

Rania was among the youngest of the women I met in the course of the research for this book. Almost immediately after completing her engineering degree, she found a high-paying job working with an international humanitarian organization, pointing to the ways in which regional conflicts and an international aid regime have created new, albeit temporary, prospects for women.[2] Although her salary was generous, the hours were long and work conditions challenging. Rania told me she learned to be tough but respectful while supervising labor crews working at her construction site. She relished the professional challenge and was quite proud that at age twenty-four she could help support her family by paying for the educational expenses of younger siblings. However, she complained that the cost of living was expensive in Amman, and even with her high salary she managed to run out of money. Still, she made clear that this would not affect her relationship with her parents: "I give them an amount every month without telling them what my situation is. I was the one who decided how much I would give them each month, until my sister and brother finish university." Rania insisted that no one asked for her help, but that it was the least she could do, given what her parents had sacrificed for her. She saw her role as provider as a temporary one: she had visions of starting her own engineering firm and getting married. Indeed, she married a few years after we first met, and she and her spouse, also an engineer, had their own plans for the future.

These are three stories among many. Each of the experiences documented in the following chapters, like those of Jihan, Rania, and Maysoon, has been shaped by the larger contexts in which my interlocutors have come of age, and the opportunities, challenges, and desires produced in these contexts. Most significant among them are educational developments and the expectations they have produced, neoliberal economic policies, increased urbanization, and increasing concentration of the population in Amman, as well as delayed marriage and related demographic shifts. Yet, the women's migration is also shaped by individual effort and desires, their families and communities, and the unpredictable circumstances that frame action, agency, and movement.[3]

I return to each of these women's stories throughout this book, as well as those of many other women who have come to Amman to make a life for themselves through migration. Each narrative provides unique insight into ways of being a young, educated woman today—insights that contribute to a more nuanced understanding of choice, agency, value, and family ties after several decades of neoliberal economic and social developments in Jordan. The women's labor migration also highlights some of the instability of gender in practice: the shifts and flows of life in a rapidly changing society, shifts that are insufficiently captured by the dominant modes of measuring, defining, and promoting women's labor.

Revisiting "Gendered Paradoxes"

One of the central development conundrums in the Middle East, often deemed a "gendered paradox," is the high rate of female education alongside relatively low rates of female labor force participation.[4] Jordan best exemplifies this "paradox," with some of the highest rates of women's education in the region, alongside some of the lowest labor force participation rates for women in the world. In earlier work, I questioned the basic assumptions that framed women's education as paradoxical, arguing that they rested upon quite narrow views about education's purpose and effect.[5] In this book, I consider how the decision by some women to migrate for work takes a similarly complicated and unpredictable trajectory.

Concerns about Jordanian women's labor force participation pervade development discourse, policies, and programs in Jordan. One of the key reasons given for women's low participation rates in formal labor involves cultural norms around gender and mobility, which is why the mobility of the women profiled in this book is so significant. It is important to situate this "object of development"[6] within a broader discourse about unemployment and especially unemployment among educated youth, which tends to represent them as unskilled (having credentials without skills) and unrealistic in their expectations (expecting the state to give them jobs, unwilling to take risks and become entrepreneurs).[7] These cultural logics are also viewed as most relevant for youth in the provinces, given the assumption that "traditional" dispositions are more prevalent there, which points to the ways in which class and geography are imbricated with notions of progress and development. This book speaks back against a dominant narrative that represents provincial youth as unskilled and passive, and provincial women as doubly disadvantaged by cultural norms that also limit their mobility. These tropes elide the lives of the women we will meet in these pages who are persistent and creative, and who aspire to better lives for themselves and their families.

After my extended conversation with Jihan about her migration to Amman, and the factors that led to her decision, I continued to meet single, university-educated women who had migrated from other parts of the country to the capital city of Amman for work. While I already knew some women who had moved to Amman for work, the numbers of women I encountered and the distances from which they came, surprised me. Internal female migration is not entirely new. Since the establishment of the state, female teachers had been needed in Jordan to educate children in villages around the country. Internal migration of single women was often short term—a temporary post until one had enough seniority and/or connections to be transferred to a school closer to home. Female teachers were also needed for the expanding school systems of the Arab Gulf countries, and some women migrated there.[8] While teaching was the primary profession that took women away from home, it was not the only one: there were nurses, doctors, and students who left home for work even though this was not the norm. I examine some of these historical migrations in the next chapter.

In 2011, however, I began to meet women who did not fit these earlier patterns of migration. A few were teachers, but most were not. Rather than moving to meet state-building needs for educational expansion in rural areas, these contemporary migrants sought opportunities that were produced by education, and responded to neoliberal economic developments that made staying in the provinces difficult and less desirable for educated young women. The stories of female professional migration I heard were many and diverse. I began to ask: *What had changed to allow these women greater mobility? Why were families willing to allow young women to go off to the capital to pursue careers even when their salaries barely covered living expenses? What hopes and aspirations did these young women bring to Amman with them? What challenges did they face in the city? What effects did their migration have on their lives as young professional women in Jordan? What hopes did they have for the future?*

The narratives of women who migrate to Amman for labor are at the center of this ethnographic study. I draw on their stories to illuminate how substantial demographic and socioeconomic shifts within Jordan have shaped particular lives, and how a group of young, educated women have worked to navigate these shifts. Building on fifteen years of ethnographic research in Jordan, and extensive interviews with dozens of women, including oral history interviews with women born in the early years of the state, this book considers the effects of developments such as expanded educational opportunities, urbanization, privatization, and the restructuring of the labor market on women's life trajectories, gender roles, and family relations.

Single, university-educated women are those most likely to be in the labor force, and they have been for decades. The women at the center of this text are university educated, overwhelmingly employed in the private sector, and migrate from "underdeveloped" regions of Jordan to the capital to pursue professional employment. This increase in female mobility, with the support and sometimes encouragement of families, is indicative of significant shifts in gendered expectations, as typically women rarely live apart from their families before marrying, except to attend university. This is also true for most men, unless they (like the women profiled here) move for work. My research shows that the motivation for women's labor-based migration is not always or entirely economic, but also stems from family and personal aspirations and histories, as well as perceived marriage opportunities. At the same time, the economic contexts and ongoing economic crises cannot be separated from these aspirations. Drawing on women's experiences, I argue that their migration gives us crucial insights into the incremental processes of social change. Through their aspirations, actions, and struggles, women forge a path (for themselves and often for their families) toward greater economic stability and improved social status. Although they are not always successful, their actions have important material and social effects, with implications for the prevailing gender system, its ideologies, and its practices.

Structural Contexts

The migration of these women to Amman helps illuminate the ongoing transformations wrought by education, uneven development, and neoliberalism in four key ways. First, the trajectories of these women highlight how educational structures shape individual calculations about desirable forms of labor. A hierarchical tracking system in the Jordanian public school system acts to structure educational and career pathways for young people early in their educational lives. For the young women profiled here, who have largely been successful as students, these structures have created opportunities for women in fields such as engineering and computer science. Entry into these fields is also facilitated by cultural norms that do *not* mark the study of math and science as gendered fields more suitable to men, as is the case in the United States, for example. Women's narratives about migration are closely linked to the desire to make use of their education (especially for those in fields such as engineering who view their education to be of particular value) and to a belief that educational success opens up the possibility, if not the necessity, of seeking professional opportunities, and the attendant improved social status, elsewhere.

While the quality of education in rural areas is relatively poor,[9] some students in the provinces benefit from preferential admissions to universities and greater access to scholarships, either because of where they live, or because their fathers have served in the military—a benefit not divorced from their academic achievement.[10] Preferential admissions policies will be discussed in detail in chapter 1. For now, it is sufficient to say that some women have benefited from these admissions policies. However, geographic and class-based inequities present challenges for women once they arrive in Amman, due to a lack of social capital needed to get by in certain spaces, as well as to the biases they face as women from the provinces.

Second, the migration of these women illuminates the geographic disparities in Jordan's economic development. Development and investment have been heavily concentrated on the nation's capital city, leading to significant rural–urban disparities.[11] In rural and peri-urban communities, university-educated men and women have fewer employment opportunities and thus must commute or migrate to the capital for work. Most of the jobs that are available in the governorates are public sector jobs, which have been traditionally favored by women and their families.[12] While most university graduates (male and female) still end up in the public sector, the majority of single, university-educated women in Jordan's major urban centers (Amman, Irbid, and Zarqa) are employed in the private sector.[13] Many of the women I interviewed made the move to Amman seeking private sector opportunities. These trends intensify geographical disparities as those most capable and educated migrate out of the provinces. Provincial neglect drives their move to Amman and affects how they are perceived there: they are often viewed through a lens of provincial "backwardness" that is classed, gendered, and at times read through a lens of national origins (Palestinian or East Banker). It also shapes how they come to view their own home communities. However, their migration can also challenge hegemonic narratives about the provinces, provincial values, and politics.

Third, the experiences discussed in this book cannot be viewed outside the frameworks of neoliberalism and ongoing economic crises.[14] Neoliberal economic reforms have significantly reshaped economic life in Jordan and transformed the labor market. Unemployment among the educated has been a persistent feature of these transformations. Alongside the economic restructuring of neoliberalism, a plethora of institutions and policies have worked for more than two decades to promote neoliberal norms of efficiency, entrepreneurship, and personal responsibility in Jordan as elsewhere. Chief among these institution are nongovernmental organizations (NGOs) and international development organizations that have proliferated in an aid-dependent Jordan.[15]

In some dimensions, the neoliberal logics, which today underpin educational policies globally, were part of the migration stories.[16] The women we spoke with insisted they could not waste their education by staying at home in the provinces, and they viewed a productive use of their education in very specific terms. Some were driven by a belief in their ability to fashion their own futures as successful professionals by seeking the opportunities they believe economic restructuring can provide them. Despite limited evidence that this is likely, their "success" as students in valuable fields—such as engineering and technology—propels them to strive to be the "neoliberal exceptions."[17] Nevertheless, the projects of self-fashioning cannot be reduced to neoliberal logics, as the women also strive to be respected, to marry someone who will support them, and to care for their parents and siblings. While such narratives about responsibility and care for one's family need to be situated in a context of receding state provision of welfare and the persistence of patriarchal norms, they also exist in a context of large-scale protests against neoliberal economic policies (for example, in 2018–19 and 2022).

Finally, this book and the ethnography upon which it draws highlight the complex interplay between gendered ideologies and practices. The persistence of low labor force participation rates for women is a key factor in shaping a view of Jordan as a place where gender roles are slow to change and where gender as an oppressive system is somehow stagnant or particularly traditional. Through an examination of these women's experiences, I show that seemingly rigid gender structures (notions of gendered propriety, restricted female mobility, and gendered division of labor) prove to be more pliable and negotiable than ones that can be more difficult to traverse, such as social class or status. Structural change is incremental, but the changes in these women's lives relative to women of past generations, to their peers in provincial communities, and even to older siblings are significant. This is evinced in their mobility, in the ways their families adapt to their migration, and in their shifting roles within their families. These shifts are also a product of their agency—while not limitless by any means, still a significant force in the trajectories they have pursued.

Creative Agency

Speaking about the creative nature of agency, Lois McNay argues that "a creative dimension to action is the condition of possibility of certain types of autonomous agency understood as the ability to act in unexpected fashion or to institute new and unanticipated modes of behavior . . . However, . . . any theory of agency must be placed in the context of structural, institutional or intersubjective constraints."[18] The creative work that these women engage in is future-oriented—they move with a view toward what is possible and expected. In other words, they act with not only a belief in what the future can be, but also a strong conviction that it *must* unfold in particular ways. As one woman described her decision to move to Amman, "For me, it was a matter of life and death." These visions for the future have been shaped by education, economic crisis, and neoliberal promises—the "constraints" that McNay references. The women's aspirations and expectations for progress, distinction, and mobility are at times supported by (and, in turn, support) family, and at other times resisted and constrained by them. Although economic imperatives provide a partial explanation for the women's labor migration, they do not fully account for the motivations or effects of their relocation for work. They work to fashion their own visions of what a successful trajectory can look like in a world shaped by powerful global and local forces of development, neoliberalism, and gender. But in their own lives, they too are powerful—forging new ways of being a woman in Jordan and reminding us that there are always many ways of "doing gender."[19] It is in this sense I argue that their agency is "creative."

A significant body of literature has engaged with the question of women's agency in the context of patriarchal and capitalist global systems, especially the scholarship on "Muslim women." In large part this preoccupation is driven by Western assumptions about a lack of female agency.[20] Saba Mahmood's critical intervention into this debate about agency, as well the work of Lila Abu-Lughod in this vein, has significantly informed my own conceptualization of agency and the ways in which it is shaped and limited by history, structure, and power. Mahmood urges us to see the ways in which the embracing or embodiment of norms is as much a function of one's agency as is the resistance to those norms. Abu-Lughod argues that agency as resistance produces new forms of power. In that way, resistance is best analyzed as a "diagnostic of power" that enables us to "detect historical shifts in the configuration/methods of power."[21] *Creative agency* is in a sense a melding of these two views. It acknowledges that agency is not purely or always resistance, but can be about the making of something new or unpredictable from the experiences we are given. Central to this "varied account of agency" is an attention to both the material and discursive dimensions of power, and the importance of experiences over time in understanding how the gendered subject is formed, what McNay describes as "a more *dialogical understanding of the temporal* aspects of subject formation."[22]

This book and the narratives of the young women interviewed provide critical insights into the practice of gender in ways that are typically overlooked in policy-oriented research on women and labor in the Arab world, and in much of the extant scholarship on Jordan. The women are contributing to an emerging "structure of feeling," a sense that despite the bold persistence of patriarchy, much has changed and is changing, and that in their own lives they are part of making and feeling that shift.[23]

The realities of time, and the temporal limits of this project, hinder any definitive claims about the effects of my interlocutors' experiences. Their lives and the consequences of their choices continue to unfold, and I have only been able to see a small snapshot of this ongoing process. They (like me) continue to be surprised by what life offers, divulges, gives or takes. While the women I write about in these pages are strong actors—forging new paths for themselves, persuading others of the merits of their choices, and standing up to those who assume they will fail—they acknowledge that some things are just out of their hands. But this acknowledgment does not stop them from creating what they can for themselves and their families with and despite the economic and patriarchal structures with which they must contend.

Methods

Growing up Jordanian American has provided me with some unique ethnographic insights into the questions this book takes up, and my own ethnographic journey with Jordan is central to my engagements here. Long before I lived and worked in Jordan, I learned about cultural norms and expectations in a Jordanian and Palestinian community in New York. Those who immigrated to my hometown of Yonkers in the years between 1950 and 1970 were largely Christian and came from rural communities back home as was my own family. By the time I went to live in Jordan in 1993, it seemed as if Jordanian society had changed at a pace far faster than my own community in New York. Over time I understood why and came to understand the diversity within Jordanian society that I had not experienced growing up. Nevertheless, my own upbringing and some of the struggles around gender roles and expectations resonate with the accounts in this book.

When I moved to Jordan in August 1993 at the age of twenty-two, as a Fulbright scholar, it was the first time I had lived on my own, although hardly alone as I had hundreds of relatives in Jordan. I would soon come to know this extended family whose members were very concerned about caring for me, most importantly by keeping me well fed. I had lived at home as an undergraduate, a decision I had little choice about because of both the expectations of my family and our financial situation. That I would live on my own for the first time in Jordan felt strange, given that single women in Jordan rarely lived on their own in the early 1990s. Thus, as an American coming to Jordan in 1993, I found that my living situation was seen as exceptional. "Western" women played by different rules. However, as a Jordanian with an extensive network of relatives in Jordan, I was initially met with some mild resistance. The night I arrived at Queen Alia Airport in Amman I was greeted by my paternal uncle. My uncle promptly tried to convince me to live with my grandmother, assuring me I would have no trouble getting back and forth to Amman from her home in a town not far from Amman. While I loved my family in Jordan and would relish the opportunity to get to know them better while living in Jordan, I did not want to live with them. Coming to Jordan, ironically, was part of my pursuit of some independence from family. I also feared that living with family would be looked down upon by my American peers and the Fulbright staff. I told my uncle I had no control over the matter, insisting that "the Americans" had already secured housing for us and that I was required to live in Fulbright housing. Fulbright, however, had done no such thing. After putting us up in a hotel for a few nights, the organization left us on our own to find an apartment. I spent the first few weeks nervous that my relatives would find out and pressure me to live with one of them. However, despite my concerns, no serious pressure was put upon me, even if they found it a bit odd that their female relative should be on her own, when she had plenty of decent alternatives with her vast network of family members.

By the time I began my doctoral research in 2002, I had developed a much deeper understanding of Jordan, and I have spent the last two decades engaged in ethnographic inquiry in and reflection upon Jordan. Between 2002 and 2009, I undertook ethnographic research in schools and among families in a provincial town about seventy kilometers from the capital city of Amman. That research and the relationships built in the course of that work are what led me to the women who are the focus of this book. The story of Jihan, her sister Nida, and the rest of their family with which I began this introduction help illuminate some aspects of this ethnographic journey.

In January 2011, my family and I relocated to Jordan for a sabbatical in which I was to embark on research related to the purported marriage crisis in Jordan.[24] On the plane ride over I read news of protests in Tunisia. Little did I know then that parts of the Arab world would be turned upside down in the coming weeks. My partner and I, like many of our friends, colleagues, and family, were captivated by the scenes of protest around the region; keeping track of those events became almost a full-time occupation in those first weeks. As regimes fell in Tunisia, Egypt, and Libya, and protests erupted in many other countries, I started to doubt myself and the value of my research—my ethnographic labor at this critical point in history. My research interests felt misplaced or even insignificant. I began attending protests in Jordan and closely following the news there. I also began researching the independent labor movement in Jordan.[25] However, I came back to the research I had planned to do about marriage and being single. Eventually, some of my interviews with single women led me to focus on labor and migration.

I bring this up because I want to juxtapose such events and the potential for transformative change they signal with the "continual processes of incremental social change that are always at work" even as we bear witness to tumultuous and dramatic changes.[26] Change is typically much more banal—small, gradual, and constant—and often invisible at the macro level and to outside observers. Nowhere are the limits of our change paradigms more apparent to me than in thinking about gender roles and ideologies. In the wake of the Arab Spring, many people asked how these dramatic political events would change women's roles, while others argued that women's roles had already changed dramatically through participation in revolutionary action.[27] However, as a scholar of women, gender, and development in the region, I am keenly aware that the gendered contours of daily life in the Arab world (and everywhere else) today have been shaped by centuries of socioeconomic and political transformations. From colonialism to the spread of bourgeois liberalism and Islamic reform movements, to deepening entanglements with a global capitalist system and the adoption of new technologies, the world in which men and women live has changed dramatically, and these experiences are always gendered. Yet, the ways in which the world has changed, through the slow unfolding of history, may be imperceptible to those looking only at the surface. Even as the unfolding political events continued to preoccupy me, I returned to ethnography, specifically, the ethnography of everyday experiences of young, educated women and their communities. Centering people's experiences and their own reflections on their experiences gets beyond cultural determinism and wrestles with the ways structures and ideology can be co-constitutive. It sheds light on the limits of ideas about gendered norms—ideas that do not sufficiently capture the gap or lag between changes in practice and the gendered ideologies that we have become accustomed to reproducing.

I first began to meet the women profiled in this book in the course of my research on marriage (for which I interviewed about fifty men and women). During that period, I also interviewed female engineers about their experiences in the profession, some of whom lived on their own in Amman. Ultimately, it was a conversation with Afaf Al-Khoshman, who became my primary research assistant, that led me to pursue this project. I met Afaf in 2007, when she joined a delegation of Jordanian teachers who came to Columbia University, where I was completing my doctorate. We reconnected in 2011, and I learned that she was living in Amman and working for an international organization there. As I became more interested in learning about the experiences of young women who had moved to Amman for professional opportunities, Afaf was instrumental in connecting me to a wider network of women, and became a key partner in conducting the research upon which this book is based.

Against the assumptions and expectations of many fellow Jordanians, the women I was meeting at the time overcame one of the strongest gendered norms—that of living with one's family until one married. Even if a woman did not marry, the prevailing norms dictated that she would continue to live with family, moving in with brothers once her parents were deceased. Indeed, older women often cited as one of the downsides of staying single the eventuality of having to live with a brother and his wife. As with any other norm, one could find exceptions, and among the upper classes women were more likely to leave home for education abroad or jobs in other countries. Still, the norm was a powerful one. Even young men are typically expected to live with family until they marry, unless they migrate. The experiences of the women I was meeting intrigued me.

Working very closely with Afaf, I decided to learn more about the experience of single professional women living independently of their families in Amman. In all, we interviewed forty-three women about migration.[28] All interviews were conducted entirely in Arabic. The women came from all over the country, and from communities diverse in size and distance from the capital. Jordan is a relatively small country (about the size of Indiana) with a limited transportation system, so that even relatively close towns or villages can feel significantly farther away (see map). Women came from villages hours away, or from the second-largest city, Irbid, significantly closer to Amman and decidedly urban, with a population of more than half a million.[29] The majority of women interviewed lived in female student dormitories when they came to Amman, although some in time would move into apartments with other single women. Living arrangements are part of the longer term challenge of being in Amman as a single woman, as dormitory life can become quite suffocating for women as they get older, and older women grapple with the desire for a home of their own.[30]

In terms of their family backgrounds, socioeconomic status, family size, and other demographic characteristics, the women interviewed were quite diverse, and no discernible demographic pattern could explain their migration other than their being educated and relatively successful in academic terms. They ranged in age from twenty-four to forty-eight, although the majority were in their twenties when we first interviewed them. Most of the women we interviewed were Muslim; we also interviewed several Christian women.[31] Their academic successes put them in a position to take advantage of perceived opportunities in Amman or motivated them to seek professional and academic experiences in the capital that were not available in the provinces. Even for women in fields such as education, the capital offered the possibility of upward mobility in the field or the chance for a career change. Education gave them a sense of agency—a sense that they could shape their futures in particular ways, that they had a responsibility to fulfill certain expectations, and that they had a right to certain outcomes.[32]

After the initial interviews had taken place, I continued to meet with a small group of women, at times in their dormitories and apartments, in a few cases meeting family members and continuing to correspond over social media and email. Over a period of almost five years (with several visits back to Jordan), we talked about their fears and aspirations, their jobs and how they spent their leisure time, and their experiences of life as a single woman on their own in the city. The ensuing years have provided a glimpse of their shifting fortunes, changing perspectives about the paths they have taken, and their status as their positions at work and in their families have changed. The unfolding nature of the life paths discussed helps in breaking out of the agency/control dichotomy, as changing circumstances have led to self-reflection, new strategies, different expectations and opportunities, and at times setbacks. The personal narratives and my observation of the spaces in which women socialize, commute, and live are the central data here.

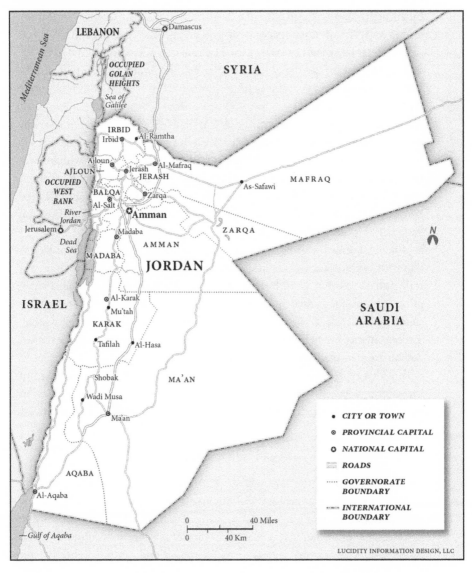

In addition to research with young women currently or recently living and working in Amman, I worked with another research collaborator, Helen Ayoub, who conducted oral history interviews with women born between 1931 and 1960 who had left home for work in earlier times. All but three of these women were teachers who went to rural areas to meet growing demands for education in the early decades of state-building.[33] This book is also informed by ethnographic research over the last two decades—in schools, in homes, and in a variety of other spaces with Jordanians of diverse backgrounds—as well as deep personal ties to Jordan. The research was also facilitated by my fluency in Arabic (especially Jordanian colloquial Arabic) and broad and diverse networks and experiences in the country (I have lived both in Amman and in the provinces).

Because the research for this book has benefited from the labor of many people, when I speak about the field research process, I use the first-person plural "we" unless I am speaking about a specific interaction in which I was the only one from my research team who was present. Throughout, I maintain the anonymity of all my interlocutors. To ensure this, I have changed some personal details (for instance, field of study). In many places, I rely on vague descriptions of place and employment for the same reason.

Finally, I draw on a vast literature about women, gender, and labor in Jordan with two goals in mind. First, I draw on extant research to situate my interlocutors' experiences within broader demographic trends in Jordan. Much of this knowledge is presented as quantitative data about educational attainment, labor trends, and research regarding barriers to women's employment. These statistics are helpful for painting a picture of the broader contexts Jordanian women navigate, although the stories of these women are absent in data of this type. I also consider the ideological assumptions that undergird the work that has emerged to address Jordan's most cited gender and development challenge, namely, low labor force participation rates for women.[34]

Organization of the Book

In chapter 1, I chart the recent history of Jordan, with particular attention to the expansion of education and attendant new labor regimes that came with state-building. While what is today Jordan has been settled for millennia, the state of Jordan is less than a century old. Education, migration, and displacement have been central to its formation and development, as have the political machinations of Western nations. Drawing on oral histories with ten women who were born in the early years of state development, as well as Jordan's historiography and more recent accounts of development in the country, the chapter sets the context for understanding female mobility and movement for work today, as well as related aspirations.

Chapter 2 centers the narratives of women who have moved to Amman to pursue professional and personal projects, and their expressed reasons for moving. At the heart of their stories is education, and the possibility and promise that is tied to their status as educated women. The sense of possibility they described was heightened by strong convictions about what their lives ought to look like given their educational success. Determined not to waste their education, women seek to pursue a personal and professional trajectory worthy of their efforts. Ideas about what such a suitable future should look like are informed by neoliberal tenets of efficiency and flexibility, but they are not entirely encapsulated by the logics of neoliberalism. Responsibility and obligation to family are key, as is a sense of obligation to their communities.

For the young women at the center of this book, the transition to Amman is initially a difficult one. In chapter 3, I consider how women navigate the spaces and places of a capital city that has seen tremendous growth and transformation in the past two decades. While the city and the diverse social relations that form its spaces pose many challenges for young women, Amman also provides opportunities for greater mobility, independence, and leisure that are not available in their provincial communities. Challenges are exacerbated by the precariousness of being single women on their own, and their felt need to prove themselves as moral beings and as competent professionals and adults capable of caring for themselves. Among their co-workers, they also must reckon with biases toward people from the provinces. Precarity is also economic, and many women are barely able to support themselves when they come to the capital, and some rely for years on financial support from family and friends. Some women are never able to save money, let alone assist their families, while others become important breadwinners for siblings and parents. Nevertheless, most women reflect on great personal growth as a result of the relocation to Amman.

My interlocutors' evolving relationships with family members, and in some cases ongoing negotiations about the need to be away from home, are the subject of chapter 4. While the move to Amman is very much about their academic achievement, determination, and creative agency, their efforts are not solo projects. Every story of migration is also a family story and, in many respects, a family project. In this chapter, I start with the move to Amman and the negotiations and struggles that this move entails for some women. For some, the transition is less contentious, and for others, moving leads to a significant redefining of their roles and relationships, with important implications for understanding how gender ideologies function in practice. I consider how the male breadwinner ideology is challenged by the reality of more diverse economic practices. Finally, I argue that for most women, autonomy and success are linked to their ability to care for families. I conclude with women's reflections on what has shifted in their communities to allow for greater female mobility for work, and their self-perception as actors who are playing a part in making these shifts.

Many young women interviewed for this book have married and settled with their spouses in Amman or in the provinces. For those who have lived as single women in Amman for many years, often in dormitory-style housing, questions about the future emerge with the passing of time. Chapter 5 focuses on marriage and the ways in which migration has shaped marriage prospects and expectations. It also illuminates the experiences of women who are older and still single, a status that has received limited attention in scholarly literature on women in the Middle East. While the numbers of single women are growing, to remain single is still deemed an unfortunate fate by many. Nevertheless, some women accept "singlehood," arguing that their social and professional experiences make marriage difficult, if not impossible, and plan for a future life accordingly.

Finally, the book concludes by returning to broader discussions about women, labor, and development in Jordan and beyond. I highlight the ways in which this ethnography works to complicate prevailing discourses about gender and development, and women's labor. Specifically, I argue that processes of social change must be sought through an analysis of everyday human practices. The creative agency of the women profiled here gives us great insight into the everyday workings of class, gender and geography in shaping the lives of people in Jordan, and the ways in which human practice (aspiring, moving, caring, laboring) constitutes, challenges, and transforms gendered norms and expectations.

Between the chapters I have included five interludes that provide a fuller story of particular women's experiences (and one man's experience). We will meet many women throughout these chapters, but in order to provide fuller accounts, I opted to thread these stories throughout.

Conclusion

As with any study about women, and particularly women in the Middle East, many people may ask if these women's lives are improved by their migration or whether they are "empowered." Because the women whose stories I share in this book come from parts of Jordan that are considered to be underdeveloped and/or culturally conservative, many Jordanians in Amman with whom I spoke assumed that the labor migration of these women must be coercive.[35] For example, when I described my research to a middle-aged female NGO professional in Amman, she argued that the migration of provincial women was dangerous and could lead to all kinds of social problems because they would be unable to cope with their newfound freedoms in Amman.[36] Ironically, while this elite urbanite framed women's movements to Amman

as dangerous, many women said their families permitted them to move because of trust. While parents had concerns about their daughters' safety and
reputations, they put faith in their daughters and their ability to navigate the
unknown.

Clearly the migration of young women to Amman creates many opportunities and challenges. The question of whether the women's lives are "better" is, in my view, an unanswerable one, primarily because what they desire,
need, and value varies and has been very much shaped by the reality of their
migration. While none of the women spoke in terms of "empowerment,"
nearly all of the women made the assessment that migration has been both
personally and professionally beneficial. But the lives they create have not
been without challenges and uncertainty. For those women for whom migration and being single looks increasingly "permanent," the achievements are
tempered by desire for families and concerns about longer term futures, even
as they assert that they will not settle.

Elias and Hoda

Long before I began the research for this book, I interviewed Elias in 2003 when I was a doctoral student. He was about seventy at the time, and I was trying out my oral history interview skills. I asked Elias about his childhood, and he told me about his interrupted education:

> I left school in sixth grade. My parents needed me to work the land. I am very embarrassed about that.
>
> *Why are you embarrassed about that?*
>
> I wanted to continue my education.

Although Elias was initially reluctant to talk about this phase of his life, he went on to tell me that his educational story did not end there. A few years later, he went back to school, traveling to a nearby town because no additional schooling was available in his village. He completed preparatory school there, walking miles on the weekends to get home and back. He eventually completed secondary school by means of a correspondence course and some ingenuity. During this oral history interview, I was surprised at the deep sense of shame Elias conveyed about having left school once. He had so embraced the idea of education as progress, status, and modernity that he was embarrassed about having been forced to leave school, albeit temporarily, at the age of eleven. His embarrassment was also linked to his inability to go on to higher education even after he had worked so hard to complete his secondary education. He had had an opportunity to study in Baghdad, Iraq, but the resources were not available to finance his education. He became a teacher in Jordan, working in several rural communities. In his early thirties, he had the opportunity to immigrate to the United States. There, he believed, he might be able to pursue his dream of higher education. But the demands of his extended family, and his own young family, meant these dreams did not materialize.

While this book is primarily about the experiences of women, I start with this conversation I had with Elias, as it was the first time I understood how transformative the spread of education was for his generation in Jordan. His sense of embarrassment or even shame about the interruption of his education was palpable in our conversation, and it surprised me. Nearly twenty years later Hoda, a ninety-year-old retired teacher, described similar struggles to complete her education:

> My father (b. 1905) attended some elementary school under the Ottomans. He knew Turkish. He was in the military. My mother (b. 1914) had no formal education. I studied until sixth grade in Husn, but then my parents took me out of school so I could help the family. At least I felt that was the main reason. I remember when it was time to harvest the wheat and barley, they took me out to the fields, me and my mother and my sister. That was my situation for six or seven years. After a while, I got books from those who had continued their studies, and I started studying them by myself, especially math. I really liked math.
>
> Two of my sisters continued after me. One was in seventh grade and one in eighth. They went to Jerash to complete their schooling [the schools in Husn at that time only went to sixth grade]. The principal of the girls' school in Irbid would not let them continue, she said the classes were full [and secondary school was not compulsory at the time]. By chance, there were girls from Husn who had gone to Jerash for school, for the same reason. There was no space for them in Irbid. I convinced my father to send my sisters. He said, "I won't send little girls there by themselves, *yatgharrabin* [to go be among strangers]." I told him, "I will take responsibility for them. I will go with them and take care of them. And I will take them to and from school" and I gave similar assurances.
>
> [Laughs] But I had other plans. I wanted to return to school. I had relatives who knew the principal in Jerash. They were friends, and I got them to write a letter on my behalf asking her to let me into the school.

Even though you had not completed the necessary grades?

Yes, even without the diploma, but I had been studying on my own and I had finished the ninth grade. I studied it all. I gave the letter to the principal in Jerash, and she kissed it and said welcome, but don't tell anyone that you are here without a diploma. Tell them you have been transferred. So that's what happened. I studied, and things went well. I hope everyone will find success as I found success. I was the first in the class at the end of that year, and I took the metric [exam at the end of third intermediate or ninth grade] and then we went to Irbid to the principal there, and she was very happy with me because I was very accomplished in math, and she taught us geometry. I finished secondary school, and after that some folks from the Ministry of Education came and they wanted teachers for the coming year.

They sent us to villages all over the country. At that time, when you were first appointed, you needed to go to the villages because they had no teachers. Most of the time we had to live in the village because there was no transportation. They appointed me to teach in a village north of Irbid. There was no transportation and there were only dirt roads. We'd be covered in dirt when we arrived. We would come home once a month to get our salary. I stayed in the first village for six months. No one was opposed to this work. Quite the opposite, they wanted only for their daughters to have the same opportunities. All the girls who graduated from Husn became teachers, but they wouldn't let her go work in a bank, for example.[1] They would say no, there are men there. A teacher is respectable and the rural communities like teachers—male and female—and they respect them more than you can imagine, much more than you can imagine.

I faced no problems in the village. In the second village I went to, the *mukhtar* [village leader] said to me, "Everything about you is good except for one thing." [Laughs] I said "Oh no, tell me. We will have to fix it." He said, "If only you wore the *shursh*[2] like our women." I told him, "That one is difficult to implement because the *shursh* makes it hard to walk and we walk around a lot in class in between desks." Like the first village I went to, I would go home once a month. Even the young men went home once a month because there was no transportation. The people in the village were very nice, in both villages, but I was in the second one for much longer, five years. But there weren't many opportunities for building relationships. They were farmers and they and their children worked in the fields.

After that I used some connections to try and move. They would not transfer me, but then a new director took over for a while and he approved my transfer to a different village. I had a good reputation as a teacher, and I could teach whatever they needed. More cars were available in this community, so me and a few other teachers hired a car to take us and return us daily. The community was very nice and supportive. I was also a principal there for a while, and they complained to the ministry when I left: "How do you take the best teacher we have ever had?"

Overall, the experience was very positive for me. The people in the villages were so welcoming and respectful. Also, since I was young, I liked to depend on myself for everything. The work and the *ghurba* [being away from my community] helped build my character. I have always been able to handle problems big and small on my own.

Hoda went on to teach in public schools in her hometown for thirteen years, and then for a few years at a parochial school in Amman, after which she retired.

A History of Education, Labor, and Migration

Elias and Hoda's educational journeys, presented in interlude 1, illustrate aspects of recent history that constitute the backdrop of this book's arguments and interventions. By the late nineteenth century, tremendous changes were under way in what is today Jordan—new systems of land registration, expanding presence of missionaries and Christian parochial schools, as well as a more extensive Ottoman bureaucracy. Within a few decades, the Ottoman Empire fell, and the British and the French carved up the Levant into their own spheres of influence, establishing the Emirate of Transjordan and the mandate system that would govern the new territory. The British had reneged on their commitments to Sharif Hussein of Mecca, the great-great-grandfather of Jordan's current king, to support the establishment of an independent Arab nation. Emir Abdullah, one of the Sharif's sons, went on to establish the Emirate of Transjordan, a move the British presented as a temporary stepping-stone to an expanded united Arab nation. This was not to be, however, and the Hashemites, as they are known, remain the ruling family only of what came to be the modern nation of Jordan.[1]

Initially, the availability of formal education was limited, especially in rural areas. However, the promise of education quickly spread, as it did throughout the world in this "age of education."[2] In Jordan, as elsewhere, modern education was bound up with visions of progress—for individuals and their families, but also for the nation and broader political projects, nationalist, anticolonial, socialist. With the expansion of state bureaucracy in Jordan and the jobs it created, promises of waged employment also acted to increase demand for more formal education. The state initially struggled to meet the demand, but education soon became more widely available.[3]

The parallels between the stories of Elias and Hoda are strong. Both were born during the British Mandate (1921–46). Both were children of farmers. Hoda's father served in the military, the first primary employer of men, when she was a child, and Elias's father sought out waged labor in the ports of Palestine for a time. Still, for both families, agriculture was central to family survival—a reality that would change dramatically in a generation's time. Men and women in rural areas struggled to access education. Elias and Hoda both had access to a parochial school in their villages through sixth grade.[4] After completing sixth grade, both wanted to continue their education, but their families needed their labor more so they left school for a time. Despite the initial interruption, both were able to gain enough education to join the ranks of teachers who spread throughout the country in the project of educational expansion. It was an era of new expectations, and for young men and women like Elias and Hoda, education was central to partaking in their country's new reality and to making history. Education, in short, was central to the state-building project.

Elias eventually left Jordan when the opportunity to immigrate to the United States emerged. He didn't really want to go. He was committed to the project of Arab nationalism and to political liberation struggles that were afoot in his time (ideas that were cultivated in the burgeoning school system), but again family pressure prevailed, and he went to the United States with the intention of returning after making enough money to help his parents and siblings and start his own family. He never returned. Hoda, who never married, was able to help support her family by staying in Jordan, where she worked as a teacher for decades.

This chapter examines the recent histories of education, labor, and migration in Jordan to consider the broader context for the migration of people like Elias and Hoda, as well as the subsequent migrations of the young women at the center of this book. As we will see throughout, education, and the potential it offered for different futures, has been central to social transformations in the twentieth century and intimately linked with new economic realities and systems of value. These transformations are also inextricably linked with the establishment of the Jordanian state (1946) and the broader political realities that informed this social history. It is with the making of the state that I begin.

Making a State

Jordan was established as an emirate in 1921 under the leadership of Emir Abdullah, with the support of the British.[5] Of course, this was not the beginning of life for the people who had inhabited the land for centuries, but it was the first formal step toward the establishment of a nation-state called Jordan. Before 1921, Jordan had been part of the Ottoman Empire for nearly four centuries but not as Jordan per se. Different parts of present-day Jordan had links to various regional centers in Syria, Palestine, and the Hijaz. In recent decades, historians have contributed significantly to our understanding of social, economic, and political life in what is today Jordan during the late Ottoman period. This scholarship has shown us that there were more continuities with the pre-nation-state past than the ruptures that Europeans had claimed. In some sense, the more significant ruptures and transformations were yet to come.

Despite such developments in the historiography of Jordan, some stale tropes still dominate how students, scholars, policy makers, and many Jordanians make sense of the present. A prominent one is the oft-repeated claim that Jordan is a fake nation with artificial borders. This argument is deployed to explain politics in Jordan as well as in nations as diverse as Iraq, Syria, or Ukraine. Another powerful trope is that what is today Jordan was populated by often violent, mostly nomadic "tribes" that resisted governing and continued to resist up to the present, and that these tribes (or "Bedouins")[6] were in constant conflict with settled peasants and townspeople. In surprising ways, a narrative of unruly, if not violent, "backward" tribes continues to color how the provinces of Jordan are conceived, represented, and imagined.[7] Similarly, it serves as a pillar of broader narratives about politics in Jordan. With little attention to class, geography, or specific family histories, the Jordanian political landscape is often still described as a struggle between the "tribes" and the Palestinians, with "tribes" standing in for East Bank Jordanians or Jordanians not of Palestinian descent. This narrative significantly oversimplifies the realities of kin-based connections and how they function in people's lives; class hierarchies; and diverse histories of migration, settlement, and pastoral and agricultural life. It also neglects the ways in which the category of "tribe" and "the tribal" is mobilized for political ends.[8]

Recognition of the tendency to see Jordan through such tropes is important for understanding the political geographies of contemporary Jordan, *and* the spaces from which the women profiled here migrate. Women, especially provincial women, have largely been left out of Jordan's historiography until recently.[9] These lingering discourses, as well as recent histories of development in the provinces, are critical to understanding why women leave the provinces to engage in particular forms of work, how they themselves frame the decision to leave, and how others view them once they arrive in Amman. More broadly, the migration of women today elucidates the ways in which class hierarchies are gendered, racialized, and grounded in spatial representations of internal others.

In this chapter, I trace the three key dimensions of state development in Jordan: education, labor, and migration/displacement. Throughout, I pay particular attention to the nodes of distinction that have been there from the start—class, geography and gender. I consider how this recent history has shaped the world these women navigate today, one seemingly rife with ongoing economic crisis and opportunity.[10]

Building an Educational System

It was very normal for a girl to go [elsewhere as a teacher]. There is not a girl who was given a post in her hometown to start with. Teachers had to go live elsewhere. You had to work in a village for a few years before you could be transferred to Irbid or even Husn [a town near Irbid].

In 1963, I finished *tawjihi*. I was seventeen and a half, and I was appointed right away. There was no wait for an appointment in those days. The West Bank needed teachers more than the East Bank.[11] All of us who graduated in 1963 were given an appointment even if the salaries were low. It was 20 dinars. We needed the money even if we were not very poor. We had land and agriculture, but you still needed money.

I liked the idea of being employed, of getting a salary. I was appointed to a village between Ramallah and Nablus. It was 50 kilometers from Nablus, but there was only one bus that left in the morning and returned in the evening. When I was appointed there, my family was a bit hesitant. My mother came with me to check out the area, and I started crying, "How am I going to live here?" But then my parents agreed because they trusted us, and in those days folks were not afraid for their daughters [that is, it was safer]. In our time, teachers were very much respected, they had status and respect.

After two years I left. The people of the village were so respectful . . . We would always be invited to people's homes. There was no objection from anyone [to the teachers being there]. It was normal. All my friends and my sister, we all went to go teach in other communities . . . After a while they stopped sending people to the West Bank after the 1967 war [i.e., when Israel occupied the West Bank]. Then they were appointed here. We all lived in the communities that we worked in because there was no means of transportation to take you back and forth each day, so you were required to sleep there even if it was close.

IMAN, retired teacher, b. 1945

In the mid-nineteenth century, schools in Jordan were scarce and took the form of community-funded religious institutions, both Muslim and Christian. The late Ottoman period saw increasing efforts to govern education and to create a tax base that would fund it.[12] During the Mandate period, local demand for education far exceeded supply. While the number of government schools slowly increased, the British invested very little in education and did not view it as a priority.[13] By the 1945–46 academic year, Lars Wählin reports that there were more private schools than government schools, although government schools (of which there were seventy-three) enrolled more students.[14] Private schools enrolled more girls and were more likely to be found in rural areas.[15] After 1946, Jordan began to make significant investment in public education for boys and girls, and undertook a big push to ensure that basic education was available in rural areas, which initially lagged. Wählin argues that the expansion of education into rural areas was made possible by several factors: demand from rural communities, the availability of an educated cadre of Palestinian teachers, the groundwork of the parochial schools in this area, and the restructuring of the economy away from agriculture.[16]

Initially state planners were concerned about the spread of education to rural areas and tried to contain aspirations for new ways of life by limiting the type of education provided in these areas. Such a strategy kept with policies (colonial, Mandate, and state) throughout the region that sought to limit the educational aspirations of rural people and curtail rural-to-urban migration.[17] Hilary Falb argues, "In the 1950s, King Abdullah and a cadre of Mandate-era officials continued to view agricultural instruction as a way of limiting social mobility and urbanization, thereby counteracting policies inducing peasants to leave farming."[18] Despite the intentions of policy makers, small-scale agriculture as a means of making a living became increasingly untenable, and cash-strapped rural families came to view education as an important avenue to sustaining families and to achieving upward mobility in a rapidly changing world. In part, this was due to the policies of the very elite who sought to keep people in rural areas, which made it more difficult for the land to sustain a family.[19] Demographic growth, enabled in large part by improved health services and the availability of vaccines, also placed pressures on rural families to diversify their economic strategies. As in the stories of Elias and Hoda, oral history interviews with provincial women born in the Mandate period, or in the first few years of independence, also pointed to the increased need for and availability of waged labor, and the concomitant demand for more education. Expanding opportunities for employment in the military contributed to these changes.

Jordan saw dramatic demographic shifts in the decades after World War II. Its population grew rapidly in large part due to the Nakba, the destruction of hundreds of Palestinian villages by Zionist forces and the forced expulsion and displacement of nearly 800,000 Palestinians when the state of Israel was created.[20] Some 70,000 fled to Jordan, which at the time had a population of about 374,000 to 400,000 people.[21] The Jordanian regime undertook a de facto annexation of the West Bank of Palestine in 1950, a move the Jordanian regime referred to as the "unity of two banks," significantly expanding its geographic domain and population as it granted citizenship to all Palestinians in the West

Bank.[22] Jordan lost control of the West Bank after the 1967 war, when Israel occupied the remainder of historic Palestine (the West Bank and the Gaza Strip),
driving out 440,000 Palestinians, many of whom were displaced for a second
time and ended up in Jordan.[23] Israel also occupied the Syrian Golan Heights.
Musa Samha argues that the sudden growth of Amman's population that resulted from the forced displacement of Palestinians in 1948 and again in 1967
led to rapid urbanization and development, which in turn attracted migrants
from other areas of the country.[24] Jordanians from all over the country also
moved for civil service opportunities and jobs in the armed services.

Despite the challenge of incorporating a rapidly growing population, the
education sector grew rapidly to meet the increasing needs and demands of
the people and the new state. This was accomplished with aid from Western
donors and multilateral organizations, as well as Arab Gulf countries, and
remittances that came from Jordanians laboring in the Arab Gulf.[25] Jordan
remains a heavily aid-dependent country today.[26] The United Nations Relief
and Works Agency for Palestine Refugees (UNRWA) became a major actor
in this field, educating Palestinian refugees in Jordan since 1950. It continues
to be a significant educational provider, and at present has about 120,000 students each year.[27] By the 1980s, Jordan had reached basic education goals and
had built several public universities, and secondary school completion rates
were on the rise. The expansion of education took on distinctly gendered patterns relatively early on, as I discuss below.

Within decades of the state's establishment, the Jordanian educational
system was viewed as one of the most effective in the region—in terms of
both its geographical and socioeconomic reach and the relative quality of the
educational system. Up until the 1990s, the vast majority of Jordanians still
considered public education to be strong, and the availability of private education was limited. However, with the growth in population and the under-
investment in the public sector precipitated by structural adjustment policies
and neoliberal economic "reforms," Jordan witnessed a deterioration in public education and increasing inequality in the education sector.[28] This was accompanied by the growth of private education at all levels, as well as a system
of private tutoring meant to compensate for the deteriorating quality of public education.[29] Most of this growth in private education has been in urban
areas, and in Amman in particular.

GENDER AND EDUCATION

In 2002, I was sitting in the home of Um Murad. I met her daughter at a local high school
where I was conducting pilot research for my PhD. I opened our first conversation

with a general inquiry about her daughter's education: "Um Murad, tell me about your daughter's education . . ." But, before I could finish my sentence, Um Murad interrupted me and said, "She's fine. Her education is fine, but let me tell you about my son . . . he refuses to repeat the *tawjihi* exam and the boys' schools . . . ," and she continued with a litany of complaints about her son's refusal to study and the state of boys' schools, complaints which I would hear often.

AUTHOR'S FIELD NOTES

The women profiled in this book are among the most successful students in their communities, and educational success figures centrally in their narratives about labor and migration. Every woman linked her story of migration to educational achievement—the long hours spent studying, the time away from family to access higher education, the sacrifices of parents to finance their education and support them as students. Some of these women were the first in their families to receive a university degree, and some were the first to go to school. About a third of the parents of women we spoke with had less than a high school education, and some had no formal education at all. Slightly over a third of parents had some postsecondary education (associate's degree or technical training, bachelor's degree, and even advanced degrees [in the case of three of the fathers]). Whether they were first-generation university students, the first generation to be schooled at all, or daughters of professionals, women who made the move to Amman in the last decade linked the investment in their education, and their own efforts to succeed academically, to particular visions of the future that they sought to fulfill through migration.

As we see from the brief history given above, levels of formal education were relatively low in the early years of the state, but within decades, the numbers of those enrolled in formal education rapidly increased, and the education of girls was not far behind the overall pattern. Linda Layne, in her research on schools in the Jordan Valley in the early 1980s, finds that "in terms of attendance, curriculum, and achievement Jordanian women seem to be enjoying relatively equal, if not privileged, educational opportunities to men."[30] Today, by all available measures, women outperform their male counterparts academically. While overall secondary enrollment rates have decreased for all children in Jordan for more than a decade,[31] girls have consistently been enrolled in secondary school at rates higher than those for boys. A Ministry of Education report for academic year 2016–17 found that gross and net enrollment rates for girls in secondary school were more than ten percentage points higher than those for boys.[32] The gap between girls and boys at the secondary level (with more girls in secondary school) is found throughout the country in nearly every province between 2009 and 2018. The female advantage in secondary school enrollment covers a broad range: in

Amman girls have outnumbered boys by more than ten percentage points in recent years, while in some of the southern provinces girls outnumber boys by more than twenty percentage points.[33] Nationally, girls also outnumbered boys in higher education enrollment and graduation rates every year between 2008 and 2020.[34] At the provincial level, there is more variation across provinces, with boys in higher education outnumbering girls in some of the provinces. Still, in a majority of the provinces, girls outnumber boys.[35]

The available data also reveal that girls are outperforming boys academically. For example, the Ministry of Education reported that girls passed the *tawjihi* (high school completion/college entry) exams at rates higher than their male peers every year between 2007 and 2020 in the scientific, literary, and information technology tracks, as well as nearly every year in all of the vocational tracks.[36] On international standardized tests, such at TIMSS (Trends in International Mathematics and Science Study) and PISA (Programme for International Student Assessment), which have become ubiquitous measures of educational quality in recent years, female students in Jordan consistently outperform male students.[37] Recently, more attention is being paid to this gender gap in Jordan, a "reverse gender divide" that has also been documented in other parts of the Arab world.[38] Parents like Um Murad, whom I met in 2004, especially those in the provinces with few educational alternatives to public schools, have long voiced concerns about their sons' education, the school environment, and the quality of education in boys' schools (public schools in Jordan are required to be segregated by sex after fifth grade). While these gender gaps are not the focus of my work here, it is important to acknowledge that the reasons for these trends vary significantly and that socioeconomic status is a significant factor in shaping the educational experiences of young men, and their decisions to leave school.[39] Despite these trends, policy makers, both local and international, have been largely dismissive of women's academic accomplishments, especially in Jordan, where their low labor force participation rates have led to a devaluing of women's educational achievements.

Academic tracking, which begins in secondary school and is officially based on academic performance, guided many of the women in this book to specialize in science, technology, engineering, and math (STEM) fields that are ostensibly in higher demand and potentially more lucrative. Nearly three-quarters of the women we interviewed had majored in STEM fields. The pathway into such fields and the professional trajectories (for instance, STEM jobs in the private sector) are laid much earlier in the lives of young women, as their educational performance early in life shapes their opportunities for postsecondary education and subsequent career choices. In Jordan, higher performing students (male and female) are typically expected to go into fields such as engineering and medicine, and may be pressured to do so even if their own interests lie elsewhere. A great deal of status is tied to these professions. Conversely, students who do not perform well in school have a difficult time getting into such fields.[40] Tracking begins in secondary school with the highest performing students being funneled into the scientific track. Students whose grades are lower are placed into the literary track. The lowest performing students are concentrated in vocational education schools.[41] One's assigned track at the secondary level also largely determines one's potential major at university.

Admission to Jordanian universities (both public and private) is based almost exclusively on the *tawjihi* exam.[42] Once exam results are in, the admissions process is managed through a centralized system at the Council of Higher Education. The council establishes minimum grade requirements for particular fields in all universities each year. However, today it is estimated that less than half of students are admitted to university through open competition at the national level.[43] In a system sometimes referred to as "exceptions," the government allocates quotas for children of those who have served in the military, public school teachers, university staff and faculty, and several other groups.[44] These students compete among themselves for reserved seats at public universities in different fields. Because they are competing within a smaller pool, their chances of gaining admittance to competitive fields are higher, although they must still meet the minimum grade requirement set by the Council for Higher Education. Students from underdeveloped regions of the country are also given a quota, as are schools with "special conditions," essentially poor and underresourced schools.[45] In addition, the top performing students in every province, district, and school are awarded preferential admissions based on their merit as measured by *tawjihi* exam scores.

Significant inequalities are built into the system, one main criticism being that the process unduly disadvantages Jordanians of Palestinian descent, as they are underrepresented in the military and public sector, two of the most prevalent routes to "exceptional" admissions. The largest quota (20 percent of seats in 2021–22) is reserved for children of those in the military and a variety of public security agencies.[46] Another source of inequality in admissions is the *muwazi*, or "parallel system." Created in the late 1990s, it is a parallel track that enables students to enter particular majors in public universities with lower grades than those required in open competition by paying higher tuition, significantly advantaging those who can pay more. Close to 30 percent of university students were in the parallel track in 2015–16.[47]

However, other policies act as a form of affirmative action for students who are disadvantaged economically and academically. Often accusations are leveled that students who enter university through these alternative pathways are given a free ticket to university without reference to merit, which is not the case. In this way, public perceptions about these students being "unworthy" mirror public bias against affirmative action policies in the United States, for example. More disturbingly, the negative view of students who are admitted to universities fuels other narratives about students from the provinces. For example, journalists, activists, and scholars at times assert that preferential admissions for so-called tribal Jordanians have led to increased violence on campuses.[48] While the various exceptions benefit students from various backgrounds and geographic origins, public discourse sometimes frames the exceptions as an issue of students who are "tribal," an amorphous term that is used as a catchall to label troublesome students, as well as many other problems in Jordanian society.[49]

Most relevant for this book is that the experience of the women profiled here gets elided by such a discourse. Policies that benefit students from underdeveloped regions and/or the children of public sector workers and members of the military have created opportunities for provincial women that might not be available otherwise. Because the women profiled here are from the provinces, where public sector employment (civilian, security, and military) is more prevalent, some have benefited from these policies—but not without their own educational achievement. While we did not explicitly ask about how they were admitted to universities, some discussed the process, and several had fathers in the military or parents who were teachers. This is not to minimize the biases that are built into the system, which are indeed significant. Disadvantaged youth in provinces are given more seats and/or larger quotas than poor youth in urban areas, for example. The quota for children of those in the military or veterans is the largest "exception." And the parallel system, the largest alternate admissions pathway, significantly advantages those with the financial resources to pay their way into particular majors. However, geographically based special admissions policies benefit students from around the country, many of whom have faced structural disadvantages, and reward the top performing students in every region of the country.[50]

For the young provincial women profiled in this book, who have been successful as students despite many educational disadvantages, these educational structures have created opportunities for access to higher education, as well as greater access to fields such as engineering and computer science. While not all of the women we spoke to were engineers or scientists, they prided themselves on their academic achievements. They came to Amman to pursue the opportunities that education could offer, and to seek ways to help support their families in projects of economic security if not upward mobility.

Women and Labor

As previously stated, Jordan has one of the world's lowest official rates of female labor force participation in the world despite relatively high rates of education for women. This apparent paradox has been a central focus of development policy in and for Jordan for decades, and concerns about low female labor participation have an even longer history.[51] At the same time, in recent years statistics show that male labor force participation rates have declined, and male unemployment has increased.[52] Women's relatively low labor force participation is often discussed without reference to male labor patterns, or the realities of the Jordanian labor market.

Despite a prevailing local narrative about the need for women to work, one that I heard constantly, a parallel discourse about men as the primary breadwinners was also predominant. This should not be surprising, given the longevity of the male breadwinner status in many societies.[53] Just as men are ideally breadwinners, taking care of home and children is still viewed as primarily women's responsibility in most of the world. Women who do work outside the home often face a "double burden," one that persists in the United States as well.[54] In large part because of the gendered division of labor in Jordan, married women are much less likely to work than their single counterparts. However, statistics about married women and labor do not sufficiently capture informal or seasonal work that women undertake. For example, research shows women are actively engaged in home-based businesses that they can manage while also taking care of other responsibilities.[55]

Exacerbating these cultural or ideational factors are the structural barriers that shape labor opportunities, as well as the increasing precariousness of new jobs—more temporary and with fewer benefits.[56] For example, the lack of quality childcare and limited public transportation both act as barriers to women's employment.[57] For women in the provinces, stable, full-time work has traditionally been in the public sector as there are few private sector opportunities outside the capital. The public sector has long been the more desirable place of employment for women, because of guaranteed maternity and family leave policies, as well as a schedule that offers greater compatibility with family life. Work in the public sector also offers greater stability and less discrimination, due to civil service guidelines that mitigate some of the workplace biases, in wages, for example. Thus, women's already low formal labor force participation has been more susceptible to the vagaries of structural adjustment policies and public sector cuts. However, even as overall labor force participation has decreased significantly in the past decade for men and women, the percentage of those employed in the public sector remains substantial.[58] Although barriers to private sector employment have been significant for women,[59] single university-educated women in urban centers are more likely to work in the private sector.[60] Reflecting this trend, the women profiled here are overwhelmingly employed in the private sector, and many talked about their migration in terms of limited employment opportunities in the governorates, especially in the private sector.

In a 2018 World Bank report entitled *Hashemite Kingdom of Jordan— Understanding How Gender Norms in MNA Impact Female Employment Outcomes*, the authors sought to understand reasons for gendered labor force patterns. A finding that the researchers considered most surprising was that Jordanian men and women assumed that many more women were working than was actually the case: "When participants were asked about percentage of women working, the majority of those interviewed gave a very high percentage of 70% on average."[61] This perception kept with what I had been hearing since I began ethnographic research on education, labor, and gender in Jordan in 2002. A common refrain I heard from men and women, high school students and parents, and others has been: "Nowadays, a man wants to marry a woman who works." This was typically explained in terms of the need for families to have two wage-earners in Jordan's current economic context. Yet, statistics still show low rates of female labor participation, and women who do work tend to drop out of the workforce after marrying, at least temporarily.

What is the source of this misperception about women's labor force participation? One answer may lie in how people understand and perceive work. I suspect Jordanians are accustomed to seeing women hard at work in ways not counted in statistical calculations of employment. For example, working at family-owned shops but not necessarily "full time," or in contract labor jobs like cooking, cleaning, tailoring, or child care.[62] In addition, because women are well represented in education and health sectors, most Jordanians will have interacted with formally employed women in one or another of these sectors throughout their lifetime. But perhaps most important is the overwhelming sense that life is too expensive and that a family could not possibly get by on one income. The assertion that a family cannot survive on one income reflects several decades of decreased investment in public services and the public service jobs that helped propel many educated families toward the middle class in earlier decades. It also led educated young parents, especially in Amman, to give up on public services like education and health care, and turn to private services in search of better quality. Of course, not all families have the financial means to do this, and many families are only able to do so by taking on a significant debt burden.[63]

The World Bank report constructs a dichotomy between broader structural barriers to employment (for instance, lack of child care or poor transportation) and the cultural norms the authors sought to measure—norms that, they state, impede the rational choice of women's entry into the workforce. In treating norms and structures as separate and unrelated phenomena, the report elides the ways they are co-constitutive of each other. For example, with respect to the beliefs of men and women about the appropriate age for a mother to leave a child in child care to pursue work outside the home, the report finds that "working women think the appropriate age is around 3.4 years on average, while for men with non-working spouses, the average is even higher at 5.2 years."[64] But this "norm" cannot be understood outside the context of a lack of quality child care options, or the reliance on female domestic labor from other countries (primarily from Asia at first, and increasingly from African countries; see below) to provide child care for the wealthier.[65] Furthermore, the bifurcation of norms and structures takes for granted universal grounds for economic action. In this sense culture, considered as norms or customs, is viewed as an impediment to the universal aims of all economic actors if they just could be freed from tradition.[66]

Perhaps even more striking in the discussion of barriers to female employment is the limited or nonexistent discussion of the types of jobs actually being created in Jordan—largely low-wage jobs filled by foreign migrant laborers who have limited rights and as a result are the workers of choice for owners of factories, construction companies, and agribusinesses who want to maximize profits.[67] Decisions, opportunities, and norms surrounding formal labor force participation cannot be understood without considering the lack of jobs overall, and particularly the kinds of jobs university-educated youth want. It also requires attention to geography, class, and wages, and how they shape perceptions about work for women and their families.[68] To reiterate, recent data show that Jordan's male labor force participation rates are among the lowest in the world as well, a fact that can hardly be irrelevant to the situation of women.[69] Key to these labor dynamics has been the movement of labor in and out of Jordan.

Migration and Displacement

Modern Jordan is a nation that has welcomed many migrants—those displaced by war, fleeing political persecution, or seeking economic opportunities in a new land. In the nineteenth century, the most significant influx was Circassian and Chechen refugees resettled by the Ottomans in and around Amman.[70] Armenians also resettled in Jordan after the Armenian genocide of 1915–17.[71] In the late nineteenth and early twentieth centuries, merchant families from Nablus, Hebron and Damascus settled in the Jordanian towns of Salt, Karak, Ajlun and eventually Amman seeking new economic opportunities.[72] In the early 1900s, Jordan was also a refuge for political dissidents from Syria and Lebanon—many of whom were among the first government ministers in the Emirate of Transjordan, eventually to be replaced by Palestinian officials more to the liking of the British.[73]

As outlined earlier, the creation of the state of Israel, the Palestinian Nakba, and the Israeli occupation of the West Bank, Gaza, and the Golan Heights in 1967 led to massive displacement of Palestinians.[74] Today more than 2 million registered Palestinian refugees (those expelled by Israel and their descendants) reside in Jordan.[75] The overwhelming majority of Palestinians in Jordan are Jordanian citizens.[76] The Gulf War of 1991 led to the expulsion of about 200,000 to 300,000 Jordanian migrant workers (most of Palestinian origin) from Kuwait to Jordan. The US invasion of Iraq in 2003 also resulted in 200,000–400,000 Iraqis fleeing war and instability.[77] As a result of the Syrian conflict, which began in 2011, nearly 1 million Syrians reside in Jordan, with about 670,000 registered as refugees.[78] All of these political events have shaped the Jordanian state's relatively short history, and migrants and the displaced have been central to the making of Jordan. While earlier groups were incorporated into the state as citizens, the state has taken a different stance toward refugees since 1967—those who came from Gaza and subsequent arrivals of large populations from Iraq and Syria, as well as some Palestinians who had citizenship when Jordan annexed the West Bank and subsequently lost it.[79]

In addition to taking in those forcibly displaced by conflict and political repression, Jordan has been a significant importer of migrant labor since the 1970s. These laborers were predominantly men, mainly from Egypt.[80] In the 1980s, Jordan saw an increase in the number of female nonnational migrant laborers, especially domestic workers/nannies coming primarily from Asia (initially from Sri Lanka and the Philippines).[81] The number of labor migrants has increased in recent decades, with female and male migrant workers from Asia employed in manufacturing. This development was in part driven by demand in new economic zones that were built in the 1990s and early 2000s. After Jordan signed a peace treaty with Israel, the US–Israel Free Trade Agreement (USIFTA) launched the Qualifying Industrial Zones (QIZs) initiative, which allowed Jordan to export items produced in the QIZs duty free to the United States, as long as a minimum of Israeli inputs was used.[82] In addition, migrant domestic workers have more recently come from Africa, with the largest numbers migrating from Ethiopia, and smaller numbers from Ghana, Uganda, and Kenya.[83]

At the same time as Jordan became a significant receiver of migrant laborers, Jordan was also becoming a major exporter of labor. Jordanians have a long history of migrating for labor. Earlier patterns of labor migration were often driven by poverty, and responded to demands for cheap labor in the ports and cities of surrounding countries. In the 1920s and 1930s, demand for labor in Palestine (especially in Haifa and Jaffa), as well as drought and decreased agricultural production, caused men to seek wage labor in Palestine.[84] Some went even farther. My own family history reflects this. My paternal grandfather went to Palestine to work in Haifa. His uncle did so as well, eventually marrying a Palestinian woman and settling near Nablus. My maternal great-grandfather went farther, joining thousands from Greater Syria in the migration to North America. He did not last long there, however, finding the climate in New York too cold and the work building roads not to his liking. At the same time, education drove others to move as well, making what Betty Anderson calls "educational pilgrimages"—seeking educational opportunities in other parts of the country (such as Hoda and Elias) or abroad.[85]

With time, it was the highly educated who came to dominate migration out of Jordan, primarily as professionals moving to the Arab Gulf. A growing demand in the Arab Gulf for professional labor led to significant increases in labor migration, which contributed to heavy reliance on remittances for Jordan's economic growth.[86] While migrants to the Gulf were primarily men, women did migrate to the Gulf for work, especially as teachers. Decreasing oil prices, the Iraqi invasion of Kuwait, and subsequent Gulf War led to a significant decrease in the numbers of migrants working in the Gulf, although numbers increased again in subsequent years, and remittances endured as an important source of income.[87] Labor migration in and out of Jordan is a key factor shaping labor market dynamics today.

HISTORIES OF FEMALE MIGRATION

My mother told me that her favorite teacher was a young woman named Sarah. Sarah was a single woman who came to my mother's village of Ajloun in the 1960s to teach in the local school for girls. Many women of my mother's generation spoke fondly of such teachers—women who had been educated in the teachers' colleges in Jordan or the West Bank [Palestine]. Balqis told me about two sisters from Salt, who together traveled to the south to teach in Maan—how they had had a hand in teaching a generation.[88]

AUTHOR'S FIELD NOTES

Mainstream literature about women and development in Jordan represents women as constrained, immobile, and utterly dependent on male relatives. Their migration is impossible to imagine, even though migration has long been part of the story of women's education and labor in Jordan. As the epigraph above indicates, there have long been women who relocated for work (both to and from Jordan), and in the case of teachers in the early years of the establishment of Jordan, to help educate youth of the newly constructed nation.[89]

In the early years of public education in Jordan, teachers from around the Arab world were critical for staffing. According to a historical guide published in 2016 entitled *The First Hundred Teachers*, many of these first teachers, including several of the country's first female teachers, came from outside Jordan (for example, from Syria, Palestine, and Lebanon).[90] The 1950s saw a rapid expansion of public education. That expansion, especially in rural areas, relied heavily on the availability of Palestinian teachers, male and female, as well as smaller numbers of teachers from other parts of Jordan.[91] The demand for teachers persisted, and with time these teachers could be found within Jordan. Women whom we interviewed about those early years were often the first in their families to finish secondary school and might support younger siblings in doing so as well. They reported that their first assignments were typically to remote villages with limited transportation, requiring them to take up residence in those villages. Najwa's (b. 1961) first appointment, in the late 1960s, was to a village near the Syrian border:

> After *tawjihi* I looked for work. In those days you needed to find work. You didn't need college education. I went to the Ministry of Education and said I need a job. I was appointed and went to work near the Syrian border. They said I had to go to this village. Everyone supported me. My mother, my siblings, and my brother-in-law who would sometimes drive me. There was no transportation, only a car (Rover) that went weekly to Irbid. It was an unpaved road and very difficult to get to the village, but the people in the village were very nice. They welcomed us and there was a big feast with animals slaughtered and members of the community recited poetry in our honor.

Some teachers, male and female, went abroad to teach in other Arab countries, mostly in the Arab Gulf countries. An older woman we interviewed went to Algeria as a young teacher to help in postcolonial Arabization efforts. The Jordan Ministry of Education maintained a policy of sending educators to Arab Gulf countries, with the majority going to Kuwait.[92] Batool spoke with us about her mother (born in 1931), who, after finishing her training in Palestine, went to work as a teacher in Kuwait in the 1950s:

Both of my parents sacrificed a lot for the others. Around that time many women left home to work in Kuwait. Even my mother and her sister, both of whom went there to work and used their salaries to pay for their brothers' college tuition. Later, my aunt got a master's degree in Arabic. My father's case was also similar. After what happened in 1948 [al Nakba], he went to Kuwait to work with my grandfather and spent his money on his siblings' education.

When my mother went to teach in Kuwait, she was young. She studied at a teacher's college in Tulkarm and then she was off to Kuwait in 1950. She lived in the female teachers' housing. I remember my mother telling me that when she arrived in Kuwait, she was met at the airport by a Kuwaiti family who took her to the teacher housing. Things were simpler then, and Kuwait itself was much smaller. At the time, Kuwait had a need for all kinds of professionals from around the Arab world like doctors, engineers, and especially teachers.

Several researchers have highlighted the migration of women like Batool's mother, especially Palestinian women, to the Arab Gulf countries as teachers.[93] Ian Seccombe reports that 2,330 Jordanian teachers were seconded to Arab Gulf countries in 1983, although it is unclear how many of them were female.[94] While there is a history of female migration for work, more recent cases, examined at length in this book, are distinct.

THE INTERNAL MIGRATION OF WOMEN TODAY

Until the 1980s, women's migration was largely ignored in the prevailing literature.[95] Most of the migration literature focused on international migration, and initially viewed women as accidental migrants, traveling with their spouses but not necessarily for labor.[96] In the last two decades, scholars of migration have paid greater attention to gendered patterns of migration and the unique insights that a critical feminist approach can bring to understanding the multiscalar social and political effects of migration.[97] Furthermore, recent studies have shown that the reasons for migration are diverse, that goals may shift over time, and that female migration does not always fit neatly into a migration discourse with masculinized assumptions.[98] Understanding *internal* migration and the ways in which it is gendered poses its own set of methodological challenges.[99] A robust ethnographic literature on rural-to-urban migration of women in Asian countries has made critical inroads into better understanding the gendered dimensions of migration.[100]

The literature on female migration in the Middle East is limited for many of the same reasons. Much of the existing literature is focused on the experiences of female migration into the region, especially among domestic workers,[101] or women who are left behind when men migrate for extended periods of time.[102] With respect to international migration among Jordanian women, there is some evidence that professional women continue migrating to the Gulf for work with their families or on their own.[103] In the course of my research for this project, as well as my ongoing connections and research in Jordan, I have come to know several single women who worked in the Gulf (in technology, consulting, education, and health, among other fields), or had worked in an Arab Gulf country for a time. Research on female migration from Palestine and North Africa has also pointed to this phenomenon.[104]

MIGRATION AND GHURBA

A *mughtarib* is somebody who lives in *ghurba*, which means the sense of being abroad in a strange place among strangers, separated from the familial connections and safety of home . . . One can live in *ghurba* for decades and never feel that the place one inhabits is home.

SAMULI SCHIELKE, *Migrant Dreams*[105]

With respect to previous migration of women, the path of those who have moved to Amman in recent decades is unique in several respects. Many of them come from rural communities, where women's relocation for work was not the norm. And rather than making a temporary migration to a rural placement required by the Ministry of Education, these women have moved to urban centers seeking a life shift—both professional and social—that for many becomes permanent as they settle in the capital city. Unlike their predecessors, they are also much more on their own in a major metropolis that in many respects feels very foreign to them at first.

Despite the qualitatively distinct nature of their migration to Amman, none of the women we spoke with used the word "migration" (*hijra*) to describe their move to Amman (nor did the research team). Rather, they used terms such *intiqal* or *raheel* (moving) to describe their move. In part, this may be explained by the many foreign migrant laborers in Jordan who (especially the women) are a distinct and racialized other in the Jordanian context, as well as the many Jordanians who migrate abroad for work. As Samuli Schielke points out, *hijra* also implies that one is settling permanently elsewhere.[106] Schielke argues that the term *mughtarib* is a more apt description of the migrations of Egyptian men to the Arab Gulf as laborers, because of the perpetual feeling of being among strangers (and being a stranger) and the assumption of temporariness, however long one's stay.[107]

The term *ghurba* emerged in some of our discussions—both explicitly and implicitly. Um Wijdan, a mother from a town in the south, whom we will meet in interlude 4, talks about her concern for her daughter in *al ghurba*—away from the care and support of family and community living in Amman. This may sound strange, as the distances are relatively short (relative to those traversing national borders, for example) and Amman is after all the capital of Jordan. One way we can understand it is to think about the distance traversed when a person leaves a small, rural community where they are known, and ostensibly protected (or monitored or both) by their community, for a big city away from their connections. Thus, where they left from (how rural, how distant, how seemingly underdeveloped or underresourced) could exacerbate the feeling of strangeness. Yet, even those who came from relatively nearby provincial cities might find that Amman feels like a "foreign country" at first, until they acclimate and begin to make a place for themselves. Some are more easily able to make that shift, depending on class, social capital, and fortunes in the city.

I began to refer to the experiences described in this book as "migration" when I presented the results of my research to various audiences. The term "internal labor migration" put them into a category that made sense to my colleagues. Stephen Castles makes the case for using the term "migration" rather than "mobility": he argues that "mobility," and the borderlessness it implies, assumes a degree of freedom that most migrants do not actually have and that "the right to be mobile is more class-specific and selective than ever."[108] He advocates for the continued use of "migration" as a concept that "better reflects real power relations" that shape both international and internal migrations through the policing of borders.[109] I have chosen to use the term here as well because it does the work of illuminating social transformations that are under way, and the power struggles that can ensue in the process. While these women do not traverse political borders that require them to negotiate citizenship and nationality, they are crossing symbolic and material borders in their movement. In this sense, they are contending with the meaning of their citizenship, as the terms of citizenship are always gendered.[110] The concept of mobility remains important, as it is central to the ways in which women's work, and their oppression, is discussed in policy literature. I elaborate further on both of these concepts—migration and mobility—in the remaining chapters. The migration of the women profiled in this book is both a product and an ongoing process of movement as they work to forge a future and make a place and space for themselves in Amman.

Conclusion

This chapter has contextualized the contemporary labor migration of women in Jordan in a longer history of state-building. Migration and displacement have been central to this history all along. In this sense, the migration of women today from the provinces to Amman in search of opportunity is part of an ongoing history of power, politics, and movement. These contemporary migrations are also a product of the decades-long project to expand formal education throughout the country, and the economic transformations that have coincided with this educational expansion. These forces have contributed to a particular view of what education is for, and what an educated person can, if not must, achieve. It is to these views and narratives about the future I turn in the next chapter.

Buthayna

We interviewed Buthayna in 2013. At the time, she was twenty-seven years old and working as a computer networker. She had been in Amman for five years already when we spoke. Buthayna, who was from village in the south, obtained her bachelor's degree from a public university in the south and lived in dormitories throughout her undergraduate education because the university was more than two hours away. Her parents were largely supportive of her move. Her mother had attended community college and worked as a secretary, while her father had not completed high school. She has four younger brothers and an older sister who is married.

I came from a village in the south. I worked very briefly at a bank in the town near my home, but I left once I found an opportunity in Amman that was more suitable to my training. I have been working at my current job for five years now. I started as a trainee and now I am a senior officer. I left the original job because my current job is closer to what I studied, and I wanted to start on my master's degree. I did my master's degree while working and I finished in 2011.

Everyone in the family was supportive of my move. My mom and I actually came up with the idea of finding a job so I could also pursue a master's degree, and my siblings were happy for me. I came because I wanted to study and be special. Everyone had a bachelor's, and I didn't want to be like the rest of the people. I wanted to do better. I would have gone on for a PhD if there was a program in Jordan, but there aren't any in my field, and my parents would not support me going overseas for this purpose.

The move to Amman and away from my family did not represent a significant change for me, because I had already been living on my own since I was eighteen in dormitories, but work was a bit more challenging. To be honest, I had a hard time in the beginning. The first six months I didn't know how to talk and to give and take with people . . . I would wait until someone gave me work to do, otherwise I was just sitting there. But little by little, I got to know my way.

Professionally there is more competition in Amman and you feel that your skills are constantly being tested. So, I keep pushing harder. At times I get discouraged and I want to give up. Then I get back up. I am a systems administrator and on the professional front I feel that I am gaining good experience. But now I want to look for different experiences and I am applying for some positions.

Buthayna discussed what is needed to succeed in Amman—pointing out that not all young women have what it takes:

Look, a girl's experience depends on her upbringing. There are people who are very sheltered, and once they get to Amman, they go wild and things don't go well for them. Others, are just slow to learn and don't know how to sort things out for themselves, so they go back because they fail. Maybe they couldn't overcome the move emotionally or they failed financially. If a girl doesn't have a strong personality, then every time she sees someone wearing name brands, she wants to imitate them. "If you imitate, then things won't work out for you, darling, your salary will fly out the window." I started with a salary of less than 300 dinars, but I made it work.

Also, girls can be taken advantage of because of their naivete. You'll find a lot of guys here are sweet-talkers who are worth nothing, but they are good at talking. "Go sell that talk to someone else." So, honestly, I don't think I would send my own daughters to live here in the dormitories. Yet, I won't go back, because I want to work. I can't sit at home. In the governorates, there aren't employment opportunities, so a girl will have to sit at home, and if the girl sits at home in our communities no one looks at her. Because the guys don't have money, and so they want a girl that works to help them in life. They tell girls, Go work, move around, do something, see something and be seen. If she sits at home, they say *hweneh* [too bad, what a loss].

I am able to take care of myself. I have a good savings account and I am fortunate financially. Thankfully, I don't need help from my parents. I like to buy gifts for my siblings on special occasions. Sometimes, I'll buy groceries or supplies for the house when I go home. And when I go home, I feel respected. They like hearing what I have to say, because it's new . . . outside their environment, especially my younger brothers. As for the community I don't know if they value my experience. Look, if you are going to wait for them to value you, then they won't. But you make yourself valuable, and they will value you.

I asked Buthayna, beyond her professional life, what her experience was like in Amman.

When I first came to Amman, I lived with some relatives for three months. I also rented an apartment with six other women for a while, but we had issues with the landlord, and bills weren't getting paid. So, things fell apart. I moved to a dormitory close to my job, and I have lived here for three years. But I feel like people think, because I am away from my parents and living in housing/a dorm, then I am an "easy" girl. So, I am careful about what I say at work. I try hard all the time to tell my friends at the bank that I come back to the house at 9:00 p.m. and don't stay out any later than that. So they don't think otherwise. Because it sticks in their mind, even though they are from Amman, and modern, and all these things, they always think that because she lives in housing and her parents aren't around, she can do whatever she wants. But I don't care.

Migration, Agency, and Aspiration

It was my idea to come to Amman. I came up with this idea because I've always considered myself a person—not out of arrogance, God forbid—but a person who always strives to do something better. This was reflected in my upbringing. My family never accepted anything other than the best from me. Ever since I was young, my father made me feel special because I was a good student. In fact, from among all of my siblings, only I and one other sister graduated from university. Since high school, I worked hard to get into university, so it would have been impossible for me to end this journey by sitting at home. My family saw how hard I worked in order to reach a certain point. I think they gave me this chance in order to see what I am capable of reaching or to allow me a small window to escape to the outside world. There is a large generational gap between us, and my life as a young girl living on a farm distant from the world was difficult. There weren't any daily enjoyments or activities that I could keep myself busy with. My parents felt this. And there was no financial motivation, because they never relied on me or were in need of my financial help. They never asked for anything.

ABEER, twenty-four-year-old engineer

My main objective [in coming to Amman] is that I have planned out a certain track for myself in my head. And this does not have to do with my marital life or whether I will be in a relationship or not; this is a track that I have set for myself to achieve. And for me to achieve this objective, I have to secure myself financially as an initial step. My main goal isn't to become rich or buy a fancy car, my main goal is to satisfy myself financially in order to move forward and do other things. Everyone has their own financial comfort level that has to be met, and we cannot keep taking money from our parents forever.

NOOR, twenty-eight-year-old engineer

Abeer's comments about coming to Amman capture many of the sentiments expressed by the young women interviewed for this book. She conveyed confidence and a sense of accomplishment as a student, which she believed entitled her to a chance to pursue her goals. Fulfilling her aspirations required her to work, and the only feasible way she could work was to migrate far from home to pursue career opportunities in Amman. Abeer characterized her move as an escape from a small village to the "outside world." Most women did *not* characterize their journey in these terms, but for Abeer—the youngest of six children, all of whom were married, and whose parents were elderly—life on a farm in a small village was particularly constraining, and her parents sympathized with this reality. Thus, she depicted her move to Amman as an escape.

In this chapter, I focus on the stories women tell about why they migrated and what made migration both possible and imperative for them. Almost without exception, their narratives of migration center their identities as educated women with professional aspirations—aspirations that, as they envision it, can only be met in Amman.[1] Like Noor, some also framed their migration as a need for financial independence and autonomy that city living would provide, although many struggled financially in Amman. While this chapter features narratives of academic success and resulting aspirations, the women profiled seek opportunities in a landscape of structural change and cultural transformation that can be difficult to navigate. Despite, or perhaps because of, high unemployment and a difficult economic situation, they set their sights on moving to Amman for better opportunities.

In chapter 1, I detailed the institutional and structural factors that form the historical context for women's labor migration today. Here, I center my interlocutors' narratives of why and how they left home. Their own agency is central to these narratives. It is reflected in educational success, past achievements that they reference in plans for the future, and determination in convincing family members of the necessity and desirability of migration for work. It is equally apparent in their strong sense of obligation and responsibility to family, as we heard from Rania and Jihan in the opening pages of the book. It is clear in their persistence despite obstacles they face at home and in Amman. It is revealed in their ability to translate these new aspirations and opportunities to others, making different potential futures legible to their loved ones and marking alternative pathways for women in their communities. And, as we shall see in the following pages, it is apparent in their insistence upon aspiring to, planning for, and pursuing a future they believe they ought to have.

Narrative is a distinct method: asking interlocutors to narrate a past inevitably invites them to present a past colored by the present and future, as well as by interactions with researchers. Narrative is also about authoring one's story to achieve a fitting ending. It is a form of "self-interpretation" critical to creative agency; paying attention to such processes of subject formation is essential to explaining how "individuals may respond in unexpected and innovative ways that may hinder, reinforce or catalyse social change."[2] Of course, these processes are never unbounded, as one's experience of time and efficacy is always shaped by power: telling a particular narrative and writing a particular story for oneself is always conditioned by structural constraints. Furthermore, the questions we asked and the assumptions we inevitably brought to the process prompted particular forms of self-reflection that also shaped these women's stories.

A key theme that undergirds their narratives is using their education in ways befitting their past efforts and future aspirations (*tumuhat*), a future they seek to fashion through migration. Education generates expectations— the belief that one has a right to pursue particular futures.[3] Nearly all the women frame their story of success as one that begins with educational achievement but cannot end there. In their telling, they must leave their natal homes to seek better opportunities in Amman—to build a better future. This is about a lack of jobs in the provinces, or a lack of suitable jobs. "Suitable" is defined by them as jobs meeting their professional aspirations with room for professional growth. Many women argued that such jobs could not be found in the public sector (the dominant sector in the governorates), so they sought private sector opportunities in Amman. Some women also framed the move to Amman as more than a matter of jobs: it was also about city living, and the opportunities for personal and professional growth that living in a city could provide.

These narratives cannot be understood without attention to neoliberalism and a longer history of defining valuable work in gendered terms. Structural adjustment and neoliberal economic policies have been the primary paradigm driving economic policy and discourses surrounding labor, unemployment, and economic growth in Jordan for more than three decades. Colin Powers argues that Jordanian elites have embraced neoliberal policies leading to a "policy convergence" around economic policies since the 1990s, with little divergence from the agendas of international financial institutions, while also reproducing cultural logics that explain the failure of these policies.[4] In other words, when these economic policies fail, the blame is cast on the people and their culture, not on the policies themselves.[5] Inseparable from these economic policies is a view of the appropriate neoliberal subject that must be cultivated in Jordan, as elsewhere—self-reliant, productive, and entrepreneurial. It is no exaggeration to say that this discourse permeates nearly every policy space in Jordan, as well as educational institutions and the aid-driven NGO world of workshops and trainings. Thus, it is no surprise that it also colors the narratives of many of these young women in distinct ways.

While the power of these policies and attendant ideology is hegemonic, it is regularly resisted through open protest against extractive policies, inequality, and elite corruption enabled by such policies.[6] At the same time, despite its hegemonic status, and as many scholars have argued, "neoliberalism as an ethos of self-governing, encounters and articulates other ethical regimes in particular contexts."[7] In other words, neoliberalism is shaped by the specificities of social relations in particular contexts: we see this clearly in the experiences of women portrayed in this book.[8]

Visions of a future shaped in part by promises of neoliberal opportunity are what lead many young women to move to Amman. Yet, while the women's aspirations for and definitions of success at times echo neoliberal discourses, they are equally shaped by particular family histories, social relations, and obligations.[9] Their move is also a response to neoliberal economic policies that have contributed to the increased marginalization of the provinces. It is their intimate knowledge of this marginalization and its gendered effects that drives women to seek opportunities elsewhere.

Not Wasting My Education

I had struggled for four years and lived away from home in order to gain a degree, and it wasn't so I can put it up on a wall and then wait for someone to come marry me and not use it. Since I worked hard, I wanted to do something for myself.

RUWEIDA, thirty-year-old in media and journalism

The economic participation of women contributes to raising the domestic product, providing a better life for her and her family, and is an important component of the progress of societies and the fight against poverty, especially in the governorates. Women's going out to work is no longer a "right" for them, but rather an economic necessity in building societies.

MUSA AL-SAKAT, "Empowering Women . . . Economically"[10]

The word waste is hard and heavy. To waste can also mean not to make use of what you have been given.

SARA AHMED, What's the Use? On the Uses of Use[11]

As Ruweida articulates in the first epigraph above, she worked hard for her educational success, leaving her family in order to pursue an education in another province, hours away from home. While this was not unheard of for students of her generation, in Ruweida's case, neither of her parents had much formal education and no university education, so her enrollment in university and move to another city to live and study was a big change for her family. That experience left Ruweida determined to make use of her education.

Young women spoke about the importance of not wasting their education or not having all their efforts studying go for naught. Like Ruweida, they felt it was not enough just to have a diploma to "hang on the wall," and insisted on forging a future that their education required. They spoke about the efforts they had expended to succeed as students at university, and earlier in school, and the type of life to which this entitled them. However, the notion of "not wasting one's education" or not missing opportunities is not just individualistic; it forms part of a complex calculus that considers how family, friends, and society more broadly view and value individuals and their labor. It is also ultimately about the role educated women want to have in shaping their communities, and in enhancing the status of their birth families now, and their own families in the future.

Notions of waste and use are historical and gendered. Ruweida captures both the relational nature of value and how notions of value and productivity have shifted over time:

> An employed woman in the community, despite everything, is seen in a different light. She's not seen as merely a consumer but a producer. And in people's perspectives, a producer is always different from just a consumer. From the beginning, I have refused to be merely a consumer, somebody who does not produce anything. Otherwise, I would be a heavy load on whomever I live with, whether it's my father or husband or anyone. Therefore, I refuse this [status], and as long as I produce, people will view me differently. Even if I am not doing well financially and my salary is not enough, people still see you and say, "She's receiving a salary," and that means that you are capable of doing this or that . . . you are capable of doing things. You are valued in the eyes of others, and this perspective empowers you because you want to be seen in a better light.

Speaking about the notion of use and waste, Sara Ahmed argues that "disuse becomes degeneracy when something is not being used that is supposed to be used. It is this 'supposed to' that renders useful a morally weighted term even when it appears to be neutral or at least just a matter of what happens."[12] Ruweida conveys this moral weight—a sentiment that she has internalized about the need to be productive lest she be viewed as someone who wastes or is a waste—someone who is not doing what she is supposed to do.

Ideas about work, labor, and productivity are deeply gendered, shaped by a modern history of capitalist and colonial transformations, as well as more recent neoliberal economic interventions. Ruweida comes from a village in the south. Up until at least the mid-twentieth century, the overwhelming majority of families (women, men, and children) in communities such as hers would have been engaged in subsistence agriculture and/or pastoralism, with some family members engaged in waged labor. Ruweida's categorization of women outside the labor force as not productive is ahistorical, but reflective of how contemporary narratives about the past sometimes erase realities that do not fit into contemporary categories and value hierarchies.[13] In this case, it reflects contemporary views of domestic or reproductive work as not really work.

Throughout the region, deepening incorporation of countries into the global capitalist system and increased reliance on waged labor significantly changed how societies defined work and economic activity, and the value placed upon different forms of labor.[14] These processes were profoundly gendered and led to the demarcation of women's labor as not work but merely domestic and reproductive activity. Feminist scholarship has long challenged this binary—the delineation of reproductive work as private and domestic, and waged labor as productive and public—arguing that reproductive work is critical labor, and that the boundary between reproductive and productive work is blurry at best.[15] It is particularly ironic to think about the novelty and constructed nature of these categories in a context where women's domestic work produced the basic essentials for survival of the family only a few decades ago and where the shift to complete dependence on wages is relatively new.

I suspect that there is something else involved in the gendering of work and productivity in some of the migration narratives. Women did not reference their mothers, aunts, or grandmothers in reflections on wasted potential, but rather their peers, and specifically their educated peers.[16] Several women specially distinguished themselves from peers or siblings who, upon finishing their education, "just sat at home." Single female peers and relatives were often engaged in labor in their homes, such as caring for members of their family, including sick or elderly parents, younger siblings, and nieces and nephews. So, in most cases, they were not "just sitting at home." But the notion of being "useful" or "productive" here is very much shaped by the expectations created by education, and by neoliberal policies that equate value with narrowly defined economic contributions. Ideas about valuable labor have been shaped by decades of defining women's nonwaged labor in all its varieties as nonproductive, even when it is critical to family survival.

In recent decades, neoliberal economic reforms and an attendant neoliberal ideology have also led to a focus on individual productivity and responsibility.[17] In a context of high unemployment and stagnant economic growth, individuals are encouraged by local and global policy makers to find their own solutions—to produce the jobs that are needed—rather than waiting for a public sector job. Young people are repeatedly told they must take risks, fail, innovate, and not wait around for someone else to solve their problems.[18] This neoliberal discourse seeks to shift responsibility from the state onto the individual despite the structural limitations that render it increasingly difficult to make a living. International education development policy and discourse have closely mirrored these shifts, as individual "rates of return" and employment have become synonymous with educational value.[19]

For more than two decades, development discourse has framed Jordanian women's education as paradoxical, because not enough women are employed outside the home.[20] This discourse has roots in a human capital view of development, which assesses investments in education in terms of growth of

GDP or rates of return to individuals in future earnings. This discourse is ubiquitous in discussions about education and labor in Jordan.[21] While not synonymous with the aspirations and yearnings of these young women, the discourse surrounding wasted education provides an important context. Low numbers of women in the labor force are often framed by policy makers as an economic inefficiency—because the resources invested in their education have gone to waste, and because of the lost potential for economic growth.[22] International organizations regularly frame low rates of female labor participation in terms of lost GDP potential.[23] Even in the United States, where we find significantly higher rates of female labor force participation, such gendered discourse of education, value, and waste prevails. For example, when Joni Hersch found that women with MBAs from elite institutions are 30 percent less likely to be in the workforce than their counterparts at nonelite universities, some commentators wondered whether elite education was wasted on these women, while others took issue with such a characterization.[24] Linda Hirshman's *Get to Work . . . and Get a Life, Before It's Too Late* created quite a stir when she argued that women were wasting their potential being stay-at-home mothers and housewives.[25] The notion of "waste" associated with educated women staying at home has been both fundamentally interrogated, and simultaneously reinforced by the COVID-19 pandemic, as the critical importance and economic "value" of domestic labor has become abundantly clear.[26] At the same time, the sudden acknowledgment of domestic labor's worth was short-lived and overshadowed by concerns about the "real crisis" of women leaving the workforce. This is not to deny that women leaving the workforce is a source of concern, but rather to point to the ways in which other forms of labor necessary for the survival of families are so quickly delinked from issues of formal waged labor.

While the narratives of women we spoke with often drew on the language of wasted potential, their sense of use and waste was nuanced—embedded in their own experiences and awareness of the structures that shaped what was possible for them. At the same time, a call to being useful can be a call to action. As Ahmed argues, "to be useful can be a way of addressing a world . . . that faces many directions . . . [and] that can animate a life, too."[27] I understand this to mean in part the undetermined or unexpected "use" of their education, or the ways in which these young women are animated to move through the world in unexpected ways and with unexpected outcomes. What they valued and aspired to changed over time in response to their experiences after moving to Amman—an assessment and reassessment of the possible and desirable, as well as the changing desires and needs of their family members, and their evolving relationship to family. As Joan DeJaeghere contends, drawing on her research with Tanzanian women, aspirations and agency are closely linked, forming a dialectical relationship, in which the ability to see a way forward is intimately tied to opportunities for action and agency that in turn inform future aspirations.[28]

Neoliberal policies and ideology are powerful constitutive structures, which have in many ways propelled women forward, even as these policies also create barriers to fulfilling their aspirations. Women mobilize some of the terms of this ideology to make things happen for themselves and their families. The desire to be "productive" or to succeed professionally is about proving themselves to their families and about forging a potentially different future in the gendered uncertainty produced by social and economic changes.[29] In the process they are contributing to shaping what these futures may be.

Education's Future: Aspirations and Agency

Every person struggles to achieve a certain something in their life. So, my goal might have been to realize my dream and see the fruits of my hard work and studies. The objective that I struggled to achieve this whole time was independence and some liberty . . . To live on my own and to prove myself.

HANNAN, twenty-five-year-old in media

In their volume *Anthropology of the Future*, Rebecca Bryant and Daniel M. Knight distinguish between the "ought" of promise and the "ought" of potential: "expectation does not contain the same sense (i.e., as anticipation) of the future pulling me forward. Rather it awakens a sense of how things *ought* to be given particular conditions."[30] In narrating the "why" of migration women drew on both senses of "ought." Their education meant that working was possible (potential), but their narratives conveyed a strong sense of what "ought to happen" (promise)—something to which they had a right. Abeer captures this well in the first epigraph to this chapter when she says, "No one ever told me to come here or gave me the initial idea that led me to think about moving to Amman. I got this idea because I've always considered myself a person—not out of arrogance, God forbid—but a person who always strives to do something better." She goes on to say, "I worked hard to get into university so it would have been impossible for me to end this journey and sit at home." Abeer's comments capture both sides of "ought." She studied hard so she could not end her journey at home—and education meant that she should not just "sit at home." At the same time, her expectations were tied up with her view of herself and her potential as a person who "strives to do something better" or, as Hannan says in the epigraph to this section, "to achieve a certain something in their life." Professional aspirations are imbricated with the personal and moral—as one woman put it, "being who I was meant to be." The "ought" of promise means orienting oneself to the future rather than just feeling a sense of possibility. It's what one does to pursue that possibility.

Gowri Vijayakumar frames aspiration as a "gendered symbolic resource."[31] She argues that the "flexible aspirations" of her lower-middle-class interlocutors in India account for the unpredictability of their futures and the realization that the future is not completely in their hands, given the realities of patriarchal marriage. At the same time, she posits that "even if the future holds uncertainty, the act of aspiring itself can help produce gendered class distinction in this small-town setting."[32] In Jordan, many of the women we spoke with were quite explicit about their own sense of distinction as women not willing to settle for sitting at home, for mediocre jobs, or for marriages that were less than they expected. They believed that this distinguished them from their peers who did not have the same aspirations. At the same time, they recognized that many of their peers faced significant obstacles due to patriarchal norms and economic barriers that not everyone could surmount, and they were met with their own challenges once they moved to Amman.

For our interlocutors, women who migrated for work, it was clear that aspirations could not be fulfilled at home—aspiring required pursuing opportunities elsewhere. They gave many reasons for the need to relocate. First was the lack of jobs: some women had no professional opportunities in their home community, so that staying there meant "just sitting at home," a fate they refused to accept. Comments about "just sitting at home" conveyed a sense of time-passing or waiting, a way of conceptualizing prolonged youth in social science literature, which has tended to focus on young men.[33] Women who experienced a period of unemployment expressed most strongly the fear of sitting at home. Describing a period of eight months in which she had been unemployed between jobs, Noor said, "Sitting at home took a huge psychological toll on me. I felt empty. All I could do was eat, drink and sleep." Ruweida, whom we have heard saying she did not study at university so she could just hang her diploma on the wall, described a period in which she had to return home because she was unemployed. She describes being depressed during that time and driving her family crazy:

> Sometimes I miss my family, or I am having a bad day and I might get the feeling that I want to go back home. But just for quick passing moments, and this thought quickly fades away because then I start thinking about sitting at home, which means that you lose your sense of worth, especially because

you've tried it [working and living in Amman] and you know what you're
capable of. If I hadn't had this experience already, then maybe I would have
just accepted the situation I found myself in. I was unemployed at my parents'
house for a whole year. That year was a disaster for my parents, and that's why
they let me do what I wanted. I would cry to them every day, all day. I would
annoy them all day, telling them over and over, "I will not sit in the house. I
will die here. I have energy that I need to release."

A refusal to "sit at home" propelled women to forge a different path. They
were not willing to wait for something to happen, but insisted on taking steps
toward a future they wanted and believed ought to be. Staying in home communities was a barrier to the types of self-fulfillment they sought and the
aspirations they held, because of limited economic opportunities, as well as
the spatial constraints of provincial living.

The problem of sitting at home could be compounded by the isolation
they felt if they lived in villages and small towns far from any urban centers
(for example, Abeer lived on a farm from which even the nearest provincial
town was not easily accessible). Even women from communities that were
geographically closer or relatively large argued that these places were professionally and socially limiting. Thus, women from Irbid—a city whose population is estimated to be about 600,000 (with more than 2 million people in
the governorate), but which had been a small town with a public university in
the 1990s—talked about the need to move to Amman for greater professional
opportunity, emphasizing the ways in which Amman's professional environment was different or better, especially for a woman. These assessments reflect the ways in which gender, class, and geography are imbricated in capital-
centric economic development in Jordan. Amman provided not only jobs,
but also the possibility of upward mobility and an urban style of life.

Even when jobs were available, many women described these employment opportunities as unfit for them and the professional lives to which they
aspired. Given that the overwhelming majority of jobs available in the provinces are in the public sector, and for women primarily in the public education sector, women's dissatisfaction with job opportunities available in the
provinces was also explicitly a critique of the public sector.[34] Several women
stated expressly that they did not want to work in the public sector. Abeer
elaborated in her interview:

The types of opportunities in the governorates are really bad. Employment is
very limited there; jobs are limited to the public sector. Families are reassured
in regard to the public sector because of the job security, but we all know what
the environment of the governorates is like and what the limitations are. So,

if you want to work, you can either work in education as a teacher, or for the municipality. When we're talking about someone who has graduated with an engineering degree . . . I don't want to judge, but we all know the nature of governmental employees. A person who works in this sector will feel that their opportunities to grow and advance are minimal. They feel as though they are cogs in a machine that come and do the same task every day and go home. That is, if there are any tasks at all. I feel that the private sector can open up doors for professional growth and improvement.

Abeer expounds at length about the professional deprivation of work in the public sector, especially in the governorates. She emphasizes that, particularly for engineers, the public sector is an unbecoming fate. Women in fields like computing and engineering argued that the professionally rewarding and lucrative jobs were to be found in Amman (or in the Arab Gulf countries) and tended to be concentrated in the private sector. Here again we see how assessments of value and waste colored the aspirations of these young women. Just as not working is a waste of one's education, working in the public sector is conceptualized as a potential waste of one's professional potential. They aspired to something different.

The characterization of the public sector as bloated or stagnant is a powerful dimension of neoliberal ideology, and the need to shrink the public sector has been a key tenet of neoliberal economic policies since the 1980s.[35] At the same time, neoliberal economic policies have significantly weakened the public sector. Thus, the rejection of the public sector as a viable option for a woman with aspirations echoes this neoliberal tenet and reflects the reality of depreciated wages and fewer employment options in the public sector, even if, in practice, the majority of educated women (and men) end up in the public sector.[36] An examination of broader labor patterns shows that where men and women work varies significantly by level of education, marriage status, geography, and citizenship status.[37] Women with little to no education are overwhelmingly in the private sector, reflecting the sector's informality in Jordan and the preponderance of low-wage, precarious jobs not requiring high levels of education.[38] However, *single* university-educated women are more likely to be in the private sector (in addition to being much more likely to be in the labor force) than married women. Life course matters here, as women in the public sector are more likely to stay in the workforce after marrying, and there is some evidence of movement from the private to the public sector after women marry.[39] The public sector offers shorter work hours and guaranteed maternity leave, and is in many respects much more accommodating of work/home life balance. It provides a more appealing alternative to young families, and especially mothers, who still bear the majority of the responsibility for care of children and the home.

While many women we spoke with sought what they viewed as qualitatively better opportunities in the private sector, they struggled to make ends meet once they got to Amman (see chapter 3). Real wages have stagnated in the private sector since 2009, and by 2019, wages were significantly higher in the public sector.[40] Nevertheless, many of the young women we spoke with were convinced that their professional aspirations could only be met in the private sector. Indeed, the majority of the women we interviewed worked in the private sector, in keeping with the trends for single university-educated women. The move to Amman, then, was motivated both by the lack of public sector opportunities at home and the perception that there might be more and better opportunities in the private sector in Amman.

While women characterized work in the public sector as professionally limiting, they also spoke more broadly about the environment for women in the workplace and in their communities. For some women, especially those who had already lived in Amman, the prospects of greater mobility within the city of Amman were appealing due to the substantive differences in the spatial configuration of leisure spaces in the provinces, and greater access for women to these spaces in Amman. Amman also provided some anonymity, which also facilitated mobility and autonomy in their everyday lives. This could be a motivating factor for seeking out opportunities in the capital, but nonetheless, being independent in Amman could be a lonely life. At home, at least they had family, and social life is still so family-centered in Jordan that women missed these connections in Amman. In addition, though presumably more spaces were accessible to them as women in Amman, they were also limited in how often and where they could go out because of money, and class or moral sensibilities about appropriate places.

In interlude 2, Buthayna points to other opportunities she hoped to pursue in Amman, namely, further education. She was not alone in pursuing multiple goals with her migration to Amman. Wijdan initially took a leave of absence from her position as a public school teacher to study full time in Amman. She saved money for her master's degree by providing private tutoring. For Jude, who came to Amman to work for a local NGO soon after completing university, one of her goals in coming to Amman was the financial independence needed to pursue a master's degree. The desire for postgraduate education was no surprise, given my interlocutors' previous achievements as students and the ways in which education opened up certain pathways for them. It also provided a reason for leaving home that some families found acceptable. Thus, the migration of these women to Amman is often part of larger future-oriented projects—projects that evolved over time, including starting one's own business, buying a car or a home, marriage, getting a job abroad, or running for political office. While families were generally support-ive, relatives and colleagues could be critical if they considered the profes-sional gains insufficient to warrant leaving home, a judgment most evident for women working in education.

More Than "Just" a Teacher

A key theme evidenced in the oral history interviews with an earlier gen-eration of women was the great respect people had for teachers. As teachers are wont to tell you today, they don't enjoy the same status they once did. A survey about professions conducted by USAID corroborates the claim.[41] Jor-danians ranked private sector teaching as the lowest status profession, with government sector employees and public school teachers a close second and third to last. Nevertheless, when asked whether they would support a male or female relative in pursuing teaching, more than half of respondents said yes, reflecting perhaps that, despite a clear professional status hierarchy, teaching remains an important and stable profession for many.[42]

In Jordan, as in numerous other places, teaching is often viewed as one of the most acceptable and accessible jobs for women because the profes-sion allows them to balance work with care for their children.[43] For more so-cially conservative families in Jordan, the appeal of teaching also stems from the female-dominated nature of the workplace, as public schools are sex-segregated after fifth grade, and teaching and administrative staff are over-whelmingly of the same gender as well. Ironically, measures of gender eq-uity implicitly mark female-dominated fields like education as being of lesser value. For example, in the World Economic Forum's annual report on the "Global Gender Gap," the fact that women who are in the formal labor force are overrepresented in education acts as a liability in measuring equity, be-cause employment sectors are only valued (that is, relevant as a measure of equity) if they have an equal number of men and women.[44] In this frame-work, the presence of too many women makes a field less valuable while hav-ing too many men gives the field inflated status, reinforcing the lower status of education as a profession on a global scale.

Several women working in education came to Amman looking for op-portunities for upward mobility in the field, or to pursue a career change altogether. When I asked Intisar, who previously worked as a teacher and staff developer in her provincial town in the south, what prompted her move to Amman at the age of thirty, she explained:

> Initially it was the family's idea. We moved to Amman as a family and then a year later they went back home, so I stayed alone. They saw that my work in Amman was a sort of promotion for me. In my previous job, I interacted primarily with school teachers, but now my work is with principals and heads of departments and teacher supervisors. Working at the ministry is different than working in one of its field offices. Here I am in the center of it all, where they do educational planning and training.

Intisar felt supported in her decision to move for her job, and professionally satisfied with the opportunities she had at the ministry in Amman. Her experience also reveals how public sector jobs in the capital provide more professional opportunities than such jobs in the periphery. Salam, who came to Amman to teach, had a different experience. Her co-workers in Amman conveyed skepticism about her decision to leave her family and live independently to pursue employment as a teacher. Salam, who was unable to get a job in the public sector in her hometown in the south, had worked at a small private school, but the job was unfulfilling and bereft of opportunities for professional growth:[45]

> The job I had at home didn't meet my aspirations. I wanted something better, better in terms of developing my personality and living independently. Then the opportunity came for me to live on my own and work in a private school in Amman. My parents supported me because there are no jobs in our governorate, and even the schools that are there are of low quality. My aspirations did not permit me to settle for that, and my parents have supported me.

Nevertheless, Salam lamented that some co-workers, and friends and family at home, questioned the motivations and legitimacy of her decision to come to Amman to "just be a teacher":

> My parents see that I have built something for myself. I am not dependent on them, I am working, independent, and comfortable. So, my parents see me as someone who is very successful. Yet from the perspective of the community, I am merely a teacher in Amman. They think, "What's forcing you [to live there alone in Amman]?"

While Salam's parents support her in her ambitions to "build something for myself," Salam finds some members of her community less supportive. In their assessment, her migration was unnecessary as she is not doing anything "better" in Amman. She has left her family home to teach, a profession she could pursue at home. Thus, what makes women's migration acceptable in this example are not abstract notions of gendered norms but rather an assessment of value and professional accomplishments.

Engineering provides an interesting contrast with education. Among the women we interviewed, eighteen had bachelor's degrees in engineering, a professional status that several women argued made it more imperative that they pursue opportunities in Amman. Siba, a twenty-five-year-old engineer from a town in the south, emphasized this point: "A person doesn't study engineering for five years in order to just sit at home." According to Siba, her parents' support for her migration stemmed from her hard work, particularly given the challenging nature of her studies. "What pushed them to accept my move to Amman was that I studied a difficult topic and spent a lot of time studying. So, I had to gain some experience in this field." Siba emphasized that as an engineer, she felt that sitting at home or settling for a mediocre job would be particularly wasteful.

Many women living on their own in Amman felt that their motivations and moral stature were subject to scrutiny by co-workers and others whom they encountered in the city. Salam felt her own professional trajectory as "merely" a teacher left her more susceptible to criticism. Undeterred, she flourished in her career as an educator. After a year in a less-than-promising school, she moved to a larger, well-regarded private school. In time, she was promoted to a supervisory role, and she supplemented her income by offering private lessons after school. In this way, she was able to fund her master's degree and purchase a car, both symbols of upward mobility. In 2015, soon after completing her master's degree, she accepted a job offer in an Arab Gulf state. As an educator, Salam is a female professional in a field viewed as traditional by external commentators and policy makers, and as lower status by many of her fellow citizens. Yet she too had aspirations for something more than what her home community could offer. She pursued her goals in Amman, and eventually abroad—a path many teachers have taken before her. In Salam's case, her professional aspirations were fulfilled as an educator, but for others success required leaving the field altogether.

For some educators, the move to Amman was a decision to leave the field of education, which was deemed to be too limiting and even too traditional or predictable for a woman. For example, Leen, who was initially on a waiting list for a job as a public school physics teacher, was working in an NGO in Amman when she was offered a position as a teacher back home. Leen described the dilemma she faced in considering the opportunity:

> Before I refused the offer, I sat with myself to think. I asked myself what did
> I really want. I felt that this [working in the NGO sector in Amman] is what

I wanted. I wanted to progress as a person. I wanted to be able to think more deeply about issues, and I felt that if I were to stay a teacher, I would have plateaued and become the typical woman. And I had other ambitions.

Thus, for Leen, who had already experienced life working in Amman for more than a year while waiting for a position in the public education sector, the job as a public school teacher in her hometown was no longer desirable. Her uncle, who had facilitated the teaching appointment through his connections, was surprised when she turned down the job, and tried to convince her to change her mind.[46] But her father left the decision to her, and she decided to continue working in Amman. As Leen articulates it here, her work in the NGO sector held greater potential for her growth as a person—for "progress." Again, professional choices are closely tied up with visions for personal progress and fulfillment, which Leen felt teaching in the provinces could not satisfy. Her year in Amman and the opportunities she found there led her to form different aspirations.

Similarly, Wijdan was determined to find opportunities beyond teaching in her hometown in the south. Initially she took a leave from her public sector teaching job, but eventually, and to the surprise of her family members, she resigned:

Initially I hid my resignation from them, but one of my siblings found out and informed my father. He asked me, "How could you resign? This is a civil service job with the government." I said "Yaba [Dad], I don't want to work for the government. It does not pay enough, and there are better opportunities in Amman, and I will do well." Then he told me, "I trust your judgment." My mother freaked out, as did the rest of the family because they viewed the public sector as more secure. They have the perception that people are exploited in the private sector.

When I asked if she was referring to being exploited as a woman, she responded:

No. It's not about gender. They exploit you in the private sector. They make you work long hours. So, they might give you a good salary but with inhumane conditions. That's the impression people have. And people can't understand the idea of working until five.[47] To them this is not a life—it's too much.

The concerns of Wijdan's family about her leaving a secure job in the public sector reflect the uncertainties created by new economic realities in Jordan. Neoliberal economic policies have promoted the growth of the private sector, with related investments targeted to the capital city of Amman. Despite state and global financial institutions' policies prioritizing private sector growth,

growth in this sector has been less than officials projected, and much of the work in this sector is precarious. As a result, for many Jordanians, public sector employment still represents the more secure and stable option, if one can obtain such a job. Another small but significant sector that has grown under this economic regime, due to aid-dependency, conflict, and humanitarian crises in the region, is employment with international aid organizations or aid-funded NGOs.[48] Since 2011, international NGOs and aid to local NGOs outside of Amman have increased, given the significant number of Syrian refugees in the provinces. Nevertheless, the government is still the main employer in the provinces by far, and many people still view these jobs as the most stable and desirable.[49]

Wijdan, with the support of her father, stayed in Amman and built a career in the NGO world. After a brief period of unemployment, she began working for international development organizations. This work was far more lucrative than her previous job as a teacher. After four years of teaching, she made 260 dinars per month. Four months after completing her master's degree she made more than 800 dinars with a foreign aid agency, and soon thereafter more than 1,000 dinars.[50] Thus, the move to the private sector, and specifically with an international organization, in a different career, changed her economic status dramatically.

Beyond well-founded concerns that families had about the private sector and risk, in some cases parents were unfamiliar with the new professional opportunities available in Amman. They had difficulty understanding the world of NGOs and professional opportunities newly created by foreign aid, and the growth of international development and humanitarianism as an industry in Jordan. When Wijdan told family members she was working for an American organization, some voiced suspicion about what such an organization was really doing in Jordan. For Hannan (see interlude 4), who also gave up an opportunity in the public sector, the challenge was explaining to her father the nature of being a consultant for multiple organizations—a position that demanded flexibility, willingness to travel around Jordan, and odd work hours. Both Wijdan's and Hannan's parents had little to no formal education, nor did they have much direct experience with the new dynamics of the labor market, and this made it especially difficult for them to understand and accept the pathways their daughters wanted to take. This lack of knowledge left them concerned for their daughters' future, as their daughters forged a path unfamiliar to them. It is important to recognize, however, that family objections or resistance were motivated by concern for daughters' livelihoods and security, contradicting the image of families strictly motivated by patriarchal norms.

Conclusion

Throughout this chapter, I have highlighted the aspirations at the center of the women's migration narratives. These visions for the future are necessarily a product of the circumstances and the social and economic contexts in which they have emerged as young, educated women in Jordan. In these circumstances—female educational achievement, changing labor market dynamics, increased centralization and capital-centered development, and the dominance of neoliberal economic policies and discourses—women see the possibility, if not necessity, to develop different futures, and they work to make these futures possible by leaving for Amman.

Development discourses and assessments can flatten the issue of women's labor force participation as one of simple gender parity within particular labor sectors, devaluing fields such as education in the process. The aspirations of these women—their trajectories, successes, and failures—reveal that new opportunities for women's migration, labor, and imagining are forged not only within shifting moral rubrics related to gender but also within broad socioeconomic structures and concomitant ideologies, and new regimes of value where the terms of "worth," "use," and "waste" are and continue to be reconfigured.

While I have focused here on the self-fashioning projects of these young women and how they chose to narrate their projects to us as researchers, the work of setting forth on this path of moving to Amman required a great deal of negotiation with parents and other family members. In a few cases, tensions surrounding their leaving home persisted for years, and could be a regular source of concern. Part of this tension stems from different views of what parents considered possible and desirable for their daughter's futures. Young women needed to translate what they understood to be their new personal and professional opportunities for their parents who were less familiar with the prospects that might be available in a shifting socioeconomic terrain. As I argue throughout this book, in doing this work, they became part of these shifts. Their narratives and the labor of making these stories legible to their families are part of the larger story of transforming gendered expectation, economic livelihoods, and social life in Jordan. I turn to these negotiations with family and shifting social relations in chapter 4. In the next chapter, I focus on their experiences living and working in Amman.

Rania

When we first met Rania, she was twenty-four and had been living in a dormitory in Amman for about a year. She is originally from Irbid. She received a bachelor's degree in engineering from a top-ranked engineering program in Jordan and moved to Amman as soon as she found work. Both of her parents are educators with university degrees. We spoke with her on multiple occasions about her experiences living and working in Amman.

> It was my idea to come to Amman originally, and eventually my father encouraged me to go for it. I wanted to prove myself . . . to show what I am capable of. And, I didn't want my education to go to waste.
>
> Of course, it was difficult at first. It's difficult to come by yourself, to get used to people. You come to a big city that you don't know anything about, and my heart was racing all the time. I was afraid. But each time I found myself in such a situation, I would call my father, and he would tell me which way to go, where to get off [public transportation], and which mode of transportation to take. He would reassure me, "You will get to the place you want and don't look scared when you're in a taxi so they don't know that you're not from Amman." These were my biggest fears, then things became normal, and the fear went away.
>
> After coming to Amman, my personality changed completely. My mind opened up to so much more. You even feel like you've added to your education and everything you previously learned. You learn to deal with people, you interact with people your whole life, but work teaches you how to interact with people properly. And when you go to an unfamiliar place, it forces you to be strong, so no one steps on your toes. When you go to a strange place, people think you're weak and not up to the challenge. So, you have to prove it to yourself first, and then to others.
>
> There was a period of time when the job became very stressful. Each day I thought to myself, I am going to go to the project manager and resign. But

then I would reconsider and say to myself, I have made it all the way here, and I have to continue. I complain a lot to my parents when I go home, but my mother says that my field of work is difficult, and any job I take in my line of work is going to be challenging. Then they say, "If you want to quit do it," which makes me say, "No. I don't want to quit."

After these reflections on her own move, we asked Rania to discuss why she believes Jordanian families seem to be more accepting now of the idea that their daughters move to Amman for work, larger forces that she relates to her own experience.

The economic situation has precipitated these changes. Prices for everything have increased, but salaries remain the same. There are no services, so people look at their children and say, how am I going to feed them, clothe them, educate them? So, this is what drives people to change. In my family, for example, my sister and brother are currently in university. I see my parents working hard and providing for us, as they did when I was in university, and I always said that as soon as I got a job . . . I would assist them. So, I did my training in Amman for the university and I kept in mind the idea of coming to Amman for work. I kept telling my father that I wanted to find work in Amman and try out the dormitory life. After I graduated, I kept looking for work until I found something. I worked in an office in Irbid for a while, but it wasn't a comfortable situation. The person I was working for wasn't pleasant, so I left without taking money or anything.

My parents consented because I insisted that this is what I wanted. When I was offered the job, I insisted that I wanted to take the job. My father was surprised by the high salary [almost 1,000 dinars] they offered me, given I had only recently graduated, and he realized this was an opportunity I could not pass up.

I have enjoyed being independent of my parents. When you live with them, you have to do as they say. When I was at university, I would come straight home from the university—only university to home. I would not go out to eat or visit friends without getting permission from my parents a week in advance, and they would not always agree. I still can't believe they agreed to let me go to Amman. I have changed a lot. Now I express my opinion, tell them what I want and think. I used to be too embarrassed to express myself; I would just do what I was told.

The Workplace

At work, I supervise as many as a hundred laborers at a time. I also work with contractors and other engineers. We are under pressure to complete our project, so there is a lot of stress. It's a struggle, but I have become much stronger.

No one can challenge me anymore! [Laughs] I have become more realistic—less naive about how people are and how they treat you. You realize not everyone is going to be nice to you. Especially in my line of work, where I deal with many laborers and different people who can be difficult, so you have to be very strong. You have to be tough. They call me *al bint al gawiyyeh* [the strong or tough girl]. If someone violates my rights, my response is strong.

But you have to be nice with the workers. I am on good terms with them. I joke around with them. I think that I and the laborer are the same—we're both people working to make money and put food on the table. Our work conditions are the same, it's just they didn't have the chance to study, and I did. So, if they work hard, I tell them to sit down and that it's enough, we'll pick up in an hour . . . I even argue with my manager. I told him, these are human beings, and they need a break.

Salary and Making a Living

I pay 150 dinars per month for my shared room. It can be a burden sometimes. It depends on how much I give my parents and how much I spend. Some months I have enough and some left over, the past two months I have saved some.

Amman is so expensive that if they were to raise the cost of the dorm even by 10 dinars, many of the girls would have to look elsewhere for something less expensive. I don't go out much, and buying groceries and household goods in Amman is expensive. I can buy the same products in Irbid for half the price. Sometimes I run out of money, but I am too embarrassed to ask for help from my parents. I give them 200 dinars each month, but I will not ask them for money. Last winter I bought a lot of clothes because it's cold out at my work site. So, I borrowed from a friend.

When you come to Amman, there is more to spend your money on—more events and outings. I was spending a lot and found myself with nothing in the bank recently. You have social pressures to do so. But I have decided, I am going to start saving no matter what. I keep working for everyone else but not for myself. I have to save for myself. I would never tell my parents that my financial situation is difficult. I will still give my family their amount every month without telling them what my situation is. I was the one who decided I should give them 200 dinars each month—until my sister and brother finish university. I will cut back on things that aren't necessary until then.

Making a Life in Amman

Living in Amman made me. I became an independent person. I don't need a single person except God. I needed my parents' moral support to be here, and I thank God for that. But, financially, I can take care of myself. Sometimes there are hard times, but I'm able to overcome them and things improve. So as for the long-term benefits . . . I have become someone else completely. I am really happy with who I have become.

SALAM, teacher in her thirties

Much of the literature on women's labor force participation centers on the issue of mobility (or lack of mobility) as an important explanatory factor for female labor force participation rates. An underlying assumption in this literature is that labor outside of the home is itself a critical form of mobility toward independence, gender equality, and gendered agency, or decision-making power. Emphasizing the multiscalar nature of mobilities—physical, symbolic, and embodied in practice—Tim Creswell offers a productive framework for thinking about the experiences of young women profiled in this book.[1] In representational terms, he argues, "some of the foundational narratives of modernity have been constructed around the brute fact of moving. Mobility as liberty, mobility as progress."[2] However, an attention to mobility in practice reveals the ways in which mobilities are "implicated in the production of power and relations of domination."[3] Ethnographic research in the region extends these broader reflections and delves more deeply into the specific experiences of mobility—grounding them in particular spaces and socioeconomic realities—and the material and discursive construction of gendered space.[4]

In this chapter, I consider how physical movement to Amman is linked to the desire for other forms of mobility—professional, personal, and classed. The experiences of women in Amman highlight the way movement, of all kinds, is always a struggle shaped by the power of dominant social and economic relations. I discuss three such struggles the women face and engage. First, they must contend with gender norms that leave them subject to moral scrutiny because they have left home. Second, they face class bias that is embedded in stereotypes about the provinces. Finally, given the high cost of living in Amman, they often struggle to make ends meet in Amman—a formidable material challenge. One important finding is the role of some families in mitigating financial challenges. This chapter, then, is about these mobilities: place-based movement and shifting perceptions of place, changing perceptions of self and of others, and, shifting perceptions of what types of movement are possible or even desirable.

Class, Gender, and Mobilities

While women's labor migration, especially among teachers, has long been a reality in the region (albeit on a smaller scale relative to men), the experiences of women today reflect different scales of mobility—symbolically and materially.[5] The older generation of women we spoke with typically went to a rural village for a temporary placement and then moved home again, or closer to home, as soon as they could. The majority of women we interviewed of the current generation had already been in Amman for several years, and some for more than a decade. Of those who married, many stayed in Amman because they tended to marry other professionals—men whose work was based in Amman, or men whom they had met in the course of their own work in Amman. Thus, their move to Amman was potentially a more permanent one. Their migration has also been marked by a time of high unemployment and a seemingly perpetual economic crisis. They come to Amman as university-educated professionals seeking professional mobility and access to the spaces that life in a large urban center ostensibly opens to them.

Gendered mobility and the accessibility of spaces are shaped by class, and markers of social and cultural capital, such as clothing, language (or dialect), and modes of transport available. In her close ethnography of the lives of a brother and sister from a working-class community in Cairo, Farha Ghannam shows us that mobility also changes over the life course with one's educational status, professional opportunities, and community expectations surrounding marriage.[6] She pays particular attention to how mobility is embodied through gender and class, painting a vivid picture of the ways in which power and inequality shape the possibilities for movement (both physical and social) for two young adults in Egypt, upsetting common assumptions about movement and gender.[7] Anouk De Koning, examining a different classed experience in Cairo, shows how social and material capital can make spaces more accessible to upper-middle-class women and closed off to those less socially desirable who jeopardize the respectability of these spaces.[8] Use of a private car, for example, was one means women employed to secure access to and protect respectability in public spaces. Still, De Koning argues, women could not completely shield themselves from risks associated with moving about the city because space is relational.

In sheer scale, Amman is a considerably different space than the provincial capitals, towns, and villages from which the women profiled here have traveled. Living in Amman, they must learn to navigate the rapidly expanding urban capital both physically and socially. They must negotiate new professional and social situations, while dealing with the preconceptions they face as women from the provinces. These biases are deeply classed, and despite their education and professional status, women were often read through the lens of rural or provincial backwardness—a type of internal orientalizing that is not unique to Jordan by any means. In the Jordanian context, such biases were layered with stereotypes about Bedouin (especially for those from the south) and "tribes" as uncultured or traditional, stereotypes that were also tied to Palestinian Jordanian/East Bank Jordanian chauvinisms.[9] This was the case even if they were from relatively large towns and provincial cities. Such stereotypes also subsume assumptions about class and gendered subjectivities. Class and geography are co-constitutive, and the provinces are often associated with poverty and lack of development. When I first began conducting research in a provincial town in the north in 2002, a colleague in Amman joked that "everyone there still lives in tents." As women, our interlocutors faced additional scrutiny. Some members of their community or co-workers viewed them as morally suspect, in keeping with a long and global history of societies viewing single women living apart from their families as presenting a threat to morality or as motivated by frivolous or less than noble aims in their migration to cities.[10] This was also often tinged with rural bias, and a sense that provincial women were ill-equipped for life in the city, and would be easily taken advantage of.

While young women discussed great personal growth and professional opportunities, they also articulated a sense of precariousness related to being single women on their own, and their need to prove themselves to colleagues and/or family as moral beings, competent professionals, and people capable of caring for themselves. They had to simultaneously reckon with sociocultural norms that could be significantly different from norms in their home communities, while also contesting stereotypes others held about them. The cost of living in Amman posed other difficulties. Amman is one of the most expensive cities in the Middle East,[11] and the financial challenges to independent living there came as a shock to many young women. Many initially struggled just to cover essentials such as housing, food, and transportation. While opportunities for leisure may not have been the central motivator for most women in coming to Amman, or at least not what they chose to center in their narratives of migration, with time they came to value the independence they developed by virtue of living and working in Amman, and leisure space with its attendant need for consumption in the capital. Participation in leisure opportunities was constrained by financial status, although some women found affordable or free activities to participate in, such as walking or reading groups. Nevertheless the financial barriers could be a source of frustration, as expressed by many of the women in this chapter.

Beyond professional or financial aspirations, many women spoke about their migration, and the life that they were making for themselves in Amman, in terms of self-development. Women we spoke with were proud of their accomplishments and their perseverance in the face of hardships. Rania, whom we met in interlude 3, spoke with obvious pride about her strength. She remarked that on the worksite she was called *al bint al gawiyyeh* (tough girl), a designation that could be used to praise a women for being strong and able to hold her ground, but could also be deployed to criticize her as overly aggressive, defiant, or masculine, echoing the double standards professional women often face in the workplace.[12] Some women—in a kind of self-reification—tied their toughness to their provincial or rural roots. For example, Hannan attributed her strength in overcoming challenges in Amman to being from the south: "I always feel like girls from the south have different personalities. Even when they are in a public space, you can single them out. So as far as I'm concerned, the harshness of our area—the desert—has given us stronger personalities."

Much like stories of single women going to the big city in other places and other times, the women I spoke with had visions of what a life in the capital city could provide them with—a vision that itself shifted and transformed after a period of living in the city gave them different views of what was possible. Their experiences living and working in Amman changed them, as they acclimated to a new place and learned to reckon with social relations central to the making of space.[13] At the same time, the economic changes wrought by decades of economic restructuring also meant that many faced economic precarity.

"Amman Cosmopolitan"

> The question of cosmopolitanism is not about a world without borders, but a world full of borders, inhabited by people who try to overcome them. To study cosmopolitanism as a state of aspiration is therefore to study class, and economic and political inequality.
> SAMULI SCHIELKE, "Surfaces of Longing"[14]

In the 1920s Amman was a small town with a population estimated at between 3,000 and 5,000.[15] By 1947, the year of Jordan's independence, the city's population was estimated to be between 45,000 and 60,000.[16] However, it was the Nakba, and the forced expulsion of more than 300,000 Palestinians by the new Israeli state, that led to the first round of rapid growth in Amman's population, which increased by 100,000 after 1948.[17] The Arab uprisings and conflicts in Iraq, Syria, Libya, and Yemen contributed to another round of large growth in population. In the last two decades, Amman's population has more than doubled, with more than 40 percent of Jordanians now living in the capital region.[18]

With the centralization of population and increased urbanization, Amman has been the object of high-profile urban development projects. Three decades of neoliberal economic development policies and investments have led to physical changes in the urban environment that have left parts of the city visually transformed.[19] Increased economic inequality is marked on the city in deeper and more visible ways.[20] Much has been written about the new spaces within the city for leisure and consumption, as well as a significant reshaping of public space.[21] Scholars have pointed to the exclusionary effects of commodification of city spaces and places, open only to those who can afford to partake in new forms of consumption, often beyond the means of most residents.[22] Nevertheless, the city's transformations have also created new spaces for people to gather, to move about parts of the city in different ways for labor and leisure, for men and women to meet and get to know each other and to socialize in groups.[23] This "urban life," or what Jillian Schwedler terms "Amman cosmopolitan," was a feature of city living women appreciated, even if not all parts of the city were accessible to them.[24]

Relatively new to the city, Rania complained that she still barely knew how to get around: "I don't know my way around Amman well. I know my way from the dormitory to the bus stop." The demanding nature of her work left Rania little time to explore the city, even though she had been in Amman for a year and a half. On the weekends, Rania mostly caught up on sleep; she only went home to Irbid once a month. Rania, however, was lucky that her job provided transportation, as one major challenge women face upon arrival to Amman is learning to navigate a city with a limited or inaccessible public transportation system, albeit one that city officials have been working to improve (the rapid transit bus project being the most recent example of these efforts).[25] Many women gave up on public transportation and resorted to taxis, or shared taxis, but these could get expensive and were not always easily available.[26] Yara, a twenty-six-year-old computer engineer, expounded upon transportation struggles:

> It was very difficult living in Amman at first. You either have to keep going despite the pressures or quit and go back home, and no one wants to miss out and go back, so you have to endure the work conditions. My personality has

completely changed . . . Before I didn't even know how to buy things . . . or use public transportation . . . I've become completely independent. And I take public transportation.

Yara's comments capture the everyday nature of challenges faced by women in the city who live on their own for the first time. While such challenges may seem minor, for a young woman living independently they are important milestones—the ability to navigate the city is a sign of her growing independence.[27] For Yara, the challenges were also financial, as her salary was very low when she first started working in Amman.

The challenges of navigation were not purely physical or financial in nature. Women who made the move to Amman also had to reckon with greater cultural diversity, and lifestyles that were, in the eyes of some women, "too open" or even immoral by ethical standards they had lived with before coming to Amman.[28] For example, some women were surprised to see other women "dating" or meeting with men without the knowledge of their families. While they sought to change and adapt, many women were also wary of being taken advantage of, or failing to live up to moral standards they and their families held dear, especially because their families had placed trust in them by giving their blessing for the daughters' move to Amman. At the same time, women also found many dimensions of the more socially liberal spaces they occupied in Amman appealing and discussed their process of exploration, growth, and learning. One major challenge was learning to give less weight to the perceptions of others—something the relative anonymity of the city facilitates.

Managing One's Reputation: Dormitory Living

The thing I hate about living on my own is that people always tend to judge you in a worse way than a girl who lives with her parents. For example, today I was late going home. In the same scenario no one would say anything because I would be going home to my parents. But since I am on my own, then it's like, "Oh, she's late. Where has she been?" It could be the owner of the store, or the guard, or maybe the dormitory supervisor herself, or maybe my friends. So [it is] everyone around you. People will more likely judge you based on your situation [that is, living in a dormitory] than on who you are as a person. They do not think to say, "I know this girl and she's very well mannered, so it is impossible that she would do something wrong." They don't see it like that, but rather, "Why would she be late?" They always judge her by her surroundings and try to bring out something negative or wrong about her. So, this is what bothers me most—that one is always under the spotlight.

NOOR, twenty-eight-year-old engineer

When Noor first came to Amman, like many of her peers she lived with a relative to satisfy her parents' concerns about her living on her own. However, after a short while she made it clear to her parents that she could no longer live with her relatives—she needed her privacy and she felt like a burden. After much back and forth, her parents relented and agreed to her living in a dormitory. Why did parents, and sometimes young women, convey trepidation about dormitory life? Their concerns were in part fueled by a rumor mill that sometimes characterizes female dormitories as spaces of loose morals, and the subsequent stereotypes about *banat al sakanat* (dormitory girls).[29] The concerns about dormitories were also linked to broader anxieties about women living on their own—anxieties that have accompanied the movement of single women out of their natal homes throughout the world.[30]

Despite the rumors, most families believed that dormitories provided greater safety and security than living on one's own, and almost all the women interviewed had spent considerable time in female dormitories. Some had been living in dormitories for more than a decade, while others eventually moved into their own apartments, a more affordable alternative. All of these dormitories were privately owned female student dormitories with one exception, namely, the YWCA hostel, established in 1958.[31] The overwhelming majority of the dormitories were in the neighborhood in and around the University of Jordan.[32] While these private dormitories are officially registered as student dormitories, female workers also live in them. Dormitories have on-site supervision, with women as live-in dormitory supervisors. Some have security guards outside or at the front entrance and all have curfews, typically between 10:00 p.m. and 11:00 p.m. We interviewed several dormitory supervisors and gathered data about policies at other dormitories. It was clear from these interviews that dormitory staff were concerned with maintaining the reputation of their dormitories as respectable spaces. Some would not accept women who worked nights, limiting residency to women whose occupations enabled them to make curfew. Two dormitory supervisors gave the example of flight attendants as a group they could not accept, given their irregular hours, while a third said they could work with women's schedules if need be. One dormitory supervisor joked that she could tell by "the way they looked" (style of clothing, hairstyle, or makeup) whether women would be a good fit for the dormitory, signaling other markers of suitability.

Like many changes in gender roles and expectations, the presence of single women in Amman, and the proliferation of housing for them, was precipitated by necessity. Generally speaking, young professional women whose families are in Amman do not live on their own, as the presence of their families makes this unnecessary and even unacceptable. By moving to Amman, the young women profiled here have created new conditions that have led to new calculations about what is or is not acceptable. The availability of female student dormitories, despite associated rumors and concerns, facilitated this change. Another factor is the experience some women already had of living in dormitories as students. The number of dormitories has mushroomed in recent decades to meet increased demand from students—many of whom are from other Arab countries—and female employees. Some women preferred apartment living as it was more affordable and the conditions more to their liking. However, many parents preferred the nominal supervision and perceived security of dormitory living.

Trepidation about the moral hazards of dormitory life continued to be a concern for some women, even if their families had agreed to the living arrangement, because of their concern about how people viewed them as "dormitory girls." This was conveyed clearly by Noor in the epigraph to this section, and such concerns were shared by others as well. At times these concerns were related to how the behavior of some could reflect poorly on other, more "upright" dorm mates. Thus, parents like Noor's wanted some assurance about their daughters' potential roommates. Sometimes, the women or their families found a dormitory where the supervisor was from the same town or village as themselves, offering familiarity and further assurances.

Salam was a few years older than Noor, and she reflected on her initial anxieties about her dorm mates and how she learned to let go of those fears. After leaving an employer-provided living space for teachers that she described as a "prison," Salam moved into a student dormitory at the suggestion of a friend.

> I entered the dormitory complex not knowing about its reputation or anyone in it. My friend said, "Let's move there," and so I did. But after a week of living there, I wanted to leave because I saw a lot of problematic activity. So, I was in an awkward position. I said to myself that this place isn't good and the people here aren't good, but I'm a good person, so I won't let them be a bad influence on me. It was cheap—since I only paid 100 dinars it was not a big difference from the 70 dinars I paid before, so I could make do. And it was very close to my school. I got to know some of the girls, and after the first month I started to see the problematic behaviors I had seen in a different light. I started to view what they were doing as really funny. Girls would fight and swear at each other and tease each other; it was a circus, honestly. They would fight over guys in front us. For me it was really funny . . . I also found another group of girls who were really nice and were also really sick of these conditions, and we made our own group of friends. We were about ten girls, a couple were from my town, one was from Irbid, another was Iraqi, and we had a really nice group of friends, and the memories I have from that first dormitory are really nice and had a big effect on me.

Salam's initial concerns about her dorm dissipated as she came to see the behavior of the other girls in a different light—as a product of immaturity, if not different values. She also decided that other girls did not need to reflect on her. When I met her last, she was living in one of the quieter dormitories and had more space to herself.

Many women complained about conditions in the dormitories, although not all dormitories were alike and the ability to pay more could buy you better conditions. In my visits to several dormitories, one quickly got the sense of the differences. Some dormitories were crowded, and the living space shared by young women quite small. Even the common areas in lower quality dormitories were cramped. They could also be quite noisy, as was the street where many of the older dormitories are located, Ṭluʿ Neveen. A bustling ascent from the university road, the street was packed with restaurants, cafés, dormitories, and apartments, and was buzzing with activity night and day. In contrast, there were newer dormitories a kilometer or so east on the same road, located in quieter areas even if they were close to the road.

Jude complained of the lack of privacy and the conditions in the dormitories. Initially she lived with a married cousin for a few months, but, like most of the women we spoke with, she found it difficult to live with family—not because of anything their family members did, but rather because they felt that they were imposing and thus never felt totally comfortable with the arrangement. Jude left and moved into a dormitory for a month, then switched to commuting from her home in Irbid. After six months of a difficult commute, she moved into an apartment with her sister in the Jabal Amman area. When asked why she moved into an apartment, she talked about the difficult of dormitory life:

When I first came to Amman, I used to think that I would live somewhere close to my job and that's it. I thought that would be the most important thing. But then you get here . . . You think, I want to go out, I want a change of scenery, but when you first get here your salary is not very high. And the dorm is so noisy you can't read. A private room at my dormitory is 300–350 dinars each, so I needed a roommate. The dormitories are exploitative in every sense of the word. Honestly, parents send their daughters from outside the city and they feel secure in the fact that there is female-only housing and that it's safe. But that wasn't the case at all, and it wasn't secure. Suddenly you find yourself thinking, "What have I gotten myself into here?" You start asking yourself, "What got me here?" People are not clean, and in the winter we were cold and they wouldn't put the heaters on, even though we paid money. Once they found an electric heater that my friends and I had, and they took it away. We got it back eventually, but we went crazy from the cold. We were turning on hair dryers for heat. Eventually, we resorted to turning the oven on and closing all the doors to keep warm, though we were scared of suffocating from the gas because the smell of gas would be all over the place.

Some of the issues related to one's living situation could be addressed by moving to a different dormitory or just learning to ignore the behavior of others and even developing a thicker skin against gossip. However, a more difficult challenge was the cost of dormitory living. Dormitory rooms can be quite expensive relative to entry-level salaries, ranging from about 150 dinars per month to as much as 350 for a private room in a nicer dormitory.[33] Indeed, the high costs of dormitories have pushed some women to move into their own apartments, or to give up and return home altogether. Fatima, who worked in software development, commuted from Mafraq for the first two years, as her salary was too low to pay for a dormitory. Only after gaining experience and changing jobs could she afford to live in a dormitory. Others borrowed from friends and even employers, concealing their financial difficulties from their families, lest they be pressured to come home or to avoid embarrassment at having failed to manage their own affairs. At the same time, other families helped their daughters cover their living expenses.

Life in a dormitory could be discouraging, given how women visualized this move for themselves—as university-educated women pursuing professional opportunity in the capital city. Their assessment of dormitory life was shaped by the alternatives available, and the length of their stay. Eventually, women whose financial situation improved could pay for better rooms and for their privacy. Others were able to move to the comfort of their own apartments at less expense, but some families found apartment living to be unacceptable and insisted their daughters stay in dormitories where there was some security and nominal supervision. For those who did not marry and had been living in a dormitory for more a decade, dormitory living could be tedious and lonely (see chapter 5).

Amman: "It gave me life"

The place I work in went through a crisis and they started letting employees go, and many people left and I wasn't paid for a while . . . But I managed. For example, I talked to the management of my dormitory and told them I was going through difficult times and asked if they could wait on me for a bit. During this time, my parents were not aware that I was struggling financially. I didn't visit them that much. So, as far as they knew everything was going well with me. They didn't know what my financial situation was like, and I never ever asked them for money. I would calculate very accurately where every dinar went.

But with all this, it was worth it. Coming to Amman gave me life. Instead of me not having an opinion, I am the one making up my mind, and everything that I am living

is because of me. Other people in the same conditions I went through would have quit
a long time ago, but I was up for the challenge. I felt a sense of calling—that I could do
something in a place, in a situation where not everyone could.

                              R I H A M , engineer in her early thirties

Reflecting on their experiences in Amman, almost without exception the
women we spoke with described their own personal growth as one of the most
significant outcomes of their move to Amman. As Riham states in the epigraph to this section, "Amman gave me life." The type of personal progress
they discussed had to do in part with learning to overcome what they described as naivete in their dealings with others, whether in the workplace
or the dormitory, or in merely moving about the city. In interlude 3, Rania
captures this well when she talks about learning to be strong "so no one steps
on your toes." But the personal growth the women described goes beyond
standing up for themselves. Growth was connected to the ability to interact
and work with people of diverse backgrounds. That diversity figured centrally
in reflections on initial challenges. So did personal transformations, which
were often attributed to the "cosmopolitan" nature of the city, although no
one quite used this word.

While some women spoke fondly of their home communities and wished
that there were similar opportunities in the provinces so they could stay
closer to home, most believed it would be difficult to go back despite ongoing challenges of being on their own. Gender was an important element in
making this assessment, for not only would being in the provinces limit their
professional opportunities, it would also limit their mobility. But this calcula-
tion was also more broadly about everyday experiences, and a belief some
women expressly conveyed that being in the capital expanded their world-
view in ways that affected all dimensions of their lives. When asked if she
would go back and do things differently, Leen, who worked for an NGO in
Amman, responded:

> Definitely not. If you don't try, you won't know what you have missed. When
> you stay where you are, you don't know what the possibilities are. For people—
> men and women—who stay in small villages or towns, you don't see what op-
> tions there are in life. Girls don't get a chance to develop independence. Right
> now my fiancé and I are planning for the future together. If I were the same
> person I was in the past, I would just be following his lead. He would be the
> leader and I would follow. Now we are a pair.

Learning how to communicate and interact with people of diverse backgrounds was frequently cited as one the greatest benefits of having come to
Amman. Leen relates this to the difference between rural and urban life—or

more precisely provincial life versus the more cosmopolitan life in the capital. While she speaks of "village life," she herself is from a provincial city, so the geographic distinctions are also about distances from the capital and forms of sociality tied to urban living. Again, this is linked to a view of the provinces as traditional and the ways in which gendered and classed subjectivities are assumed to be grounded in geography. She argues that life in the capital city presents more diverse possibilities, or even awareness of possibilities, especially for women. Leen extends the benefits of her experiences in Amman to her ability to navigate her relationship with her fiancé, seeing direct benefit from her experience living independently in Amman for her future married life. Thus, the benefits of living in Amman that women such as Leen and Riham point to go far beyond getting a salary, although valuable work is part of the equation.

Such diversity of norms and ways of living could also pose a challenge, as young women struggled with new forms of sociality in the workplace, to which they were not accustomed. For example, Buthayna talked about dealing with different people and the lessons "I wouldn't have learned had I stayed in my hometown." For Buthayna, these experiences were tied specifically to the workplace:

> Here in Amman, you feel that they are really cool. When I would see people high-five each other, I would find it very strange . . . "Hey, why are they like that, how are they so open-minded?" I wasn't like that. So, I found my co-workers a bit strange, and I would keep my distance. But little by little I got to know people, and I learned important lessons that I wouldn't have had I stayed in my province, or at my first job.

The open-mindedness that Buthayna described was about comportment and modes of communication at work.[34] She mentions co-workers high-fiving each other as an example of openness. Coming from her town in the south—and having worked there for a period before transferring to Amman—Buthayna found this familiarity strange (and high-fiving is not a local form of expression, although it has traveled into some spaces in Jordan), but in time she became accustomed to her workplace culture in Amman.[35] At the same time, she remained somewhat guarded about her interactions with others, as she was worried that too much familiarity might lead to her being taken advantage of:

> On the personal side, I used to be very shy. Then I stopped being so shy. I am braver now, and anyone that steps on my toes I answer right away. I don't like looking weak. Because I feel that here if a girl is respectful and nice and smiles

a lot, then they take it the wrong way. So, in order for them not to misunderstand my intentions, I don't smile in anyone's face.

Rania also talked about overcoming naivete in the workplace, although she faced significantly different challenges—dealing with managers with whom she was somewhat at odds, and managing large groups of laborers in the field who were under her supervision, a significant hurdle for a young employee, especially a woman, in any context.

Leen spoke extensively about culture shock in Amman, especially in her workplace. The workplace challenges she faced were particularly gendered and reflected a larger "internal conflict," as she labeled it, "between the conservative girl and the environment I came from and the girl I wanted to be." She described the initial difficulties she faced in feeling comfortable interacting with male colleagues:

> For instance, before coming to work in Amman, it was among my principles that I would not sit with guys in a public space and laugh and I don't know what. Yet from the nature of my work, it became natural to interact with men, because my colleagues were guys. It is only natural that you and your colleague sit and talk and laugh and even go out. Sometimes, in our line of work you have to partner with someone for events out of the office. Also, you have to network with people.

While at university, Leen prided herself on never speaking to male students outside of the requirements of classwork, let alone doing social things with them in public. This was in part a function of the university she attended, which had regulations meant to limit interactions between the young men and women. This is not the case at most public universities, although some men and women might self-impose similar standards in practice. However, her workplace situation demanded she change her views, and, as she reports, her attitudes shifted significantly as a result of living and working in Amman. In a later discussion, Leen shared that the change in herself was even more far-reaching:

> When I first came to Amman for work it was very difficult. The *infitah* [openness] in Amman didn't exist for us. For example, now I smoke *argileh* [a tobacco pipe also known as a hookah in English]. In the past, I could never have imagined myself smoking *argileh*. Now, as I said, my parents . . . my father is the type that gives a lot of freedom to his children. He says, "As long as you are educated, I know who I raised." But Amman was a big change for me because I was a totally different person then. I was really closed . . . I worried a lot about what was shameful [*ayb*] or sinful [*haram*]: "*Ayb, haram, ayb, haram.*" That

was the way we were raised . . . So, when I went to Amman, I found the *infitah* frightening. For the girls there everything was *a 'adi* [normal].

In my research with high school girls in Jordan, I found that adolescence was a time of religious introspection and experimentation. In and around schools, girls grappling with their religious identities actively debated norms of modesty related to dress and interaction with men, among other things.[36] Not all of the high school students were similarly preoccupied, but in the soul searching that often happens at this age, some young women worked hard to cultivate a sense of what being a proper Muslim meant. However, norms surrounding interaction with men in public were not strictly or always about religious sensibilities; they were also linked to ideas about propriety and gendered respectability that could be different in the context of a small town or village where a young woman would be recognizable as a member of a local family and thus might have more concerns about her reputation This was a reality women faced irrespective of their religious background. In this sense, Leen's reflections on her strong convictions about interacting with men, and how her views had changed, reflected her new experiences in Amman.

Leen also generalizes about young women in Amman and her initial impressions that "anything goes" for women in Amman, when in fact norms surrounding interaction between men and women are quite varied in Amman itself—shaped by a range of factors, such as class, age, religiosity, and neighborhood of residence.[37] Leen's employment in the local office of an international NGO also meant that her experience in Amman was largely defined by working in such spaces, which were mixed, often involved engagement with the public, and had multinational staff. As she explains here, interacting with a variety of people in Amman led her to rethink her ideas about religion, morality, and her peers:

> In the past, I thought it was a really big deal if someone did not fast for Ramadan. Now I've changed. I can deal with that person. I used to deal with people through a religious lens or prism. Is this person a [proper] Muslim? Now I am no longer this way. Now I look for someone's morals. Do they deal with others morally regardless of their religion? . . . What matters is that he/she acts morally and interacts with me in a respectful way. This is something I gained from living in Amman.

Again, Leen discusses the effect of exposure to different ideas and experiences, and how such experiences fundamentally changed her views and norms. Age and experience also contributed to the changes she cites, but her coming of age as a professional in Amman in an international organization were part and parcel of this development. As discussed earlier (see chapter 2),

Leen was convinced that had she taken a position as a teacher in the provinces, her opportunities for personal development would have been severely curtailed—reflecting a broader discourse about teaching as an insufficient aspiration for an educated woman with ambitions. Like Leen, others reflected on similar shifts or movements in their own ideas or beliefs—or their ability to understand diverse perspectives of others—and their own sense of self-efficacy. However, some felt stymied and excluded due to their provincial origins and class differences.

The Limits of Mobility

Amira was one of the women who discussed the personal benefits that taking a job in Amman produced. She had previously worked as a teacher in a village in the south. Since coming to Amman in 2008, she had moved to a position at the Ministry of Education. In this position, she worked with schools throughout the country, and she described the diversity of experiences that her position, as well as city living, fostered:

> The advantages to living in Amman are many—many that I have experienced personally. I developed my social skills and got to know more people. Within your environment, which is the environment at home in the south, you are mostly around your family, even your neighbors are from the same family, and they have the same habits and traditions. Here in Amman, they're not. I got to know different types of people from different places, and I built relationships with them through studying and traveling. And since you travel from one place to another every day, you meet different people and you learn a lot of new things . . . So, a person develops on many fronts. My knowledge expanded in the education sector, and socially I also built relationships through work outside the community.

In my first extended discussion with Amira in 2014, her overall assessment of her experiences in Amman was quite positive. She found the opportunities to travel around the country and learn from other educators to be professionally and personally transformative. Like Leen, she talked about exposure to new ideas and perspectives. She was enthusiastic about her new position (she had been at the ministry for about a year) and expressed both professional and personal satisfaction. In contrast to Leen's assertions about the education sector, it was employment in the education sector, albeit not as a teacher, that afforded Amira these experiences.

For women who came to Amman with less cultural and financial capital, however, stories of success were tempered by the challenges of structural barriers and biases they faced. Amira's migration project was closely tied to her ambition to pursue a PhD, which she believed was critical to her upward mobility and improved social status, given her family background. In 2015, I met up with Amira in the lobby of the hostel where I was staying. She was less optimistic about her situation this time around and seemed discouraged. She was struggling to pay off the debt she had incurred to finance her PhD—a degree that enabled her to make her career move. She was much more pessimistic about her job. The salary was relatively low (despite the new credentials), and she described a workplace environment that was stagnant and provided little opportunity for professional development. She complained that she was often involved in very routine and mundane tasks, and she asserted that one needed connections to get pulled into more interesting initiatives at work. Amira also protested that English-language skills were increasingly required for professional development opportunities:

> The ministry offers lots of professional development opportunities, but they require English. The jobs I see all require English now, even if doing the job itself does not require English. It's also very difficult to get a job teaching at a university without teaching experience, but where will I get the experience? When it comes to English, we were very disadvantaged in our village in the south.

Amira's initial joy at being in Amman stemmed from the opportunity to achieve a PhD and to pursue better career opportunities. However, as she accumulated debt, and as the professional growth she sought seemed unattainable, she became discouraged. With increasing inequality in types of education Jordanians have access to—evinced, for example, by the proliferation of private schools in Amman, the overcrowding in urban public schools, and poor educational outcomes in rural schools—being educated does not in and of itself guarantee the types of social and cultural capital needed to access opportunities.[38] Amira references her lack of English-language skills—a form of social capital that has become ubiquitous in Amman. While in the early 1990s, only a select elite used English in their daily lives or in certain professions, today the use of English in education, and in professional and social life, has become a central marker of status. English-language competency is increasingly a prerequisite for employment even if, as in the case of Amira, it is not necessary for performing one's job. It has become a critical marker of distinction and a form of exclusion in the context of high unemployment among university graduates.

The professional stagnation that Amira references echoes critiques of the public sector (discussed in chapter 2). But Amira was also being excluded from professional opportunities in the public sector because she did not have English skills. For Amira, the only alternative to a ministry job was to teach at a university, and these jobs were hard to come by—requiring teaching experience that was difficult to obtain if one could not get hired, and connections she did not have. Amira's glum assessment of her situation was also tied to her concerns about the future and getting married (as I will discuss in chapter 5). When I saw Amira a third time in 2016, she seemed less discouraged. Things were picking up professionally, and she talked about trying to publish some of her research. Nevertheless, she was still concerned about paying off her debts and saving for the future.

Despite many challenges in the workplace, living arrangements, finances, and in navigating the social realities of the city, only one woman we interviewed expressed significant regret about the move to Amman. Sana', an engineer in her forties, was unwilling to fully elaborate, but one reason for her regret was that she never married (and at forty was not likely to marry). While Amira and many others talked about challenges, they still described their move as necessary—for personal and professional growth and self-fulfillment—if not positive. The "ought" that flowed from their education and their aspirations—their beliefs about the future they ought to have and had to work toward—pushed them to make the move and to reassess and reenvision the future in light of challenges they faced. Even Sana' acknowledged some benefits from her time working and living independently in the capital, though she implied it was not her choice to be there. Most women emphasized how much they valued the independence they had gained and the decision-making authority that a salary and independent living gave them. Nevertheless, their narratives were never black and white, and they acknowledged many challenges and compromises— financial challenges, distance from family and community, and the experience of being stereotyped as "provincial girls" in Amman. These stereotypes are deeply classed, as made evident in the difficult social relations some faced.

Your Salary Flies Away

When I met Nisreen in early 2011, I was interviewing female engineers about their experiences in the workplace. She was a twenty-three-year-old computer engineer from the south living in a dormitory in Amman. All of the women I had interviewed up until that point were Amman-based and living with their families (parents or spouses and children). While I had started to hear about working women in dormitories (among them one of my younger cousins), this was my first time visiting a female dormitory and speaking to a woman about her experience. Nisreen came from a small town in the south and was working as a paid trainee in the public sector for 120 dinars per month. She initially completed two months of unpaid training in a private company, which was required for her degree. While the company offered to extend her training, they did not offer to pay her and did not promise her a regular job. In the meantime, she heard about a government program through which she could be paid to work as a trainee (or intern) in the public sector. She found a job that she liked very much, but had been working for nearly a year on a very modest stipend. When I asked her how she managed to afford this, she said:

> My father is supporting me financially, and he totally supports me in every-thing. He thinks like me. [Here she is alluding to what she called the "logical thinking" of an engineer. She is the only one of her ten siblings who went into the science track in high school and received a high grade on her *tawjihi* exam.] Even though he never had a chance to finish his education. He encourages me, even though I am not getting paid. He says, "At least you are getting some experience."

Many women struggled to cover their expenses when they first came to Amman, and for some, financial difficulties persisted even as they gained additional professional experience or educational credentials. Indeed, one of the most surprising findings of our research was that some women came to Amman and relied on their families' financial help to survive in the city. Nearly 40 percent of the women we spoke with relied on their parents, at some point, to cover regular expenses. That women should have a hard time making ends meet in Amman is not surprising, given the cost of living, new expectations for consumption, and in some cases the precarity of their jobs. Amman was prohibitively expensive for most young women when they first came because their salaries were often low, and dormitories were expensive. The fact that their families financially supported them went against many assumptions about why single women work and why families should accept their migration.

The situation was most dire for young women who came to Amman on the promise of full-time employment but who continued to be hired and paid as trainees. In Jordan, university students in certain fields, such as engineering, are required to complete a certain number of hours of on-the-job training, typically without pay, in order to graduate. In addition, professional syndicates may require a training period before licensure (for instance, law and accounting). However, in recent years, this status of "trainee" (or "intern") has extended beyond graduation or licensing requirements, as companies hire young people without experience and offer to give them experience as trainees at low pay (more akin to a stipend). According to Nisreen, the Jordanian government sponsored such a program for new graduates to gain experience in the public sector, in which she participated. Young people who took on these paid trainee positions hoped that doing so would lead to more permanent employment or at least give them some experience that would make them more competitive for jobs elsewhere. But such programs did not necessarily lead to permanent employment[39] and are contributing to greater precarity for youth newly entering the labor market.

Nisreen benefited from such a program, but her father had to pay her expenses. Nisreen's family was not a wealthy, and she was the eighth child of ten, but still the family figured out a way to support her in the belief that this investment in her professional experience was critical for her future.

Like Nisreen, Yara was a computer engineer who had taken a position as a "trainee" at a private firm for two years when she initially came to Amman. She looked for work unsuccessfully for a year after graduation, and she spent this period of unemployment at home in a small town in the south. As a trainee, Yara was barely getting by when she first arrived, but this was not something she shared with her family:

> Honestly my first challenge was a financial one. For almost two years, I was in training at work. I kept looking for work but could not find anything. Everyone had openings, but you had to work to have experience. So, on the financial side, my salary was very little. Between food and transportation, I would have nothing left . . . And if you ask for help, everyone tells you, "Why did you put yourself in this position in the first place?" They would say, "Come back and we will give you an allowance." But the issue isn't a financial one, it's that one wants to succeed and work. But they understand work as being only about salary.
>
> So, you have to deal with that challenge. It was very difficult, and you either have to keep going despite the pressures or quit and go back. But no one wants to miss out and go back, so you have to endure the conditions. I thought about leaving my work and returning home. But then I said no. It's about being productive and achieving something.

Unlike Nisreen, whose father supported her, Yara was on her own to navigate financial challenges. She didn't tell her family, lest they pressure her to come home, and they even offered to give her an allowance if she went home. Yara argued that her presence in Amman was not just about money, but also about accomplishing something. She took inspiration from older engineers in her dormitory who had successful careers, although she did worry that if a woman stayed too long, she might not ever marry (an issue I take up later).

Even women with regular employment struggle to make ends meet in Amman. Khuzama, a physical therapist, who lived in Amman for about seven years before marrying, talked about the abrupt financial wakeup call she got when she first arrived in Amman:

I think that because we are young [when we come to Amman], we think that
life is really easy. We then face reality and realize that it's not an easy thing. For
example, when you first get your salary and watch it fly away in the first two
weeks, you end up thinking, "What am I going to do?" You end up just waiting until the end of the month for the next salary. What eventually happens is
that you lose your motivation to do bigger things. You say to yourself, I'm just
going to get by and keep going at that rate.

Khuzama's disappointments were also fueled by her expectations. Khuzama's
older sister had migrated to Amman first, as did a cousin, and they had re-
galed her with stories of having fun in Amman. However, Khuzama was
surprised at how expensive even seemingly modest leisure activities were,
although she admitted that part of the issue was that their tastes had changed:
"We've changed. We used to shop in Jabal Hussein, but now it is not good
enough for us. Today we want to buy things from Zara and Mango." Jabal
Hussein is a more popular neighborhood, which in the early 1990s, when I
lived in Amman, was a place for many middle-class families to shop and stroll
in the evenings and maybe eat some *kannafeh*. While many families still do
walk through the streets of Jabal Hussein and shop there, its social status has
shifted in the spatial and consumer realities of the last two decades. Khuzama's remarks point to the new spaces of consumption—malls and designer
shops that have become ubiquitous in Amman and unattainable to many—
and the ways in which they have come to mark higher status.[40]

Like many upwardly mobile young people in the region, Khuzama believed that a college degree and a job in the city would help her accumulate
the resources needed to live a good middle-class life in Amman—to take advantage of the new leisure and consumption opportunities that abounded in
the city and the promises of neoliberal development. With time, the women
who stay in Amman become more discerning about how to traverse the city
and its leisure opportunities. This awareness is informed by financial calculations, as well as a sense that some spaces are more hospitable and thus desirable.[41] Khuzama frames this as "getting by" and not aspiring for "bigger
things." But others continued to aspire. Those who have been in the city longer, and whose financial situation improves, begin to invest in new projects
or plans—more education, a car, a home, or marriage. They could also enjoy
more leisure opportunities.

Dressing the Part: Cultural Capital

An important marker of cultural capital, critical to fitting into certain spaces,
is clothing.[42] Dressing appropriately was a particular challenge for women

who worked with wealthier peers, as they struggled to keep up with expectations and in some cases to adopt more liberal forms of dress. Several women talked about the pressures to conform to the tastes of their colleagues and peers. Leen, whom we heard earlier in this chapter talking about the changes in her beliefs and norms surrounding gender propriety and religion as a result of her time in Amman, also talked about her struggles to dress to fit into her new milieu:

> Beside the personal and social challenges, I found clothing to be a challenge as well. For example, while I don't wear an *abaya*—I wear pants and dress normally—the type of clothing and the quality of clothing [were different]. For instance, [back home] you would just wear anything and not care what brand it was or where it was from. Now you became part of a society where everyone around you is talking about where they buy their clothes.

Like Leen, Maysoon, an information technology (IT) specialist, had managed to find stable work in an international firm but still struggled to maintain a lifestyle she believed her profession and migration should provide. She talked about the embarrassment she felt asking her parents for money when she was a working woman and a professional who should be able to support herself: "When you're in Amman and run out of money it's a catastrophe. Because however much your parents are willing to help, it's not right to keep taking money from them while you're working." While her parents were well off (solidly middle class and living in a provincial city) and could help support her, she felt like a failure for having to ask for their support, and she was not alone in this. For Maysoon, the struggle was not about meeting basic needs. While some women had to borrow money just to cover the cost of their dormitory or food, and others relied on their parents to pay for their housing, Maysoon struggled to maintain a quality of life and attendant leisure activities that she felt she was entitled to, as an educated professional with a good job. However, she (and others) also complained about class expectations and the pressures to consume in her workplace, an international technology company:

> My team was very rich (unlike some of the other teams). They looked down on me because I am from Irbid and they are from Amman. There was also some discrimination of the Jordanian/Palestinian sort but not very explicit.[43] But the main issue was not Palestinian/Jordanian but Irbid/Amman. They think the people from Irbid are villagers who are ignorant [*mā bifhamu*]. They think if you are from Irbid that you are lower-class. They are from neighborhoods like Dabouq, and they spend their whole time talking about money, and they judge people.[44] I didn't change my style of dress. But if we went out,

they would pick an expensive place for lunch. For a lunch break! But I felt as
if I had to do it. On my own I might spend 5 dinars on lunch. With them it
would be 25 dinars and for nothing . . . But I did not want them to think that
I was lesser than them.

Several markers of difference that shaped these women's experiences are
encapsulated in Maysoon's comments here—geography, class, and national
origin. First was the characterization of provincial people as ignorant—a sentiment that other women faced while living in Amman. Their clothing, comportment, and at times skills, such as English-language abilities, all marked
them as different when they arrived. While Maysoon dressed fashionably, she
also wore a headscarf (as did Leen, who also raised the issue of clothing),
which contributed to her co-workers' assessment of her as unsuitable for her
job. While one finds a plethora of research on why women veil, and contro-
versies surrounding veiling in countries like France and Turkey, much less
attention is paid to the ostensibly global or international spaces in a country
like Jordan and to the ways veiled women are deliberately excluded or mar-
ginalized in some contexts.[45] On one occasion, the manager of a restaurant
bar in a five-star hotel asked Maysoon to leave, even though she was there for
a meeting with a team from work. When she questioned the manager, he told
her, "You won't be comfortable here"—a reference to the sale of alcohol in this
establishment but also to the desired aesthetic being produced in such places.
Like Leen, Maysoon was in a workplace that was more global in orientation,
but the forms of distinction they faced were a product of local class hierarchies that were mapped onto place and national identity in Jordan. Maysoon did not change her style of dress, but she did feel pressured to keep up
with the consumption habits of her team so they would not think her "lesser
than them."

Coming to Amman created new economic expectations and many more
ways to consume. The growth of new leisure spaces—spaces of consumption—in Jordan (such as cafés, restaurants, and malls) is largely concentrated
in Amman, especially those spaces accessible to women, although even this is
changing.[46] While in some respects these pressures to consume could be oppressive, women had a variety of experiences and appreciated new opportunities for leisure. There was enough diversity in the social and cultural milieu
of cafés, restaurants, and the like that women eventually found spaces they
were comfortable in and avoided the leisure spaces that were too expensive or
alienating in other dimensions (moral sensibilities and/or class).[47] However,
the geographical and class-based stereotypes of their co-workers were harder
to overcome.

Conclusion

I was sitting in a café with Wijdan, Sumaya, Sahar, and Sumaya's sister who was visiting from home. In the rapidly shifting currency of popular new places, Rainbow Street, where we were, had already become yesterday's hot spot for many young people, especially those with more resources. But these women, in their thirties, were quite comfortable in this setting and found the café to be inviting and affordable. We sat for a couple of hours, having *argileh*, tea, and coffee. These were the spaces women had come to appreciate while living in Amman.

AUTHOR'S FIELD NOTES

In her reflections on Amman's status as a city, Seteney Shami asks, "Who is invested in denying Amman's citiness and why?"[48] Ultimately, she argues that "the making of cities always takes place through struggles over space, struggles that manifest themselves in different locales and are undertaken by different segments of the population."[49] Young women come to Amman because they believe it will provide the necessary setting for the futures they expect and seek. They also come to the city in the hope of some financial independence. Many of the women we spoke with sought these opportunities in the spaces of global aid institutions, international corporations, and in the promises of privatization and investment. Others sought professional opportunity in the upper echelons of the public sector, which they could not access in the governorates. For these women, Amman is most definitely a city—bigger, diverse, bustling, relatively anonymous, daunting, expensive, enticing. The stories told in this chapter are about their struggles to identify with its spaces and places, and to make a home for themselves in Amman should they stay.

In this chapter, we have seen how the migration to Amman for work is also a story of multiple mobilities—gendered and classed, professional and personal. Because movement is constrained by dominant forces,[50] their trajectories are not without obstacles, and I have shared some of their experiences here with particular attention to gendered and classed structures that they must navigate as they make a place for themselves in Amman. As we saw, some of these challenges are mundane and everyday—learning the transportation system—while others concern the "moral rubrics" needed to negotiate spaces and their attendant social relations, and protect their own moral standing in Amman.[51] Most challenging were the material and social constraints they faced. Women worked to forge a way forward and to build a life for themselves that was authentic—in keeping with their values—and befitting the professional and social status they desired. Still, their migration and future plans were always in some sense family projects, whether they depended on their families financially (or were depended upon) or not.

Um Wijdan, Hannan, and Hala

Wijdan had moved to Amman, after working in her hometown in the south for a time as a teacher, to pursue other opportunities—academic and professional. Here I share excerpts from an interview conducted with her mother about her move to Amman. Um Wijdan's perspectives are followed by excerpts from the narratives of Hannan and Hala, two women who had very different experiences with their families.

A Mother's Perspective: Um Wijdan

It was my daughter's idea to move to Amman, and I was opposed at first because I wanted her to be in her community, close to us, and I was also convinced that she had a good job here. But I could not prevent her. In the end, I saw that she was happy, and I was happy. But it was very difficult for me to accept at first . . . to accept the situation, and it was tiring [for her] living in the dormitory. It is tiring living on your own, sleeping all alone, being all alone and isolated . . . till now it would not be my preference. I am still not happy about the situation, to be honest.

What do you think her goal was in going to Amman?

She wanted to change her profession, and she had a desire and ability to do something better [higher status] and more challenging.

Where does she work?

In an international organization, but it's a job more suited to a man because it's mixed [co-ed] and it's far—far from her family and community [*fi al ghurba*].

Was it the right decision for her?

To be honest, I don't think it was the right decision, but I was forced to be quiet. Maybe financially it was a good decision, but still it's tiring and she is *fi al ghurba*, far from her family and home. And she is alone. There are others from the community who went—two or three—but they did not have good jobs here like she did. If they got a job as teachers today, they would come home right away. It's tiring for her, and she goes to the dorm at the end of the day tired and there is no food or drink for her.

Did you ever ask her to come home?

If I knew she would listen, I would, but I haven't. She won't listen. Today is not like before. A girl has started to come and go. Not all families accept this, but their daughters insist. They say, "I am going." People see how things have developed—girls study outside [the community, or abroad], they come and go, they go out, and they have started to think if others are doing it, she can do it as well.

Why did you as a family agree?

We couldn't make her upset or angry. We didn't want to be too strict with her or put too much pressure on her. So, we said, Let her do what she wants and maybe she will be satisfied.

Do you think a young woman leaving home for work affects her prospects for marriage?

Marriage is in God's hands. Sometimes they go to Amman and get married. Marriage is in God's hands. It's fate [*nasib*]. If she is destined to marry, she will find someone in Amman or at home. It's all the same.

So, do you think your daughter's move was fruitful?

Yes, she thinks it's better. I feel like she's happy and her life is better . . . She is a stronger person.

Does she provide you any financial help?

Yes. When we need it, she does.

Do you think working improves a woman's place in society?

Yes, of course. She is stronger, bolder, confident in herself. Work is good. It improves a woman's status. It's better than just sitting at home. Even if she leaves home . . . if that is what she wants.

Hannan: "Every person struggles to achieve
a certain something in their life"

Hannan was twenty-five from a village in the south when we interviewed her in 2013. She completed her bachelor's degree close to home at one of the provincial universities. While she was university educated, her parents had limited formal education. She was one of ten siblings. When we met her, she described ongoing conflict with her father about her presence in Amman, as well as the ways in which her salary mitigated this conflict.

> I thought about coming to Amman because there were no job opportunities in my province. As much as you try to develop yourself, job opportunities are limited. So, I felt that there would be more opportunities in Amman. I decided to leave. I had some communication with people in Amman, and when I felt the time was right, I left . . . about a year after graduating.
>
> I worked throughout my time at university to cover tuition. Then I saw an advertisement for a training course with an American NGO. It was very competitive. About 250 students applied, and only four of us made it to the final stage. We worked to initiate a community-based media project, and this was all still while I was a student. Then, when I was trying to transition after graduation [to a job], the path to this type of employment (in NGO sector) still wasn't clear to me. I had some contacts, but you could say the qualifications required were high, and our area didn't provide the type of qualifications needed, like English-language courses and these sorts of qualifications. These organizations were all searching for fluent English-speakers to translate, and Arabic was secondary. So, I found it difficult to get a position and I pursued media work in the public sector. I took a civil service exam, and they accepted me. I worked for them [in the public sector] for a monthly salary of about 140 dinars. I felt I shouldn't pass up this opportunity, but I decided to work with them on a contract basis so that I could do consulting with other organizations. I am still committed to them, but I have my free will to move as I please. I started working on a youth program for an international NGO.
>
> Another reason I wanted to come to Amman is that when I worked in my home province, I couldn't go out at certain hours, and my work required different shifts to get the news. I was subject to certain hours [by my family] . . . Then, as people came to know my work, everyone started telling me, "Why are you only working in the provinces? Try leaving."
>
> So, I spoke to my family about this. When I first told them that I wanted to go to Amman, they refused. But when they knew it was to work in the public sector, they approved. But then I got an opportunity at an NGO. It created some . . . conflict with them. I wanted both positions, and my parents only wanted me to work at one, in the public sector. For them, securing a full-time

position is the most important thing for a girl, that way the time she comes and goes and leaves work is all predictable. For them it was better all around, but not for me. I wanted the flexibility to pursue different options.

At first, I would commute back and forth, but mostly I would telework . . . For me to move to Amman at that time would have been a big leap. It wasn't until 2012 that I became fully independent. Before that I would stay some nights with an aunt who lived in Amman, but, you know, I didn't want to be a burden on other people. There was a lot of opposition to my move. I was the first girl in the family to complete university . . . So, I experienced strong opposition because we don't have many educated people, male or female, in our family. You feel at times that a girl in our rural communities almost has to be extraordinary, an overachiever, or unique in order to overcome these obstacles.

I wanted to live on my own and to prove myself. I wanted certain freedoms, but I stay away from what we can call damaging aspects of liberalism, because for me traditions are things to be respected. At the same time, a large portion of these traditions don't fit the contemporary world. It's not that I am seeking the freedom to go out and about, no . . . For instance, sometimes you just want to eat lunch on your own without someone bothering you. So, it gives you independence in everything you do, and at the same time I am helping my parents, but after a certain period that stops being a goal. I feel that now I have served a lot of people and worked for a lot of people, and now it's my turn.

How was living in Amman?

I had never really spent time in Amman before. It was a very different life than my community. Here things are more complicated, and initially I felt like Amman wasn't for me and I wanted to go back. But then I was working with people from different governorates, and I started thinking that maybe, given my experience, I can make the best of it. In the beginning, I was very scared of interacting with anyone. I think any person who comes from far away, especially a village, they feel like the person in front of them doesn't really want to talk to them or doesn't like them . . . you feel, this other person is looking at me funny so I don't want to interact with them . . . I think this fear is instilled in us. Maybe because people from the village are unsophisticated and so they're scared.

Still . . . my presence in Amman gives me opportunities, while my presence in my province impedes my progress because opportunities are limited. The cost of living in Amman is high, but you are also able to live your life simply . . . I felt somewhat defeated in the beginning, because the finances play a large role in creating a positive or negative experience and in determining whether you will progress or not. When a person feels secure enough to spend, they will be okay, but if they feel that their finances aren't improving, or professional opportunities aren't improving, or personal life isn't improving, they won't be happy and won't be able to proceed.

After my sister graduated, she came here to take a professional course . . . then worked as a public relations manager for fast food places. She met a lot of challenges from my family but also because she wore a hijab. It was very difficult, especially in her position.[1] Even though she started making a higher salary due to securing more projects and making important contacts, she came back home and got married. Now she doesn't leave the house. Other than her, I do not know any others who have gone to Amman. Our area is very conservative, and to them I have stepped out of the social norms and rules. Not many people are convinced of what I am doing, but I am convinced of my work . . . My father is one of those people who likes to be in control. He doesn't want anyone to rebel against him. Rebellion, not in the sense that I will rebel against our norms and traditions, but why should Hannan be any different than anyone else in the house?

My parents don't understand my work or why I volunteer my time in some cases. You feel that there is a major gap between you and your parents' generation and their education. For example, until today my father's salary is less than 300 dinars. So, the portion I give him is very significant. I insisted on going to Amman. It was forced on them. But, it was partly facilitated by the fact that I was a source of income. I said, "Okay, you don't want to me to go out to work, well, there's no money at the end of the month." Also, they accepted it because of my reputation. People started saying, "Hannan this and Hannan that" [praising her work], so I would use that to pressure my father. They accept things from outsiders that they don't accept from us.

From a professional perspective, I feel like I am gaining experience that will benefit me greatly in the future. I am interested in running for office, but I don't know when or for which office . . . There are people that speak English perfectly and everything, but they lack my experience. My experience is an advantage on that front, and I can work with any organization.

I don't think my family appreciates my progress. Because it's hard to reach a person who is illiterate. A person needs to be able to read in order for them to know what you are and to talk to you in order to know that you have progressed. Maybe members of my community do.

A couple of years after I had this extended discussion with Hannan, she married, and as a married woman she continues to work in her field.

Hala: "My family is not the difficult type"

I first encountered Hala in 2011, when I met with a group of single women in their dormitory to discuss being single, the purported marriage crisis, and what it was like for them to live and work in Amman. I sat down with Hala again in 2014 at a local coffee shop to further discuss her decision to come to Amman and her experiences there. By that time, she was thirty and a successful engineer living a relatively comfortable life in Amman, given her professional success and good salary.

I came to work in Amman because there were no real work opportunities for someone with my degree in Irbid. So, my parents had no problem with my working in Amman because they knew the professional opportunities in Irbid were limited . . . no decent or respectable jobs for a woman in Irbid. So, from the start, I was applying for jobs in Amman. I would come to Amman for interviews . . . my brother would take me to Amman . . . until I found a job in December the year after I graduated. As soon as I got the job, I moved to a dorm. I had a private room, and I got to know some girls there but not very well. I roomed with some different folks during the first year. After a year, I quit my job and went home to Irbid for three months, and then I came back to Amman again. Then I ran into a friend I knew from university, and we decided to room together. We stayed in the same dorm for a while and then we moved to another one.

My parents don't like the idea of me living in an apartment because they are afraid for my safety, not because of moral reasons. My mother is more fearful than my father. My father would not mind if I lived in an apartment. What concerns him is who am I living with. My mother says, "Don't leave the dormitory." I am even a bit afraid myself. And who will change the propane gas canisters for me? [Laughs] Even after my roommate got married last year, I stayed in the dormitory. I have my own room, and I am not looking for an apartment. I am very comfortable, and I am used to living by myself now. I can't imagine looking for an apartment with roommates now. When my friend first got married, I was kind of depressed, as I was used to always being with her. But now I am used to it, and I changed my jobs. A lot has changed.

My current job is my fourth. I stayed in the first job for a year and the second job for one and half years. Then I worked for a multinational corporation for four years, and now I work for a different one. I have been with them for nine months. I moved to my current job because the pay is better. Plus, I had been with the other company for four years already, and it lost its excitement for me. I needed a change. I was recently promoted, so there are opportunities, and they invest in people.

I have always worked in factories [as an engineer] where you interact with a lot of people. In my first job, there was no differentiating between men and women at all. In my second job, it was a bit more challenging. The factory itself was a challenging environment . . . the people were a bit "strange." They did not do anything, but you could tell from the way they looked at you that they didn't accept you, even though there were many women who worked there. I had no issues at my third job—I left for more money. You feel as if people have just gotten used to women in the workplace.

My parents were very supportive. They did not object to my specialization or to my line of work. They are not that way. Even when it comes to travel—I see an ad for a trip, and I tell them I want to go on a trip. My mother predictably is worried, and my father is like, "Go, have fun, who are you going with?" No issues. I am the youngest of six, and my parents have changed somewhat over time. But my parents have always been flexible people. I see other people—my friends—and see how they interact with their families, and I see that my parents are really flexible. Even when it comes to marriage, I have seen a lot of friends get pressured by their parents. They would say, "That's it. You have a good suitor. What's wrong with him. It's time to get married."

I am not married, and we do not have this mentality in the house that you must get married . . . If it happens, it happens [*nasib*]. I have an unmarried sister at home, and no one puts pressure on her. I was the only one of my sisters who moved to Amman as a single woman, but there were no objections.

Being in Amman changes you, your personality changes. If I were at my parents, they would, of course, have some influence on me and would get involved in my decisions. Here I am all on my own, and I make my decisions on my own. I am independent. Even my parents depend on me. They ask me to take care of things for them in Amman. My mother was saying the other day how happy my father is that I am self-reliant. Even if I could find work in Irbid, I would not go back. I prefer to live here. Irbid has changed . . . the mentality is different from Amman. It's more conservative and there are only two main roads . . . I can't even cruise and listen to music as I like to do in Amman.

When I first came, my salary was very low, but it covered the basics. I would spend it all each month. I am the type who is a good manager, and I managed my money well so whatever salary I had, I would make it work. My salary was 350 dinars. I would pay the dorm around 110 dinars, and transportation to and from work was provided so transportation expenses were limited. So, it was just enough. I never had to borrow money. With time my salary increased, but then I had new expenses. I bought a car three years ago and I started having car payments. But I still managed to have enough each month. Now I am able to save. So, I have managed my situation throughout based on what my salary was. I never asked for financial assistance. Now I pay 220 dinars per month for my room. I want to buy a home in Amman. Once I pay off the car loan, I will look for a home. That's the next step.

The culture is slowly changing in Jordan. People are changing. What is not *a'adi* [ordinary or normal] now in two years becomes *a'adi*. Sure, some people want their daughters to work for financial reasons. But some families are struggling financially but will not let their daughters work or come to Amman. I know some girls who would commute between Irbid and Amman because their parents did not want them living in Amman. Sometimes, though, you see change even among siblings . . . the older sister may have to commute because her older brother is opposed to her living in Amman. But then the younger brother is more open-minded, and a younger sister wants to live in Amman, and he supports her, so they let her. So, you see the generational change within the family.

I don't have much more to say because my case is a positive one. [Laughs]

4

Family, Power, and Change

While this book centers the stories of young women who migrate, migration is necessarily a family project, as most major life decisions are for young people in Jordan. What do I mean by this? Very few consequential decisions are made by young people, male or female, without a discussion with parents and in some cases with siblings and even extended family. Some of the women profiled here, like Hannan (interlude 4), come from small villages, where most members of the community are extended kin—that is, from the same tribe or clan. Other women, such as Hala, come from provincial urban centers, where close kin may or may not be in proximity and have less of a say or an effect on family deliberations about education, jobs, and marriage. So, who exactly constitutes "family" in the contexts of the narratives of migration here varied, although for most women "family" meant the nuclear family, even if parents might be concerned about what other family members think.

Maya Rosenfeld, in her study of multigenerational family efforts to educate members who in turn help support the family, argues that scholars must be attuned to the ways in which power and patriarchy shape the division of labor within family projects.[1] The experiences of her interlocutors in the Dheisha camp in Palestine are strongly shaped by displacement, colonial violence, and Israeli occupation, but her work also echoes the work of feminist economists and economic anthropologists who critiqued earlier models of the household as a cooperative and altruistic unit, arguing that they were overly simplistic and did not sufficiently account for power and the gendered division of labor.[2] Mary Kawar, writing about women's labor force participation in Jordan, contributes to this critique by arguing that households are not static, and that, just as the economic and social roles of family members shift over the course of their lifetime, so do household relations and structures.[3] The experience of the women we interviewed is complicated further by their leaving their natal homes, and in some cases living on their own for many years. These migration projects are family projects in another sense. While the women profiled were motivated by individual aspirations and ambitions, these aspirations were also shaped by family needs, values, and expectations. Indeed, it is at times difficult to untangle the two, especially in instances where the woman's migration ends up shaping the course of family fortunes in significant ways.[4]

I begin by discussing the initial decisions to migrate and the at times extensive negotiations with family that were involved in making this move. In most cases women told us that they had to work to convince their families of their need to move to Amman for work. As we saw with Hannan's story in the interlude, for some women, the move to Amman was quite contentious and led to a significant amount of conflict with their families. Hala's family, although concerned about her safety, encouraged and supported her. For Jihan, whom we met in the opening pages of this book, the story is a different one—one of need and a family project to improve the opportunities for everyone. These stories and others will help us delve into the specificities of change—what does it look like when we focus on the experience of particular families, and how do their experiences help us better understand how change happens? We asked all of the women to reflect on these transformations as well. What had changed to enable women to leave home and live on their own? What did they think were the most important factors in their own family, in their provincial communities, and in Jordan more broadly? In addition to negotiating their departure and the terms of agreement with their families, women continued to negotiate their roles within their families over time. Some faced pressure to marry, others felt that their families grew to rely on them to navigate the capital and make important decisions, and some women became important contributors to the needs of varied members of their family. In this way, their migration and labor contributed to shifts in gender roles and expectations, albeit not without some tensions.

Negotiating Family

The women who are the focus of this book could not have moved to Amman without the consent of their parents. Young men and women in Jordan typically consult their families about major life decisions related to their choice of major at university, employment, migration, or the choice of a marriage partner. In practice, for many young people, the involvement of family members goes beyond consultation. Parents, and in some cases older siblings and extended family members, may be actively involved in decision-making processes for younger relatives, if they do not actually make such decisions for them. Both men and women are subject to the advice and intervention of family members in important life decisions, but women have less liberty (and greater potential repercussions) in opposing family, particularly when it comes to migration and marriage. The role of family is not necessarily viewed as oppressive or intrusive. To the contrary: young adults typically trust that their family members have more knowledge and experience than they do, and have their best interests at heart. Of course, at times family members don't see eye to eye and conflict emerges, but the guidance and significant involvement of multiple family members is standard for most people.

Among the women profiled in this book, only one was in direct conflict with her family about her living in Amman, and even she had initially gone to Amman with her family's permission. While many had to do some convincing and cajoling (in some instances over months or years), all went to Amman with the permission of their families. In some cases, parents had no objections at all. For instance, when asked whether any family members were opposed to her relocation to Amman, Abeer commented:

> My father was never the frustrating type. On the contrary, he was in support of the idea. My mother never prevented me from doing anything unless it protected me, but I always felt as though she left these issues to my father to judge. She avoided taking the responsibility for major decisions such as these.

Abeer emphasized that her father had been supportive of her and her sister throughout their lives. "What has helped me my whole life is that my father is the type that enjoys seeing his daughters excel and grow, and he would say, Work hard because I want to see you reach high places." According to Abeer, her mother left such decisions to her father, but in some families, mothers and even siblings could be instrumental in facilitating or standing in the way of a young woman who wanted to migrate. Abeer also mentioned that an older brother who lived in Saudi Arabia had expressed his displeasure about her living arrangement, but Abeer put little stock in his disapproval, and he was unable to exert any influence on her or her parents.

Amira discussed the role of women in her family when she proposed the idea of moving to Amman:

> It wasn't that I faced opposition from my family, but it was a struggle. Because it was the first time, and it was a new idea for them. I had to work to convince them, and thankfully it went okay . . . It is usually the women [of the family] who oppose it [moving or migration] more because they feel like the men won't accept it. But I am very close to one of my uncles, and he helped me a lot

in convincing my father and convincing my grandmother. The old women always worry about you and where you go. They worry about dormitories, and they think, "You have a job here, so what's the point of going somewhere else."

Not all the women in Amira's family played the same role. For example, Amira, who comes from a village in the south, had an aunt who had lived in a dormitory for university and for the mandated professional training for engineering degrees. Although this aunt married soon afterward, her experience of living and working in Amman was a precedent Amira could reference, and her aunt encouraged her to make the move. But Amira also gave herself credit for convincing her family:

> They might have felt the drive within me—that I really wanted this. Even if most people in my environment don't let girls go to work, they still hear about other girls from other areas. They feel great pride when they hear that a girl from the south becomes a doctor or that she travels abroad. They realize that they have to be more open-minded.

Women were not passive actors. Family was central, but they were active parties to these family dynamics and agents within the broader structural changes under way in Jordan.

Maysoon, an IT specialist, had the full support of her family when she was offered her first job in Amman and wanted to move there. Maysoon said they would support her in any decision, even going abroad for a job or to get a higher degree if she so desired. Salam similarly had the backing of her family:

> My family has never been of the mentality to refuse or forbid. So, there wasn't a need to convince them. It was a very simple issue. My father is a very intelligent man. Even though he's a somewhat religious individual, he is democratic and he saw my need to work. He saw me sitting at home unemployed or working at schools where they would pay me 100 dinars. My aspirations did not permit me to settle for this, and my parents have supported me. My sister went through the same thing, where she was sitting at home unemployed. He hoped that we would both find work, and he would move the family to be closer to us in Amman.

Salam's sister was unable to secure a job in Amman, however, and her family never made the move to Amman with her. In a subsequent interview, I asked Salam if she ever felt pressured to return to her home in a small town in the south:

> No. Because there is no alternative. If there were, I would go back. I am living here alone. I would prefer to go home, even though life in Amman is nice. Yet, I go crazy during the summer vacations when I go home, and I have a hard

time adjusting. In Amman I can come and go as I please, and there are many opportunities for leisure. But at the same time, it's hard to live without your family. You still want them around.

Salam conveys the conflicted feelings that some women had—really missing their families and community, while at the same time determined to pursue professional and economic opportunities in the capital and their own personal growth and independence. Their loneliness is also tied to a family-centered social life that permeates Jordanian society. However, as discussed in chapter 3, rapid urbanization and population increases in Amman, as well as urban planning and related developments, have led to the creation of new leisure spaces that are not strictly family-centered—spaces that women such as Salam come to appreciate.[5]

According to Jude, whose parents were supportive of her migration, her father's primary concern was related to the financial implications of her move:

> Initially there was some opposition from my family to my moving to Amman. I remember in one conversation, my father was like, "How are you going to go to Amman for 300 dinars?" I would get offers for 300 dinars, and he would say that will not be enough, that it is impossible for me to make do with less than 400. In reality, his words were a hundred percent accurate.
>
> My parents are understanding, but they were worried about me leaving, since I am a girl and I have a very close relationship with my parents. For instance, I remember the first day I left my parents' house. I kept crying all day, and my mom called me and she was crying, and we were both crying. I couldn't stand it.

Even though Jude was determined to move to Amman, the move was an emotional one for her and her mother. She was very close to her parents, and her compassion for them came through in her interview. Even though Amman was relatively close to her home in Irbid, she said it felt like "living in another country," recalling Um Wijdan's references to *al ghurba*, and the way such phrases demarcated Amman as so distant and/or different as to feel like a foreign place to some. Most centrally, this was about being away from family and community. The initial experience of living on her own was difficult both because of the distance from family and the financial challenges she would face in Amman.

Like Jude's father, parents needed to be reassured that their daughters would be secure in Amman (female dormitories being a central piece of this), but they were also worried about the financial implications of the move. These two concerns were related. Giving their daughter permission to leave home and live on her own involved some risk and some courage to go against the grain despite what others might say. However, supporting such a move also entailed a realistic assessment of the financial feasibility of her moving out on her own. Jude's father wondered if she would be able to support herself on the low salaries she was being offered. Ultimately, he supported her move, even though the salary she eventually accepted was quite low. In Jude's case, the fact that she lived with relatives at first helped in the initial transition—a strategy many young women employ to make their transition to independent living in the city more palatable to their parents.

Noor, who came to Amman from a provincial town in the south, initially lived with a relative as well. However, like many of the women who started out living with relatives, she was not comfortable with her living arrangements, so she talked with her parents about moving to a dormitory.

> I decided to live on my own, and I was positive that my parents would oppose it completely because you know how others view the reputation of girls living independently . . . But with consistent persuasion—and thank God, I have open-minded parents—they were convinced of my point of view, and they let me get independent housing.
>
> In the beginning, my mother was the most opposed to my moving. She would say, "We have to find another solution." So, it's not that she was against me working but that we had to find an alternative solution to me living on my own. I had not yet talked about this issue with my father, because I knew I had to convince my mother and then he would be convinced. So, I sat down with my mother and explained my situation to her, and I made her feel how much of an impact this had on me, and she agreed. I feel like it came down from God because I thought it would never work out. But in the end, she said, "I think you're right. I wouldn't want you to be uncomfortable at anyone's house or anything." So, we sat down again with my father, and we came to an agreement. Their condition was that I would live with girls that I knew, who were well mannered, principled, and moral. So, it turned out that my friends from home were coming to live in Amman, and my parents knew their parents, so all of this helped my parents ease into the situation.

Noor's recollections capture the incremental ways in which some women moved toward greater independence in their living arrangements in Amman, through repeated negotiations with family members and larger networks of kin. As Noor's story shows, the more women migrate to the city, the more they have each other to turn to, and parents feel reassured about the presence of young women from families they know and with whom they share values.

Similar to Noor, Ruweida also had a family that initially opposed her living in a dormitory. In Ruweida's case, it was because her brother was married and living in Amman, and her parents wanted her to live with him:

My father completely rejected the idea of me not living with my brother. He just couldn't understand how I would live anywhere else when my brother lived in Amman. He kept saying I would not be a burden on my brother and his wife—that I was only one person whose food and additional expenses were not that significant. "How can it happen that you have brothers in Amman and you go out to live in separate housing?" But in the end, when I couldn't take it anymore, I told him that I work to support myself. That I'm not looking to save or build something . . . I just want to spend on myself. I want to be comfortable.

Interestingly, part of Ruweida's argument was that she did not need to save money—she just wanted to live alone comfortably and be able to support herself. This argument served two goals. First, she made it clear that she did not need anyone to support her financially. Also, the cost of the dormitory was not an issue, she argued, as she did not need to save money. But what of her assertion that she did not want to "save or build anything"? In my experience conducting research in Jordan, a number of women used this rhetorical device to minimize cultural or ideological objections to their paid labor. Specifically, rather than directly challenge the role of a father as *the* provider, working women sometimes minimized their own economic roles or frame their desire to work in noneconomic terms, lest their fathers feel their role as breadwinner was being disputed, or their capabilities in fulfilling this role questioned. In other words, some women felt the need to clarify to others (including the researchers) that their decision to work was not reflective of their father's ability to support the family, and sometimes, as with Ruweida, their assurances were directed to fathers themselves. In this case, Ruweida also used this argument to justify her desire to live alone in the comfort of her own place. Thus, she argued, she needed to work so that she could live the way she wanted to. Hannan's experience with her father (related in interlude 4) was a stark contrast.

The material realities that demand changes in social roles and practices often precede shifts in ideology. The stories we tell about ourselves do not necessarily match the compromises and adaptations that people make in everyday life. Relatedly, the categories social scientists often use to try and measure things like labor, household decision making, and the like often significantly oversimplify the complexity of social life and/or use an idealized middle-class norm as a benchmark.[6] For this reason, the migration of these women is nearly invisible in discussions about women and labor in Jordan. It goes against dominant stereotypes about their provincial communities and their families. At the same time, Ruweida's case also reveals that there is no simple story to be told here about gender roles. While Ruweida was not supporting her family, she was supporting herself, and given that she was likely to stay single, she would continue to do so throughout her life—a role that prevailing gender ideology insists her father and then brothers should assume. Ruweida's words capture this lag in some sense, but don't really challenge it. Indeed, she gives her father an out and allows him to save face. However, such a narrative is also about status, and the status of these women is tied to that of their families. Women, too, had an interest in asserting that their families were financially well off and not in need of their labor. Thus, for some, it was important to present their migration for work as a function of choice rather than need.

In diverse contexts, scholars have found that the realities of who contributes to a family's economic well-being is much more varied than static models of the household, which often serve to reinforce male breadwinner ideologies, allow for.[7] As we will see in this chapter, some women did become significant breadwinners, while others helped their families regularly even if significant need was not there, and some supported a particular sibling for a period of time. The variety of these experiences speaks to realities of who contributes to family projects, and how the contributions of these women may or may not challenge prevailing gender ideologies.

Managing Family Struggles

For some women, the move to Amman was much more contentious, reminding us that change is often a product of struggle. This was especially the case given prevalent norms surrounding female mobility and the expectation that unmarried children live at home until they marry. While these gendered norms and family dynamics contributed to some of the conflict and resistance on the part of families, the disagreements and their negotiation also often involved other issues and concerns. In some cases, families were opposed to the move primarily because of the nature of the job their daughter was taking. As we saw above with Jude, the issue might be about salaries and the financial feasibility of living on one's own in Amman. However, especially in cases where women had opportunities to work closer to home in what were viewed as more stable and secure jobs, family members could not understand why their daughter or sister would take such risks. As they viewed it, their daughter or sister was acting rashly and against her own interest, in addition to going against cultural sensibilities about the appropriateness of a young, unmarried woman leaving home.

Here I focus on the experiences of women who sought opportunities in the development and humanitarian aid sector. Young women dominate this sector in Jordan.[8] As articulated by the women who chose this path, these jobs provide both meaningful professional opportunities and relatively high salaries. However, the sector is not without its issues. As other researchers have shown, the jobs provided by aid agencies and the NGOs they fund could be quite precarious and professionally or politically disappointing.[9] Local staff of international organizations criticize the hierarchies within these organizations, relegating them to cultural "fixers" or translators for "international" staff who often do not know the local language or social context.[10] In a particularly strong critique of such dynamics in Jordan, Ayah Al-Oballi points to the ethical dilemmas such work poses: " 'humanitarian' work in its current form requires either a daily state of active resistance, or the acceptance of losing some of our own humanity and voices to be able to continue working within it."[11]

In their research on NGO workers in Jordan (most of whom were female), Janine Clark and Wacheke Michuki found that people sought out these jobs because they were committed to the issues the NGOs were advocating for and wanted to do something more meaningful and professionally challenging. Female respondents in particular cited the importance of the issues, flexibility of the work, and the problem of discrimination in other sectors.[12] Many had left other jobs to work in the NGO sector, including 23 percent who were formerly teachers.[13] At the same time, NGO employees cited "low pay, limited benefits, and limited job security" as among the greatest challenges to this type of work.[14]

Hannan (interlude 4) was one young woman who had sought out opportunities in the aid-funded development sector, after working for such an initiative as an undergraduate. After initially working on local media projects funded by an international aid agency, she sought opportunities beyond her local community as a consultant in the capital. Hannan's father regularly raised the issue of her returning home, and her residence in Amman was a constant source of conflict with him. Nevertheless, her growing status in her community, as well as her role as an important breadwinner in the family, offered important leverage against concerted opposition from her father to her living in Amman. Locally—in her home community—she had developed a reputation for herself through a citizen media project, but she sought new and more lucrative opportunities in the capital, and the long commute from her home village was too taxing. However, her father was opposed to her move, as she details in interlude 4. She had this to say about her decision to move to Amman and her family's reaction:

> When I first told them that I wanted to go to Amman, they refused. But when they knew it was to work for a government media outlet, they approved. But

I decided not to take the permanent job with the government-affiliated out-
let and decided instead to pursue the opportunities with an NGO because I
wanted to keep my options open. They couldn't understand how I could give
up a secure job. But there were other concerns as well. I was the first girl in
the family to complete university, and in their perspective, as much as a girl
studies, her place is still to come back home.

The resistance Hannan faced from her father was related to the career decisions she was making. From his perspective, she was passing up an opportunity for a stable job and one that enabled her to commute from home, however arduous that commute.[15] Her move contravened ideas about propriety
and gendered mobilities in her family, and she was also passing up a stable
job with benefits in the public sector. This decision was difficult for her family to fathom, given their limited exposure to such sectors and forms of work.
Furthermore, as Wijdan conveyed in an earlier chapter, the private sector was
viewed as exploitative, a real concern given the precarity of much private sector work.

What women such as Hannan viewed as opportunity could make little sense to their families. Women had to do the work of translating labor
market opportunities to parents who believed in the superiority of steady
public sector jobs. Given the overall picture of the labor market, and the
precarity of private sector jobs, parents were correct in trusting in the stability of public sector jobs. Rather than translate, perhaps it might be more
accurate to say that they shifted the terms of discussion, to idioms of aspiration and the need to take risks for success in order to convince their parents that they should go to Amman. The work that women do to make these
choices legible and acceptable to their parents also supports the view articulated by some that they themselves are forging new ground. When I asked
Hannan how she managed to convince her family to accept her move, she
responded:

In part it was my success . . . I had built a strong network and relations with
important people in my community through my work, such as the police chief
and the governor . . . This power put some pressure on them. It wasn't through
arguing or words . . . I received several awards for my programming. So, you
could say that this provided me with some leverage—the seriousness of my
objectives and the results gave my parents the impression that "Hey, maybe
our daughter is able to get somewhere." Perhaps they felt I might be able to
help with any problems we might have . . . Also, I was a source of income.

Hannan's growing reputation in her community, and the powerful connections her family might benefit from, all helped to convince her father to

accept her move. Nevertheless, the conflict with her father would regularly flare up. Hannan was also the only woman interviewed who discussed conflict with her family surrounding her income—her father did not want her in Amman but needed her financial contributions to meet the family's needs. She leveraged these tensions to insist on staying in Amman.

Like Hannan, Ibtisam and Leen both gave up stable public sector jobs. In the case of Ibtisam, this decision created some conflict with her family when they realized she had resigned from her public sector job. In Leen's case, while her uncle was surprised she would give up the opportunity for a job as a teacher close to home, her parents were supportive. In part this was facilitated by her sister, who had preceded her and was also working in the NGO sector. Also, her father was university educated and had a professional job, which perhaps explained his familiarity with opportunities outside the public sector, and willingness to support his daughter in her decision.

Sumaya and Riham faced sustained resistance from their families over their migration to Amman. For Sumaya, who commuted to Amman from her village, it took years of convincing for her father and brothers to finally accept her move to Amman. Sumaya began work as an engineer at a public ministry in Amman shortly after finishing university. However, soon after getting her job in Amman, she was offered an opportunity to transfer to Irbid—a city much closer to her village. After a very brief stint in the Irbid office, she decided that the workplace and career opportunities in Amman were superior, and she transferred back to the Amman post. Her family members—and especially her father—were disturbed by this. Why would she leave a job that was much more convenient, enabling her to live at home with her family, to keep a job that involved a long and arduous commute?

> My father was disappointed, and we would always argue. Our relationship was fragile for two years because he wanted me to take the job in Irbid. For example, in the morning, before I bought a car, he would give me a ride to the bus depot. If it was raining and he didn't want me to go to work, he would wake up yelling and cursing . . . And I would go to work devastated and keep crying the whole way . . . And when I would be late to work, I would get told off. But what could I do? Sometimes I couldn't get transportation. At night sometimes I would get to the Irbid junction and not find a bus, and I would have to go sleep at my uncle's house.

While the majority of the women we interviewed moved to Amman because of lack of work at home, and their refusal to accept the reality of sitting at home unemployed, women such as Sumaya are making the case to their families that better professional opportunities (in this case in the public sector) matter, even if that ultimately necessitates leaving home. In real terms, Sumaya did not live as far from Amman as some of the other women we interviewed. However, the sense of distance had much to do with transportation and the limits of the existing infrastructure. She was from a small village not on a main transportation artery, and transportation could be very limited and unpredictable, even if in real terms the village is closer to the capital city.

After Sumaya purchased a car (with a loan from her parents), commuting became easier. Note that while her father made much of not wanting her to work in Amman, he did help her purchase a car. It's hard to know exactly how her father came to that seemingly contradictory decision. Yet in thinking about it, one is reminded that parents (people) don't always act in consistent ways, or may be negotiating competing impulses, or succumbing to the pressures of other family members or societal pressures, or their strong-willed daughters. Sumaya's mother may have given her father an earful along the lines of "how can you leave her to struggle with the transportation system and get stuck in the bus station with no way home?" Or her father himself may have been trying to give her fewer excuses for spending so much time in Amman, or he may had had enough of dropping her off at the bus stop each day. Perhaps one of his brothers may have made a remark about his stinginess, or many other scenarios that are easy to imagine. Sumaya's family was relatively well off, and owning a car, rather than struggling with public transportation, would better reflect her family's status. All of this is to say that, like the young women themselves, their parents too had to weigh competing demands and shifting realities, and their own decision making was not always predictable or linear. Sometimes it was driven by mundane, everyday considerations.

Even after she purchased a car, Sumaya would stay with friends in Amman two or three nights a week, but her father remained opposed to her living in a dormitory. When we asked her why he was so opposed, given that she was already staying in Amman in dormitories or apartments with friends from time to time, she responded, "They worry about the reaction from my brothers. That's our problem, in short. My two older brothers won't accept my moving out." She went on to say that she blamed her parents for giving her brothers so much say and allowing her to be so miserable for so long.[16] The hurt was apparent in Sumaya's voice when she described the preferential treatment her brother received when he started working in Amman:

> My father was the one who was most strongly opposed to me working in Amman, but when my brother . . . when his male child graduated as an engineer and wanted to go work in Amman, he would wake him up gently in the

morning so he wouldn't be late. He supported him and kept talking about how important work is. So, when my brother first started working with me, I would remember those hard times a lot. When I wanted to go to work in the morning and he would tell me off because he didn't want me to work in Amman because I am a girl . . . I don't know, maybe it's fear. Mostly it's fear, I think.

Sumaya eventually moved out on her own into an apartment with two other women in Amman. When I met up with Sumaya just a few weeks after she had moved into her apartment, she was ecstatic. I asked her how she did it, and she said, "I made a revolution. It is the greatest accomplishment of my life." She admitted that her mother had a hand in finally convincing her father to relent:

> I think in the end, my father stopped opposing me [in my desire to live in Amman] because my mother must have interceded. She decided to get involved. I know my mother has influence over him, and she figured, what's the difference if I sleep in Amman or in my home. I was already sleeping in Amman two or three nights a week, and when I didn't, I would not get home until seven, so what was the difference. I would just come home to sleep. Now that I live in Amman, they do not see any difference . . . little has changed. I lost ten years going back and forth . . . Irbid, Amman, Zarqa, Sweileh [towns she had travel through on her commute].

Mothers, brothers, fathers all potentially had a say, and their role was not necessarily predictable. One constant, however, was that fathers needed to be on board. Given that fathers are the official heads of family and are culturally and legally accorded rights over dependents as heads of household, this is no surprise, even if they were not the sole decision makers in practice. Also, at times, while fathers were supportive, mothers were the ones needing more convincing because they were concerned about safety, reputation, and marriage prospects for their daughters. Women are sometimes those who guard gendered traditions more closely, fearful of the dangers of rocking the boat, and cognizant that the stakes are high for women should things go wrong.

Sumaya's family, despite coming from a small village, was relatively well off. Thus, for Sumaya, unlike for Hannan, money was never an issue. She did give her mother some money on a monthly basis, but this was more about the status she sought as an independent adult than any need on the part of her mother. However, given her background and the rural community in which her family resided, Sumaya's insistence on moving out of her parents' home significantly challenged notions of acceptability, leading to years of tension with her father—a reality that clearly pained her when we spoke. Her younger sister had no interest in following the same path. Sumaya told me,

"She studied computer engineering. I offered to help her find a job in Amman, but she doesn't want to put up with this kind of lifestyle." The example of Sumaya's sister is a good reminder of the great diversity of experiences, even at the family level, and how important the individual agency of the women profiled is for understanding the full story of their migration.

Of all the women we spoke with, Riham, an engineer in her early thirties, had the most conflict-ridden relationship with family when she first came to Amman. As I got to know Riham, it was clear that the disagreements with her family were not strictly about her living in Amman. Riham had long had a contentious relationship with her parents, and especially her mother, and she conveyed some bitterness about the favoritism she believed her parents showed to other siblings. When she initially came to Amman from her village in the south for work, Riham lived with a sister and a brother. Her family supported her at this stage; however, when her brother left the country and her sister married, her family wanted her to return home to their town in the south. She refused.

> When my sister got married, it ended up that I was here alone in Amman, so they started pressuring me to leave work and find something in my hometown. I told them I would only come home if they used their connections to find me a good job. My mother had good connections through her family. But my mother and I were not on good terms, and I did not expect that she would help me. So, I didn't listen to them. I kept my job in Amman, and we didn't speak for a while. To tell you the truth, I didn't feel like it made much of a difference for me that I was distant [because our relationship was strained].

Eventually, her family came to accept Riham's decision. In the meantime, Riham had gone through a very difficult financial crisis. Her company went bankrupt and was not paying her consistently for several months, again pointing to the risks involved in private sector work. Yet, she managed on her own. When I asked her if she still felt pressured to go home, she replied:

> Yes, every once in a while there is still pressure for me to go home. They say, "Why are you there? What do you want from this whole thing? Haven't you been there long enough?" They worry about us [single women in Amman] and believe that the system will never accept us. Mainly, it's from their fear. Yet that fear is added stress on us.
>
> There is no reason for them to be fearful. On the contrary, there isn't anyone in the family that can say anything negative about me. I am confident in myself, and I have maintained our traditions with high regard, and I respect my parents' old age . . . The only reason I took such a stance against them is to prove to them that I am up for the challenge, can bear the responsibility, and

that I am on the contrary stronger than my brother. So, they shouldn't be worried about me because I am a girl. I can take care of myself better than a man, and they are not going to hear anything but that which will make them proud. I think their biggest concern is that I will end up by myself and not find anyone. But I am fine with the idea of being on my own. I can take care of myself.

Parents cared for their daughters and worried about their futures should they continue to live in Amman on their own. Both Sumaya and Riham talked about their parents' fears. They were worried about what people would say, worried that their chances for marriage would lessen or that their daughters would wait too long to get married and find themselves alone in a society where family formed the core of social life. Riham understood this and insisted that in terms of what mattered—tradition, values, morals—they had nothing to fear. In addition to concerns about the reputation and moral status of their daughters, parents were also worried about their well-being and the future. Would their daughters be alone? Would they be loved and cared for? They also had everyday concerns: is she working too hard, will she eat well, is she lonely, or is she warm enough? Um Wijdan (interlude 4) conveyed such concerns poignantly. Ultimately, family members could not control these outcomes. They had to trust that their daughters would do the right thing—live by the morals held by parents and family—and be okay. And their daughters insist upon this.

As we have seen, women had to negotiate their move to Amman and at times continued to contend with family concerns over, if not objections to, their decisions. While these are very personal and familial stories, with all the diversity that specificity implies, their narratives also reflect larger structural forces in Jordan today. The structural forces that emerge most prominently in their stories are the changing labor market dynamics, the socioeconomic realities that families face, and the shifting terms of patriarchal relations and bargains in light of these socioeconomic realities.[17]

A Changing Society and Economy

Beyond the views and circumstance of their own families, we spoke with each of the women about the broader contexts for their migration. Most referenced similar demographic shifts and economic developments, such as female educational success, the difficult economic situation in the country and a family's need for more earners, new professional opportunities, and a discourse of professional aspiration that downgrades certain choices—issues that I have already discussed at length. When prompted to reflect on the broader context for their migration, nearly all of the women also talked about a changing society, one in which families thought differently about their daughters and the roles they would play in life. Amira, whose own trajectory involved a lot of struggles with her father, expressed this sentiment:

> Maybe we have started to change socially—in terms of the difference between men and women. Fathers have started taking pride in their daughters' accomplishments, just as they are proud of their sons. So, when my daughter becomes a doctor, it's the same as if my son becomes a doctor. Many fathers have changed their perspective and started wanting to send their girls to study. Indeed, maybe here in Jordan specifically, where the rate of women that are educated is higher than for men . . . Parents have started to realize that their daughters might make more of themselves than their sons.

For Amira, this reflection was in some respects aspirational, as she clearly sought her distant father's affirmation, but it also captured the sense of agency that many women conveyed about their role in facilitating change. Leen also cited societal change:

> The first thing is that the view of girls has changed. A long time ago the view of a girl that lived in dorms was really bad; people believed that this girl was not respectable . . . The second thing is the lack of employment opportunities in the governorates. There aren't employment opportunities in the governorates. Before, it used to be that most of the girls would enter the education system—be hired by the Ministry of Education. But now there are no more jobs in the ministry. The third thing is the greater openness of people in the governorates to the capital. Before, it was almost a mystery, no one really knew what happened there. Now, for instance, you are from a village, and a girl from your village left to go live in Amman. You see how she changed, and you are encouraged to leave. When people see that she has succeeded, everyone will want to go and try. I would also say the financial conditions of families have had an effect. Maybe some families would not agree with me, but I would say that, if a daughter goes out and gets a salary of 400–500 dinars, and gives you 200 or at least 150, you improve your financial situation.

Leen's explanations echo those of many others—changing views of women in Jordan, changing economic circumstances and labor opportunities, and the precedent of others who have gone before them.

The motivations of the women themselves correspond to this view of what is changing in Jordan. They saw themselves as an integral part of a shifting socioeconomic landscape that, while replete with challenges, offered them new opportunities. They saw themselves as important actors driving some of these changes. They emphasized that their accomplishments as students, daughters, and professionals have been indispensable in persuading family members to support their migration, even when this challenged norms in the extended family and in their local communities. Jude expressed this clearly when we asked her what had changed in Jordan to allow women to migrate to Amman with the support of their families. She listed many of the reasons given by others: increased openness, later marriage, precedents, education, and economic needs and desires. But she rounded out these remarks by emphasizing the importance of individual determination: "Honestly, determination gets everything done. If a girl is determined, even if her parents told her no a million times, if she wants it bad enough, she will eventually get her way." Of course, not all women had the ability or even desire to make such decisions. Such possibilities were shaped by class, geography, and particular family histories. But it is important that some women viewed themselves in these terms. They saw themselves as part of the change.

Through shifting socioeconomic structures, and the attendant changes in material realities, migration and related mobilities become more possible. The forces of political economy are powerful here. These women have come of age in an era of ongoing economic crises precipitated by neoliberal economic policies (the growth of national and personal debt, deteriorated public services, increased cost of living, and so on) and geopolitical realities that have driven the increased militarization of the entire region at the expense of other kinds of investments. These political and economic realities are driving some of the changes that the women discussed. However, these shifts cannot be contained within the sphere of the economic, as these women are also beginning to feel a sense that the social structures and gendered hierarchies are shifting, too—a "structure of feeling" of their lived experience and what it says to them about the future, however uncertain.[18]

BREADWINNERS?
FAMILY SUPPORT/SUPPORTING FAMILIES

> Structure is both medium and outcome of the reproduction of practices. Structure enters simultaneously into the constitution of the agent and social practices, and "exists" in the generating moments of this constitution.
> ANTHONY GIDDENS, *Central Problems in Social Theory*[19]

As this chapter shows, the connections between personal agency and family relations, on the one hand, and broader structural forces, on the other, are not easily teased out. The relationship between human action or practice and the reproduction—as well as the potential transformation—of structural forces is dialectical, and over time the practices of these women will constitute and reconstitute gender roles. One of the most persistent gender ideologies is that of the "male breadwinner." Specifically, male heads of household are expected to be the primary economic providers for their families. Male breadwinner ideology is not unique to Jordan, and despite its strong and persistent currency, which also has religious foundations, in practice women have always been central to the economic survival of families. The economic roles of the women profiled in this book provide interesting insights into the dialectic between this ideology or structure and actual practices.

As we heard from several women, many were barely able to support themselves when they first came to the capital. Indeed, some relied for years on the financial support of family and friends. In the long term, some women were unable to maintain their newly made lifestyles without debt, let alone assist their families. However, others became important breadwinners—supporting siblings and parents, and taking up important roles in their families. Slightly over one-third of the women we interviewed regularly gave an amount to their families, and several others reported that they occasionally supported the family in particular ways (gifts, a one-time contribution to a house improvement, paying for private tutoring for a sibling taking *tawjihi*, and the like). At the same time, another third reported needing assistance from their families, and several women talked about borrowing money from friends or getting an advance on their salary when they found themselves in a financial bind. Finally, about a third said they needed no assistance and did not give assistance to their families.

These are not mutually exclusive categories. For women who had been in Amman for several years or more than a decade, their financial situation could improve over time, with a need for family support initially and then a desire to contribute to family projects once their situation improved. Also, the situation of the family could change in ways that required more (aging parents who needed care or someone falling ill) or less assistance (siblings finishing university, a home-building project completed). Some women faced financial crisis, as in the case of Riham who wasn't paid for months when her company went bankrupt. Sahar, whom I discuss below, also went through a period in which she was not paid and had to borrow money from family and savings groups.[20] Yet, later she became the primary breadwinner for her family. These relationships of interdependence were complicated and rarely static.

Kawar argues that one reason why it is difficult to disentangle personal goals and family is that "young women's 'self interest' is intertwined with the well-being of their families as a whole and therefore their financial contributions are seen as part of their 'self interest.'"[21] Kawar links this to both the status of the family and its importance for women's marriage prospects, as well as the long-term security and support a family provides for a woman should she not marry or should she be divorced or widowed. While the women profiled here did not explicitly talk about their contributions to family in these terms, they emphasized duty and responsibility toward family, and viewed their personal success and desire for independence as tied up with their ability to support their family, if only temporarily.

This was evinced even in families where financial assistance was not needed. Even when families were relatively well off, women persisted in giving small gifts whenever they went home or giving money to their mothers as a token of their appreciation. Taking care of one's female relatives is a tradition that men typically fill. Especially on holidays, men give small amounts of money to mothers, married sisters, and at times other female relatives. Like all traditions, this has its variations and is likely changing, but I recall that my father did this annually, going to each of his sisters and nieces in New York, where we lived, and giving them an *eidiyye* (literally, a holiday gift), continuing this obligation even (or especially) in *al ghurba*. Some of the women we spoke with insisted on playing this role with their mothers as well, as a way of signaling their status as professionals and showing respect.

Rosenfeld's rich analysis of multigenerational household family projects takes up this question of duty or obligation to one's family. For example, one of the women in her book who had delayed marriage for several years to support her family explained that it was "both her choice and her duty."[22] Young men she spoke with also framed support for family as duty.[23] While Rosenfeld acknowledges that the commitment of young adults to support their natal family rather than focus on their own economic independence is "so pervasive that it might even be called normative," her analysis ultimately conveys how abnormal this appears to her as a researcher.[24] She ultimately concludes that the obligation young people feel to their families reproduce and are a product of patriarchal "control and dependency."[25] Of course, norms are always about power, and the norm of economic independence in a place like the United States is equally a product of power, and a coercive one, in a context where for many there are severe economic challenges to setting up an independent household. Never mind that this norm devalues deep traditions of intergenerational households in a range of communities in the United States. For the women profiled here, independence is valued, but it is not necessarily viewed as distinct from obligations and duties to the family. For many women, the ability to significantly support their family was evidence for them of independence—being an adult—and success. That success was about taking care of themselves, but was equally defined by meeting their obligations.

Of course, the persistence of unemployment and poverty makes this ideal hard to achieve for many.

Rania (interlude 3) captures this sentiment well. As a young engineer who was recruited by an international organization at a relatively high salary, Rania nonetheless talked about her initial struggles with saving, despite this salary. She described sometimes running out of money, in part due to poor spending decisions, but insisted that the decision to give a substantial amount of money to her parents for her younger siblings' education was her own. Rania articulated an early desire to help her parents, given how hard they had worked to finance her education. Rania was the second-oldest in her family, and at the time of our first interview she had two siblings at the university and a younger brother still in school. While her parents were both employed professionals and roughly of the middle class, putting two children through college was economically taxing and Rania wanted to help them. She framed her decision to migrate as in part motivated by a desire to pay her parents back for all that they had done for her. "I saw my parents working hard and supporting us, as they did when I was at university, and I always said that as soon as I got a job . . . I would assist them." At the same time, she had the goal of saving for herself. She spoke of future plans and the need for these savings. Her remarks conveyed some tension ("I keep working for everyone else but not for myself"), but this tension was also about her frustration with herself for not managing her money well. Assisting her parents was not a question, at least not at the time or our last meeting. Within a couple of years, Rania was engaged to someone she had met at university, and they were planning to marry when the time was right. Men have different pressures, as they are meant to save money and be able to support a household before marrying. For working-class men or those in the lower middle class, the pressures can be intense and the ability to marry severely hampered by lack of resources.[26] But women also were concerned about financing their futures. What if they didn't marry or got divorced? Even if they married, they understood that a middle-class lifestyle required both a man and a woman to work. This life-style they were working toward was not merely or even mostly about leisure or conspicuous consumption, but about the ability to access quality education and healthcare in the relatively expensive private sector, give the deterioration of public services. Women spoke about these realities and understood that securing a good life for a family was not a given.

The case of Hannan, whom we met earlier in this chapter and in interlude 4, was more contentious. Her conflicts with her family about her move to Amman and her rejection of stable employment in the public sector were tied up with demands on her income. While women felt a personal obligation to contribute to their family's income, the ongoing conflict Hannan faced was unique in my research, entangled with both the financial needs of her family and their conservatism. Her significant contributions to the financial needs of her nuclear family were a condition of her staying in Amman. Besides giving her father a regular monthly sum, she also paid for her younger sister's private tutoring lessons for the *tawjihi* exam. Nevertheless, she also framed this as her advantage:

> My father was just saying last week, "Choose a path, either you come here or stay there." I told him at the end of the day I cover my own expenses and a major portion of my work is to help the family out, not for myself. So, I told him if I lose one job, then they will lose some of the help that I'm providing. Because what I am contributing is coming out of the efforts I'm putting into both jobs.

It's important to note that Hannan's father, who had very little formal education, made much less money than she did (he made less than 300 dinars per month), and the overall financial situation of the family was difficult. For context, in 2008, the poverty line in Jordan was 323 dinars per month. In 2017, the poverty line for an average household of 4.7 people was 396 dinars per month.[27] Hannan, like several other women we spoke with, had outpaced her father in terms of income soon after finishing university. According to Hannan, her father had come to rely on her to meet the family's needs, and her monthly contributions were on par with his salary. Note that Hannan dropped out of university at first, as she was unable to afford the tuition. She reenrolled in a less expensive major at a provincial college and worked throughout her university years. It was this paid work, and trainings funded by international organizations, that set her on a professional path made possible by international development aid to Jordan. It also meant that she had some financial autonomy early on, but also financial obligations and a sense of responsibility to the family.

Although Hannan complained about the constant arguing with her father, she never expressed a reluctance to help her family. Rather, the point of contention was her presence in Amman, and she resented the ongoing conflict with her father over her living arrangements and travels. Speaking about her financial obligations, she referenced the economic pressures that made it necessary for "daughters to help, too":

> We have a financial crisis [here in Jordan], so that a man is in need of a wife to work in order to help him. And, if sons don't work . . . and most of the young men today are not joining the army as they did in the past or getting governmental positions, and so young men aren't able to help out their fathers as they used to.[28] Therefore, the daughter is obligated, from my perspective, completely obligated to help out her parents. She should help them . . . Well,

she shouldn't have to, but from my experience it becomes necessary for her to do so. In my case, I work and so I have to help my father, and if I don't want to help out, then sit at home. Therefore, it becomes a condition in order to work. You either help financially or don't work.

Here Hannan highlights broader socioeconomic changes that have led to changes in gender expectations and roles, as well as the blurred contours surrounding notions of choice, obligation, responsibility, and agency. First, she referenced the oft-repeated assertion that men want to marry women who work because of the high cost of living. While labor statistics show that women tend to drop out of the workforce when they marry or soon thereafter (unless they work in the public sector), since I began doing research on women, education, and labor in 2002, Jordanians I have spoken with about this topic have consistently asserted that changing economic realities demand that families have two wage-earners.

Hannan also delved into the expectations surrounding financial contributions of adult children. Specifically, she said that sons are expected to help out their fathers, but are no longer in a position to do so. Thus, daughters are left to fill this role. However, why should daughters be better able to find work than sons? Given the region she comes from, the importance of military and public service jobs for employing young men is well known. Furthermore, as discussed earlier, in many provincial communities, women were more highly educated than their male peers and thus might be better positioned to take advantage of new and potentially more lucrative employment opportunities. But university-educated women report high levels of unemployment, much higher than for their single male counterparts, so men are much more likely to find work. Nevertheless, unemployment among young men is also quite high, and young men of lower socioeconomic status and with less education have fared the worst in recent economic downturns.[29] In a context of increased cost of living, and deteriorating quality of public services, expectations surrounding obligations to care for parents and siblings are shifting, with women taking on an increasing role in supporting families in some cases.[30] In reality, some women have always helped support their families. Hannan filled this role for a couple of years, but then married and started her own family in the capital city. So, this role was a temporary one for her, and part of the way in which she negotiated her migration. In the long run, her position as a successful professional may work to provide upward mobility for her new family, mobility that her natal family has struggled to attain.[31]

Pressures to support family members financially could also come from siblings. Wijdan was a schoolteacher in the provinces when I first met her.

Several years after finishing her bachelor's degree, Wijdan moved to Amman to pursue a master's degree. After completing her master's degree, she found a job with an international NGO that paid more than three times her teacher's salary. Wijdan's unmarried sister, who at times resented being left at home to care for her ill, elderly father and the numerous grandchildren, pressured her to return:

> Initially I had a lot of conflict with my sister. She was older and unmarried, and home with my parents in the village. For a time, I was unemployed, and she was like, "What are you doing in Amman? You just want to avoid us and your responsibilities." She said, "Your family needs you and you are sitting there in Amman doing nothing."
>
> Even though she was harsh with me, I understood why she was angry. She hated doing the housework. She hated having to constantly serve people. It was a big house, and lots of kids [the grandchildren] would come. It was kind of unfair to her, to be honest. Just because she did not get married, she was cleaning up after these kids and caring for our parents. I promised her that as soon as I got a job, I would pay for a domestic worker to take care of the house and my parents. And I eventually did do that.

Under pressure from her sister, Wijdan made a financial commitment to help care for their parents, or more precisely to contract out this responsibility to a paid domestic worker. Again, this represents a departure from norms surrounding care for parents, even if in practice these norms have already been shifting for decades, due to migration of adult children, fewer integrational households, and women's labor outside the home. Since the 1980s, families with the resources have begun contracting with recruitment agencies to employ women from other countries as live-in domestic help. Tamkeen, a Jordanian NGO, reports that, as of 2015, there are about 50,000 legally registered domestic workers and an additional 30,000 "irregular workers."[32] Much has been written about the exploitative conditions of their work (organizations like Tamkeen regularly report on human rights and labor violations faced by migrant workers). Yet, rarely does the literature concerned with promoting women's labor in Jordan make the explicit links to the exploitation of other's women's labor as intimately connected to this project of getting more women into the formal labor force. Wijdan clearly hears her sister in ways that this literature on women's labor does not.

In Wijdan's village the hiring of a domestic worker was still novel, but the shifts happening within her family are indicative of the changing roles and expectations around care work that undergird these shifts. Wijdan was from a very large family, and all but one of her siblings were still in Jordan. She had a married brother who lived in the village and a sister-in-law who would have been expected to take on some of these responsibilities as well. However, the one brother who stayed in the village was, financially speaking, the least well off. "Success" meant getting out of the village. Also, her other sisters-in-law were in Amman and, in a world much changed from the life of extended kin in the village, not willing (or not able because of the distance) to take on such roles. Wijdan's family assumed that her unmarried sister would take on this labor as the single daughter at home, a role that single daughters take on in many societies. Wijdan, who might have been in the same position had she not moved to Amman, acknowledged her sister's unpaid labor and care for the family in ways her brothers had not.[33] As a wage earner, she sought to support her sister and relieve her of some of this responsibility. Wijdan purchased another woman's labor to do this. The ways in which some Jordanian women's labor force participation has become dependent on low-wage female labor from other countries reminds us that the global division of labor must be central to analysis of "women's work."[34] These transnational realities need to be more central to the analysis of economic developments and their gendered implications.

FAMILY CRISIS, WOMEN'S WORK, AND CHOICE

As we have seen, both the financial challenges and the obligations women were faced with were necessarily shaped by the economic status of their families and broader economic realities in Jordan, even if this did not wholly determine which families significantly resisted their daughters' migration to Amman. In a few cases, women emerged as the primary breadwinners for their families in times of crisis. Sahar, one of the older women we spoke with, fell into this category. She came to Amman at a later age (in her early thirties), and when we met, she was over forty and had been in Amman for more than a decade. Part of the reason for this late start was that her education was interrupted by the Iraqi invasion of Kuwait and the Gulf War that followed, forcing her family to relocate to Jordan. Thousands of Jordanian citizens, most of them Palestinians like Sahar's family, who had never lived in Jordan, were forced out of Arab Gulf countries where they had lived, in some cases, for two to three generations already.[35] This displacement put her family in a difficult financial situation. To add to the challenges, one of her siblings died and another had health problems. Another brother had gone abroad and only supported the family minimally. As Sahar conveyed it, "He helps out sometimes, but his situation is not that great, and he has gotten used to me taking care of things." This situation left Sahar as the primary breadwinner for her parents and her unwell brother's family.

When I last met with Sahar, she was excited by her new position as a su-pervising engineer at a major real estate development. She explained that site management was challenging, and she worked hard to get workers to take her seriously, but she was having great success. Despite this excitement, she was not getting paid regularly. In fact, she had not been paid for two months in the previous year, and this was the second time this had happened to her. The first time, she said, she was really in a jam, as she had no savings, a situation she attributed to her spending habits:

> I have four or five hundred saved now, and I am staying afloat despite losing two months of wages. It's hard to carve more out. I can't get a car, and I haven't received any raises. I just stopped spending so much—especially on clothes and makeup. I am just trying to buy what I need. I still owe the dormitory for two months' rent [220 dinars per month]. I've tried savings groups, but they don't really help when you need money in a pinch. So, when I didn't get my salary, I was stuck. I took money from my family, even though I normally give my parents money each month. My brother is ill and can't work. He lives with his family with my elderly parents. Right now, we have a project in mind to build a home for them, with a store so my brother can work close to home.

Rather than focus on the precarity of her job, despite being a supervising en-gineer at a major real estate development, Sahar focused on her own spend-ing habits as she talked about economic difficulties. Again, this was not the first time an employer had failed to pay her. Perhaps her own financial man-agement was something she felt she had more control over, but still, the types of precarity that professionals such as Sahar face is astounding.

The situation of her family—forced displacement, death, illness, and a distant brother—left Sahar in the primary role of provider even as she faced her own economic challenges. Sahar was concerned about the long run. She has Social Security, but her main preoccupation is where she will live in the long run: will she have a home? Sahar's situation can raise the question of choice. Some might ask whether it was her choice to support her family, or whether, had this obligation to support them not been there, she might have tried harder to get married. However, as Penny Johnson argues, reflecting on the life stories of single Palestinian women, "choice and responsibility are [thus] interacting poles."[36]

Jihan, whom we met in the opening pages of this book, became the pri-mary breadwinner for her family soon after finishing university. Jihan's story illuminates the difficulty of framing any move or migration as choice in a pure individualistic sense and the reality that choice is structured by conditions not of our own making. As Jihan narrates it, her choices came out of need and a strong sense of obligation to her parents and younger siblings. Choice is always constrained and shaped by circumstances, as Jihan articulated quite clearly. Jihan had been living in Amman for more than ten years when I first met her. She initially went to Amman as a university student, with a scholarship from the army to study nursing. When asked if it was her decision to join the army, she told me that without the scholarship from the military, it would have been difficult for her to complete her university education at all:

> You see, the situation in our house was such . . . my siblings were younger and my father was sick. The credit hour at the university was 35 dinars. Can you imagine? There was no money, not enough for everyday spending. My mother said, "Here you have this other option [the military]." So, you can say it was my decision, but it was shaped by very particular circumstances.

The decision at the age of eighteen to move to Amman to study nursing and commit to a career as a military nurse far from her family was one that had far-reaching implications for Jihan and her family. Jihan was successful and had great pride in her career; she had been promoted several times and was the director of a pediatrics division in a hospital. She was also proud of the opportunities she had been able to give her siblings, as she supported at least two of them in completing their education. However, these decisions did not come without sacrifices on her part.

Conclusion

Coming to Amman is a family project, even while it may be driven by individual aspirations for a particular future. While women are powerful and creative agents in making this path, their movement does not happen without family consent, and this consent, if not support, requires translation, negotiation, and a great deal of emotional work on the part of women and their parents. Sometimes, there is a great deal of tension, if not conflict, with family members—tension that women work to mitigate in a variety of ways. And, in some cases, a sense of obligation and responsibility for family (parents and siblings) is the primary driver of migration. In chapter 1, we read about the history and structural realities that have shaped possibilities for young men and women from the provinces. But smaller events and processes also shape the possibilities these young women see and pursue: family crisis, short-term needs, professional opportunities, the experience of an aunt, the desires of a younger sister. Of great importance here is also what these women feel is shifting—a "structure of feeling"—and how they must respond to these openings.[37]

While few women framed their initial decision to migrate as solely about the financial needs of their families, some, like Jihan and Sahar, came in large part to help meet the financial needs of their families. Ultimately, migration enabled many of the women we spoke with to assist their families in pursuing projects of education and upward mobility, and to finance their own such projects. Their spending could also relieve other women in the family of unpaid labor, or facilitate entry into the labor force for them. In families where the financial situation was relatively better, assistance (if given at all) was typically temporary and often related to a particular project—educating younger siblings or repairing or even building a home for one's parents. In this way, some women become critical breadwinners for the family, and this complicates the view of a strictly gendered division of labor and strictly male breadwinners. Families could also depend on their daughters to support them when they needed it—to repair a home, to hire someone to care for an elderly parent, or to help them navigate Amman for a doctor's appointment. For women like Hannan or Rania, the move to Amman helped them lay the groundwork for their own future families.

Sameera

Sameera is from a village in the north. After completing her master's degree in social psychology in 2004, she moved to Amman. She had lived in a dormitory for her bachelor's degree, which she completed at a university in the south of the country. For her master's studies, she lived with other students in a space rented out by a family. Her own parents had very little formal education. Her father, who died when she was young, had some elementary school, and her mother had attended adult literacy classes to learn to read and write. She said there were no schools available in her mother's time. Sameera comes from a large family, and many of her siblings are married. At the time of the interview, she had been in Amman for eight years and was in her early thirties.

When I first came to Amman, I worked in the private sector, but the salary was very low, and we didn't have any benefits like health insurance, or Social Security. I was working in order to gain experience, because anywhere that you go work, even if you have a master's degree, the first thing they want is experience. So, in those days, even if I had to pay out of pocket to work, it would have been fine as long as I gained experience. But after about a year, I got a position as an administrator at a public university. At first, I did not have much hope that I would get a job there. I had applied to the university, and they did not accept my credentials—they said I needed experience. The position they gave me was not in my field, so I was not sure about it. My brother is the one who encouraged me. He said you don't have to work in your field of study.

My uncles were not happy about my work in Amman, especially because I would refuse suitors who came to ask for my hand in marriage from my area. I would use the excuse that my work was in Amman and my hours were too long, and it wouldn't work. I would make up excuses.

I took the job with the goal of continuing my education. I thought, I can continue on to a PhD while I work at the university, but whenever I would apply to the director, I would get rejected. It was strange for an academic institution, but they were not interested in developing the skills of their staff. I felt I was losing my professional identity and becoming an administrator. I appealed and even said I would give up vacation days and my salary increase if they would let me study, but they refused. However, just this year, they have passed a new rule allowing staff to pursue a degree.

I worked in Irbid for a while, and it was hard. The commute from my home village was long, and I had to be in the office by eight. I would go to work with bags under my eyes. I did this for a few months, and then I came to live in Amman. I lived with my brother at first. He was single, but when he got married, I started living in apartments with different girls and in dorms . . . I was used to living on my own. I went all the way from the north of the country to the south for undergraduate, and I could only go home every month or two because it took a whole day of travel and we didn't have cellphones or internet back then. So, Amman did not feel that far.

Back in the day, people wouldn't send their girls to study in other cities . . . a girl wouldn't have the opportunity to continue her education. So, they inhibited their daughters a lot. But I feel like today it has become normal. The most important thing is for a girl to work, if she can pay for her own rent, then it's fine. Back in the old days, it used to be shameful to say you wanted to marry a girl who worked outside the house. Now they talk about it openly.

Why is that?

Because the men aren't able to cover the costs by themselves. When he has to rent a house and buy gold for the bride and all these things, he won't be able to do it on his own. Still, until now people think that if a husband can provide for the whole family, then it's a shame for the wife to work, because as a woman she is going to be working in and out of the house. Where will the mother's imprint on the child be if the child is always in daycare? . . . How is this generation going to grow up without the attention of their mothers?

Why did your family accept you leaving?

My father, may he rest in peace, when my sister went to study in Karak, many people, especially those close to us, started telling him, how are you sending your daughter to Karak? Men have fled Karak.[1] But my father used to love education. For him, as long as he raised us right and trusted us to do the right thing, then it was doable. He didn't even have a problem with us traveling abroad.

How do you think your move has affected your marriage prospects?

[My move to Amman/my job] negatively affects marriage. If I had decided to work as a teacher, then I would have been able to get married because half the day would be mine. Half at work and half at home. But now my whole time is spent at work. So, I would feel guilty if I was with someone. It would be at the expense of time spent at home. If you're someone who works from eight to five, then you need someone to take care of you, not to bring kids into the world and have to take care of them and raise them. That's aside from the housework and other responsibilities. I wouldn't be able to give my home its due attention or my children their due attention. So that's why I don't like the idea of getting engaged. Maybe, if I worked fewer hours.

My family was frustrated with me because I kept turning down suitors for this reason. Most of them were teachers in my area. At some point, they ganged up on me with a full-out campaign saying, "We don't want you to work at a university." They told me, "Stop your work and start teaching like your sisters, we don't want this work you're doing." If I were convinced of a guy, I would leave my job for him—find a more suitable job. But till now I haven't seen the person who makes me feel like I am willing to sacrifice . . . everything for him. Some people say [about me], "Oh their daughter is look-ing for a doctor," but I don't care about doctors [that is, the status or prestige of a suitor]. We see professors at the university, and they sometimes have the worst personalities. One of my uncles said to me, "If there is a guy that you like or is smart enough to convince your stubborn mind, then just tell me. I would be glad to give you to him."

I am the head of my department, but the financial benefits of living in Amman have been zero. Everyone thinks that the salaries at the university are good, but they are less than 500 dinars a month. I used to live in a dorm, and the dorms and living expenses are very high. So, financially, I haven't re-ally benefited from anything, and academically I didn't get to study (although hopefully I will next year), so in terms of a profession I don't feel like I achieved anything. Right now, I am working on a research project and I want to publish it. I also have an idea for a book. Eventually, I would also like to start a busi-ness. People told me you can get a good salary with a master's degree in Saudi Arabia, so I could do that and come back and open up a center like the one I used to work at in Amman, and my business would be great.

Being away from home was challenging, but even though I feel like I wasted eight years [not working in her field] it built up my personality. It taught me things about life. I wasn't like this before. I am able to cover my ex-penses and save a little bit here and there, but sometimes I spend my savings. My family doesn't need anything from me—there are no obligations there.

Have you ever thought of going back home, if you found an opportunity closer to there?

Yes, but not because I've grown sick of Amman or don't want to live alone, but because my mother is an elderly woman who doesn't have anyone there to help her, so I would like to be with her. I also tried bringing her here to live in Amman, but she wouldn't have it. She said she can't get used to the lifestyle in Amman and living in an apartment. But no one is pressuring me to go back.

Marriage, Staying Single, and Making a Home

I was sitting in one of the coffee shops Maysoon and I frequented. Some coffee shops were more accessible to a variety of people from different backgrounds. The ones closer to her dormitory had the feel of a public space of sorts where, for the price of a cup of coffee, one could spend hours hanging out with friends or working on a project for class. The din of these places, ironically, provides some privacy, as the buzz of voices, movement of chairs, and blare of music make it hard for anyone to hear anything beyond the person sitting near them. Maysoon and I were having one of several conversations about marriage and her views on how her move to Amman might or might not have affected her marriage prospects. Initially, she talked about the ways moving gave a woman more options:

> The only thing that changes is that if the girl doesn't leave her house, then she will accept whoever comes to ask for her hand. So, what changes [with migration] is that she won't accept anyone lower in status than her in order to get married. By moving, she realizes that marrying isn't for the sake of marriage but finding the suitable partner that will enable her to live happily. I think this is the only change that happens which is a positive change. Because, honestly, I am bothered when I see girls in my community getting divorced. Why is she divorced? Then you hear she was married to some soldier and he hit her.[1] So, you studied engineering, and okay, you don't necessarily have to marry a doctor or engineer, but at least someone that has a university degree.

In a later conversation, she said that the effects on marriage are more specifically about working and the opportunities to meet people, and not specifically about being in Amman. At the same time, in subsequent conversations,

Maysoon also captured the tensions between not wanting to settle and not wanting to be alone:

> In the long run you don't want to be alone. I want someone to care for me . . . Also, people keep asking if you are engaged yet, and these questions are tiring. Coming to Amman does not decrease marriage chances. It's fate [*nasib*]. The problem is that the more independent you are, the more you look for from marriage. When you were younger, you might have settled for much less. From my perspective, it's not that your chances are better. Again, that's about fate. But it changes your perspective on marriage. You are changed. You won't settle for just anything.

*

Up until now, I have focused upon women's reasons for migration, their experiences in Amman, and negotiations and relationships with parents and other family members. I have also discussed at length the broader structural factors that have shaped the possibilities and limits these women face. Nearly everyone spoke about migration as a logical next step in fulfilling expectations and aspirations that were in large part an outcome of educational success. Their expectations and aspirations shifted and adjusted with time, and women who had spent many years in Amman reflected on what the future held in store for a single professional woman living independently. This chapter shares their reflections on marriage and the possibility of staying single in a context where marriage is the norm for adults. Slightly over one-third of the women profiled were thirty or older when we first spoke with them, and in follow-up interviews more than half were past thirty. Most had lived independently in Amman for more than a decade, and over that time their visions for the future had evolved, informed by experiences, age, and fortunes in Amman. I address the questions of how migration has shaped their lives and possibilities for the future, how their own expectations for marriage have shifted, and what they hope for in the years to come.

Maysoon's reflections, above, capture some of the ways in which marriage figured into the experiences of the women. Initially, like many women, Maysoon thought going to Amman would open up opportunities to meet more suitable partners. At the same time, as she was entering her thirties, she grappled with the possibility that she might not marry. She insisted that marriage was fate—whether or not she was in Amman, finding a marriage partner was ultimately something she did not have control over. This was a very typical way of talking about marriage. But she also nuanced the notion of fate. According to her, it's not that your chances of finding someone are better (or worse), "that's about fate. But [your migration/work] changes your

perspective on marriage. You are changed. You won't settle for just anything."
Thinking about the intersection of these forces, fate and experience, speaks
to the interplay of the two "oughts" discussed in chapter 2.[2] It's not just the
possibility that jobs and newfound mobility might allow women to find a
more like-minded, compatible partner. It's also, and perhaps more so, that
they feel they "ought" to be with a more suitable partner—that this is a fate
they deserve.

I begin this chapter with a brief discussion of contemporary discourses
about marriage, and a purported marriage crisis, as well demographic trends
in the realm of marriage. Then I examine women's own reflections on how
migration affects their marriage prospects, sharing some of the stories women
told about dating, meeting potential suitors, and their families' expectations
surrounding marriage. I end with the reflections of women who are concerned
or who have resigned themselves to the fact that they are not likely to marry
in a context where marriage is a powerful norm for adults.[3] Ultimately, how
women experience being single is tied, not surprisingly, to both class and specific family dynamics. Furthermore, their own experiences as single women living in Amman significantly color their expectations surrounding marriage.

A Marriage Crisis?

People like to call it a [marriage] crisis. The media considers it a crisis. They focus on
spinsterhood. But maybe for those who are not married, it's not a crisis.
 SHIREEN, thirty-four-year-old engineer living in Amman

As it has in many other parts of the Arab world, the perception that the contemporary era is characterized by a "marriage crisis" has been circulating in
the Jordanian press for several decades now. The crisis is typically framed in
both economic and moral terms.[4] Researchers and commentators frequently
flag the costs of getting married and setting up a home as major obstacles
to marriage plans.[5] As early as the 1980s, kinship groups publicly released
manifestos calling on families to scale back wedding celebrations that made
it difficult for young people to marry or forced families into debt. Discourse
surrounding the economics of getting married could also be gendered. In
Jordan, it is customary for the costs of a marriage to be borne by the groom
and his family. While some women can and do contribute to household or
wedding costs, the dominant expectation is that it is the man's responsibility.
Part of the marriage crisis discourse is that material expectations of women
and their families are unreasonable, making it difficult for men to marry and
leaving women vulnerable to "spinsterhood."[6] Despite these perceptions,

recent data reveal that costs of marriage have decreased since the 1980s.[7] The perception that divorce rates are on the rise has also contributed to belief that there is a marriage crisis.

Given the widespread concerns about marriage, religious organizations, civil society groups, and the state have intervened to try to prepare young men and women for marriage, to make marriage more affordable, and to educate the broader public about appropriate expectations surrounding marriage.[8] Concerns about unmarried women persist. The 2017–18 Jordan Population and Family Health Survey (JPFHS) reported that among respondents aged forty-five to forty-nine, 9 percent of women and 4 percent of men have never been married.[9] While there has been a gradual increase in the numbers of unmarried men and women over the past decade, more than 90 percent eventually marry. Nevertheless, the number of women who do not marry is almost one in ten, and some women are marrying later than used to be the case.[10] The median age at first marriage among women in 2017–18 was 22.7 years, and the majority of women still marry in their twenties; however, in 13 percent of all marriages the women were thirty or over.[11] Indeed, many of the women profiled here married in the course of our research project, some after lamenting that they might never marry.

Migration as a Marriage Project

Several years after finishing her bachelor's degree, Ibtisam moved from her village to Amman to pursue a master's degree. She worked as a public school teacher in her hometown but sought other professional opportunities in the capital city. She began by completing her master's degree and then switched careers to take advantage of more lucrative opportunities in the NGO sector. She did not return to live in her hometown, and eventually married in her thirties. In 2016, when she was in her early thirties, Ibtisam spoke with me about her migration to Amman and how, in her view, this experience had affected her marriage prospects:

> When I first came to Amman, I thought, this is a city where I will meet like-minded people, but I was mistaken. I found that, despite the fact that they live in the city, men in the city are actually worse . . . And there is the class thing. People are like, "You are from a village" [so you are beneath us].
>
> Amman is not a good place for a woman in her thirties. People have this pity for you and keep giving you suggestions for how to get married, but the end result is that you get more and more humiliated—through proposals from men who are old, married, or divorced, and God knows what problems they

have. Everyone looks at you, because you are in your thirties and you do not have the ring, and they look for reasons [to explain why you are still single].

Ibtisam's comments convey some issues faced by single women in Jordan today (and by single women in many other societies as well). Ibtisam argues that being single in one's thirties can mark a woman for pity and for unsolicited advice about their unmarried state.[12] However, Ibtisam's labor migration to Amman also created new opportunities—for financial independence, self-development, further education, and greater mobility. In some respects, then, her migration and independent living have significantly changed the terms of being single and contributed to different perspectives on who would be suitable for marriage. Was migration a liability for getting married? Some women thought so.

Ruweida was thirty years old and working for a public relations firm when she was interviewed for this project. She lived in an apartment on her own at the time of the interview, and had been living in Amman since 2008, except for a brief period of unemployment when she went home to a town in the south. She said:

> Unfortunately, people's views toward girls who live on their own can be negative. If she lives on her own, in their perspective, this is a girl with too much freedom. This means she can express her opinion because she's open-minded and she knows her rights. This goes against the idea in our society that she should obey the man. She knows her rights, and so they say, "You can't have two roosters in one cage [dikāyn fi qāfās wāḥād]" . . . A man may not have this view himself, but his family influences him because marriage is not a decision made by two people. It's made by the whole tribe. So, it's not enough that he wants to marry you, but it's his father and mother and brother and brother's wife. They all give their opinions about the matter.
>
> Since we [girls who have migrated] have lived a life where we support ourselves financially, pay rent, water, and electricity, we do not need a man to take care of these things . . . Because we do everything by ourselves, a man is additional support in life, no more and no less. And if he is not there, it does not mean we cannot go on. I will not be broken, because I am able to stand on my own.

Women viewed their migration as a mixed bag in terms of marriage prospects. Many shared Ruweida's sentiment that people judged them as unsuited to marriage because they were living apart from their families and were too independent to submit to prevailing gender roles in marriage. Others worried that their morality was being questioned.[13]

Like Ruweida, Salam complained that people judged her unfairly because she lived in a dormitory, questioning her intentions and morals. Salam reflected:

> You always have to prove yourself to be a good person in an environment that sees you as a bad person. They always question why I came to work here, far from my hometown. They always ask, "What brings you here? What's forcing you?" This is one of the challenges I face, and now, because I am a little late in getting married, I am not viewed the same way as other girls.

Salam points to the ways in which a woman who lives apart from her family can be morally suspect from the perspective of some segments of society. When I interviewed Salam a second time, the concern about her reputation persisted. She also linked her continued single status to being far from her community: "Because I moved away from my community, people stopped knowing who I am." This point can only be understood in a context where families still have a significant role in arranging marriages, and rates of consanguineous marriage (that is, cousin marriage) are still relatively high, particularly in rural areas.[14] Thus, one's community and extended kin are often the source of potential marriage partners. Sana', an engineer who was in her forties when we interviewed her, regretted migrating. She believed that her inability to marry was due to her distance from her community: "My being in Amman definitely affected my marriage prospects. Because I was not with my family, my relatives did not know me . . . even the neighbors did not know me, and traditional marriage happens by way of the family, even if it is all fate." But even with these regrets, Sana' acknowledges that marriage and meeting a suitable marriage partner are not entirely in one's own hands, repeating the oft-cited phrase that marriage is fate or destiny. In some respects, this platitude seemed to assuage disappointment and at times even a sense of failure about marriage.

What Sana' refers to as traditional marriage usually implies interested male suitors (and their family members) coming to a woman's family home for a meeting and a quick assessment by all parties involved (potential partners and their families) about the fit for marriage. In practice this can look quite different in different communities and families within Jordan. While families actively attempt to match up potential couples, their involvement can vary from arranging for a potential suitor to meet a potential bride in her parents' home (a visit that could lead to engagement shortly thereafter), to introducing a co-worker to a relative or friend looking to get married and facilitating an initial meeting in a public place without the involvement of family. The scenarios for meeting, matchmaking, and dating are too varied to enumerate.

Still, most marriages continue to be agreements between families in many respects. Being away from one's family during one's prime marriageability age, then, can be a significant factor in whom one meets and how. However, the role of families can also change over one's life course, with involvement of family, as well as the concerns of and pressures from family, shifting.

When asked how she was meeting potential marriage partners, Sahar, an engineer in her early forties, described a shifting degree of family involvement:

> It depends, really. Most of them come through colleagues, or relatives who hear that someone is looking for a wife and they tell him about me. As for where I meet them—I went through several stages, honestly. At first, I would always have to meet them at the house, and we would sit and talk for about a half-hour, then it would be like, "Okay, well, decide." I didn't like that. The result of meeting in such a manner was that I would say no . . . Whenever a suitor came, it would be like a state of emergency at home, a crisis, and this made me not like them [the suitors]. Also, I was in love with someone else—a man I worked with—so I kept refusing, hoping it would work out with him, but he was more educated, and his parents refused.
>
> Since I came to Amman, there have been other options for meeting people. But even then, my parents initially insisted he must come meet me at our home. So, he would have to travel from Amman to my hometown in order for me to meet with him. Then there was a time where I was engaged for a bit, but that did not work out. So, the next stage became that I would meet the person at a relative's place in Amman. After that we moved on to meeting someone at a coffee shop, but I had to be with a friend; someone had to be with me. And finally, I was able to go sit with a person at a public space, or a coffee shop, on my own—then make a decision and let my parents know.

Sahar's parents were initially strict about her interactions with potential suitors who were interested in meeting with her, and she consulted her parents about such meetings. At the same time, she had feelings for a co-worker, and she hoped they would marry. But due to differences in status—she did not meet the expectations of the potential groom's family—this failed to materialize. Eventually, Sahar's family agreed to let her meet men on her own. However, as she got older, the seriousness of proposals from men waned, in her estimation:

> When you grow older and you live with your parents, the situation is different than when you are living away from them. The only opportunity to change your situation is to get married. And people start saying, "Oh she's really desperate to get married." At first people would not say this publicly, but after the first two or three meetings, it would come out in an honest conversation. Guys would say, "If I'm going to marry you, you have to provide all these things in

return because I am marrying you. You should be grateful that I am considering you at your age." And then there are the new offers that I have been getting
lately: "Let's just date." They will say, "Oh, I cannot get married, but let's date,
and I will get a studio and I'll spend [money] on you and get you gifts, etc."

Sahar's situation was particularly challenging because she was relatively older
than other women we interviewed and because her family had been displaced
by war, interrupting her education and delaying her career. When she finally
had the opportunity to get a university degree, she was uninterested in proposals for marriage, as she was determined to succeed and graduate quickly.
Furthermore, as discussed in chapter 4, health issues in her family and the
death of one of her siblings meant that her family relied on her for emotional
and financial support, so she was less focused on getting married. Also, it is
clear from Sahar's telling that, while women had opportunities to meet men
at work or through colleagues, they were also negotiating family norms and
expectations, which they often shared.

Migration to Amman significantly expands timeframes and spaces for
meeting potential marriage partners. The proliferation of cafés and restaurants in the past two decades has provided acceptable spaces for men and
women to meet, although not all women we spoke with felt comfortable doing
so, given their own and their family's moral standards.[15] The privacy afforded
by technology and social media expanded the space for meeting potential
partners.[16] The sheer fact of being in Amman also gives women a degree of
liberty (and relative anonymity) in these affairs, in some cases with the consent of their families. In Sahar's case, it took some time before her family accepted this, and she, like many other women, did not feel comfortable acting
without the consent of her family. Even with these constraints, women met
men at work in their professional lives—without "dating" per se—who could
become potential marriage partners. Others saw the move to Amman as precisely the opportunity to independently get to know potential partners before
consulting family members. Being in Amman changed the possibilities or
introduced new factors that led to adjustments in their own expectations and
behavior, and families reckoned with these new realities as well.

Even if not all of the women with whom we spoke felt comfortable meeting potential partners on their own, or "dating," many of them believed that
the move to Amman significantly expanded their marriage opportunities
and increased the likelihood that they might meet someone "different"—
unlike the men at home. Several women, like Ibtisam, expressed hope that
they would find "better options" in Amman, but were disappointed by potential partners they met, or by the ways they themselves were stereotyped.

Ammanites at times viewed those from the provinces as traditional and con-servative peasants or "Bedouin," and not suitable partners for their sons (or daughters). This opposition to partnering at times was also a function of dif-ferences of national origin (Palestinian Jordanians/East Bank Jordanians), al-though this is often difficult to disentangle from the lower status accorded to those from the provinces. Nevertheless, opportunities for meeting men were significantly expanded by the move, both because the women were working and meeting people, and by virtue of living in a large city with a more diverse population. Remaining at home, unemployed, would provide limited oppor-tunities to meet men among a significantly smaller community.

Marriage Pressures

Some of the first women I interviewed in 2011 married while we were still conducting research. For women in this category, migration to Amman was a temporary phase in which they lived as single women in Amman and worked for a few years and then married. While we did not follow up with all women who married, we know that some of those who married continue to live and work in Amman, while a smaller number, in keeping with broader labor force participation trends, leave the workforce, at least temporarily, after marriage or after having children.

Labor statistics show that women are more likely to stay in the workforce after marriage if they work in the public sector, where it is easier to balance work and family. Dima, a twenty-three-year-old engineer from a provincial city in the north whom I interviewed in 2011, quit her job just before her wed-ding, wanting to free up her time for the event. Initially, not working held some appeal for her, especially since her husband was well off. However, after a few years and the birth of her first child, she decided to go back to work, this time in the public sector. She encountered some resistance from her hus-band and his family, but she insisted she needed to work. She also enrolled in a master's program after going back to work. Fatima, a software developer who worked in Amman for four years before marrying, continued to work in Amman at first, commuting from her governorate initially, but she quit after having a child, as the long hours made it difficult to balance care for her child and work. After a period of unemployment, she found a temporary job as a teacher at a private school closer to her provincial city and hoped to find a permanent job as a teacher. These two examples show that decisions about work and family did not necessarily follow a linear or predictable pattern.

Some young women faced considerable pressure from their families to marry. Women I spoke with were of mixed opinions about the implications of staying single, and some women had begun to plan for a future with single-hood in mind. Noor, an engineer in her late twenties, said:

> I don't let [marriage] worry me, even if everyone pressures you to think about it. You see it in the eyes of your mother, and when she says, "Ya rab tkooni fi baytik" (Oh, God, may you be in your house [that is, marital home]). I used to get annoyed, but now I just smile and say, "Inshallah" (God willing).

While Noor could ignore these comments, Faizeh faced much more pressure from her family. Faizeh was twenty-six years old when I spoke with her at length about her experiences as a single woman. She worked for a management consulting firm and was from one of the northern provinces. She was one of the first women I knew who had come from the provinces to live and work in Amman. Faizeh told me her story:

> I was under a lot of pressure to marry. I had potential suitors coming to our home all the time. I would go home on the weekends to meet them, and my parents were pushing me to choose one. I had constant conflict with them. One suitor [Amjad] was particularly persistent. He had seen me at a wedding, and my parents were pressuring me to take him seriously. I told my parents that I wanted to meet him outside the home, and they agreed. They told Amjad that he was free to go talk with me . . . Over a period of a few months, we saw each other a few times, and my parents insisted that I needed to make a decision. They wanted me to get engaged.
>
> I got sick of the constant pressure, and I began to approach the subject more practically. I decided, okay, he's from a good family, he has a good job, he is well off, and everyone speaks highly of him. Maybe I should give him a chance. I gave in and got engaged even though I was not sure.
>
> After the engagement, Amjad was in a rush to get married. I was still not feeling sure, and I tried to get him to delay the wedding, but he insisted on setting a date soon and booked hotels and the like. But then he started acting weird, and he made me really uncomfortable. He was very pushy, and it made me worry about what was to come. It got to the point where I could not stand being around him, and I was becoming increasingly disturbed about marrying this guy.
>
> I decided I could not go through with the marriage. I told my parents I did not love him and was not attracted to him. They refused to accept my decision, and I spent a month trying to convince them. They were furious and very tough on me. They said things like, "You just want to keep living on your own and having fun." They threatened me, telling me they would make me quit my job and go home. I told them, "Fine, I will quit my job and I will stay at home. But I will not marry him." Then I told them I would go through with the marriage, but they would be responsible for this decision. "If I'm miserable it will be your fault." Finally, they . . . relented.

After this incident, Faizeh's parents eased up on the pressure to marry. Thereafter, Faizeh insisted she would only meet with a potential suitor at her parents' home if she was 100 percent sure she wanted to marry him. She needed to get to know him before there was any discussion between families. Eventually, she met someone a family member introduced to her. She got to know him on her own terms, and they eventually married; she was thirty-one years old at the time.

While all families hoped their daughters would marry, not all were as forceful in trying to get them married. Hala (interlude 4), a thirty-year-old engineer, had a different experience than Faizeh had. Her family was very supportive of her move to Amman in 2007 and did not express concern about her still being single. Of her family she said, "We don't have this mentality in our house that you must get married . . . If it happens, it happens. It is fate [*nasib*]." Six years after our interview Hala married after all.

Thus, families play different roles. For Faizeh, and for other women who felt a great deal of pressure from families to marry, age matters. Families tended to exert a great deal of pressure as women reached "peak" marriage age, usually in their mid- to late twenties. However, women in their thirties felt less pressure from families. Perhaps this was because, as one woman put it, "they feel bad making an issue of it since they know we are past the point of likely getting married. They do not want to hurt our feelings." This is where the oft-repeated phrase about marriage as fate also helps relieve the pressures of repeated inquiries about one's marital state. Many women acknowledged and appreciated that their parents worried about them and hated to see them alone. Parents worried about their futures, particularly given the family-oriented society they live in. Most people in Jordan get married, and those who don't almost always live with family. Living alone is rare. While women understood their parents' concerns, they resisted being pressured into marriages they did not find suitable.

"I won't settle": Marriage Expectations

Nearly all women interviewed talked about refusing to marry just to marry. As Maysoon relayed:

> Everyone assumes that you must be miserable, and if you are sad, they assume it's because you are single. They also assume that you are trying to catch any available man around you . . . I will only marry if there is a good opportunity. I hear too many negative stories. At the same time, I cannot constantly be thinking about it. It is exhausting, especially because you have so little control over the matter.

Women argued that life experiences made it difficult for them to settle for a suitor who could not offer them the quality of life they needed. Typically, this was not about material or financial needs, although there were some exceptions. Sumaya, for example, said she hoped to marry someone who was sufficiently well off that she would not have to keep working, and a few others shared her desire. Dima, who married a doctor less than two years after arriving in Amman, similarly welcomed the opportunity to be taken care of financially after struggling (and as her family struggled to maintain a middle-class lifestyle), even if she eventually returned to the workforce. For most, however, the key issue was finding a like-minded man who would respect their opinions and accomplishments in life. Some of this was colored by stories from their female friends who were in bad marriages. Maysoon, quoted above, told me about a friend who suffered domestic violence and a sister whose marriage had ended in divorce. Maysoon had also gone through a broken engagement that was quite contentious. Her family had been supportive through it all; however, her fiancé's family was angry and made her and her family's life difficult in the course of the breakup. These examples served as lessons for her. A key sentiment conveyed by women was that the options available to them were just not satisfactory.

Riham, a thirty-two-year-old engineer who had been living in Amman since 2006, expressed this sentiment in biting terms:

> The reason I am single is not that I am working or living in a dormitory. I think the problem is with the men who are currently around us . . . I do not see myself as having a problem. I see women advancing and men not making half the effort. They are intimidated by you . . . I think they see you as competition more than anything. I would consider marrying if there was a suitable person, if I found a person who would support me. Why not? Meanwhile, all I see is men concerned with themselves. They want to remain in the spotlight and for you to become a new mom. I do not need money. I can take care of myself financially. I want someone to walk alongside me. I want someone who supports my ambitions.

Last time I spoke with Riham, she told me about a few men whom she had met recently, either through family or on her own. According to Riham, none was particularly promising, except one with whom she was talking online. However, Riham seemed adamant as ever not to settle. In other dimensions of her life, things were going well. Her company, which had almost gone bankrupt (leaving her without a salary for months), was doing well, and her loyalty to the company had been rewarded. She was making a good salary and had bought a car. Also, her family, with whom she had had significant conflict over her refusal to come home to her village, had finally come around to accept her living in Amman. She was looking for an apartment and contemplating pursuing another degree. In the meantime, she socialized often and particularly enjoyed opportunities for group hikes and walks around the city. She was open to meeting people, but felt no pressure to marry.

Unlike Riham, some women were dissatisfied with their single status. As I was wrapping up my discussion with Salam, I said, "Thanks Salam. I think I'm done." She responded, "There are things you still need to know. You have not asked me if I am happy." I replied, "Are you happy?" Salam said:

> Sometimes I am, and sometimes I am not. When I am not, I try to tell myself, "Be quiet." I try to ignore the feelings of unhappiness. "It's okay. Time will pass." Some days I am so tired from work I do not even have time to ask myself this question. But then I do, and I wonder, "What am I doing? Why am I here? Why [am I] here alone?"

Part of the loneliness described by Salam has to do with dormitory living and the isolation some felt about this lifestyle. But even Salam was conflicted. She missed her family and the sociality of village life, and she was concerned about marriage:

> Some people think that Amman may improve their opportunities for marriage. I can see how it can go both ways, but for me, my coming to Amman has had more of a negative effect on my marriage prospects, because I moved away from my community. People stopped knowing who I am. Also, as a female living in a dorm, people have a particular image of you . . . "Your daughter is in a dorm, so there is a question mark on her." So, this has a negative effect.

While Salam acknowledged that being in Amman might decrease her chances of getting married, she felt strongly that she had benefited personally and professionally from being in Amman and had a hard time imagining herself back at home.

Making a Home of One's Own

For women in their thirties and forties, and who continue to live in dormitories or apartments in Amman as single women, marriage will be less likely as they get older. Given that almost one in ten women stay single, not marrying is not outside the norm. Yet, they will be single in a society that often views this as a troubling fate—even though, like all subject positions, how one's single status is viewed and experienced is colored by class, education, and one's professional status. Penny Johnson, in her research on single women in

Palestine, found that not all women viewed marriage as necessary for happiness and that "they did not necessarily locate the source of the misery in their lack of spouse, but rather in the community responses to their unmarried state."[17] Johnson points to different attitudes about singlehood across generations, with an older generation of single women benefiting from a status accorded them because of their contributions to the Palestinian national struggle. We heard some echoes of this status in the oral histories with the earlier generation of teachers who helped in the expansion of formal education in Jordan and in supporting families. The brother of Zahra, one of these early teachers, captured this sentiment well:

> If we kept on recording [the interview] for days, we wouldn't be able to pay Zahra (b. 1941) back for all that she did for us and for our community and for Jordan as well. We did not realize how accomplished she was until her friends talked about her at her funeral.

Despite later ages at first marriage in Jordan today (and in much of the region) and a growing number of single women, limited attention has been paid to single women as a category.[18] The research available on single women in the region has typically focused on women living with their families. Most of it has focused on single women working outside the home, with some reference to women migrating to Arab Gulf countries for work.[19] Here, I consider what this experience means for women who are living on their own and who believe they are not likely to marry.

> I went to Sahar's dorm room and sat with her and Amira for nearly two hours. It was Mother's Day in Jordan—a tortured holiday for each of them due to personal losses they had suffered. We sat in a small corridor that served as the common space in Sahar's dormitory suite, rectangular and so narrow that it was difficult to sit facing each other and still leave room for someone to pass through. Nevertheless, Sahar made coffee on the small stove in the corner, and we huddled around a table to drink coffee and enjoy the sweets I had purchased for our meeting. At some point, Sahar's roommate, an undergraduate at the University of Jordan, came in briefly to get some belongings. She said she was going to spend the night at her sister's. Sahar—in her midforties—was old enough to be her mother and this contrast was indicative of the difficulty of Sahar and Amira's situation. They were growing older and had reached a point in their lives very different than that of a nineteen-year-old undergraduate, yet they found themselves sharing the same space. We went on to discuss where their decision to migrate to Amman brought them and where they would go from here.

Of all the women I spoke with, Amira was the one most concerned about her future and this question of making a home for oneself. The word for home—

bayt or *dar*—is home both as a physical place (the actual house), and in a genealogical sense.[20] Single women still have a social *bayt* that they belong to, relatives who form their broader kin network, but living on their own for more than a decade left some women wondering where they would make a physical home in the future.

Amira, at thirty-three, was growing increasingly concerned about her future. She had been living in a dormitory for eight years at that time and wanted a home of her own. However, she did not think her family would approve of her leaving the security and supervision of a dormitory. Her sense of insecurity as a single woman was not strictly about her singlehood, but intimately linked to her family situation, the debt she had accumulated, and her inability to get ahead financially. Her parents had divorced when she was young, but many of the big decisions in her life required the cooperation of her male guardian—her father—who was generally absent or unwilling to facilitate her life projects. One of the last times we talked about the future, she was discouraged. When I asked her if she ever thought about going back home to her village, she replied, "The problem is that I do not have a home." Thus, the precarity of being single was tied to her family history (especially the divorce of her parents when she was still a young child), her relationship with her family, and her challenging financial situation. Amira very much wanted to get married, but given these dynamics, as well as her shy and somewhat reserved personality, she had also been reluctant to pursue or respond to several marriage proposals. In at least one case, conflict within the family derailed a potential suitor. In contrast to someone like Riham, also in her thirties after nearly a decade in Amman, she felt a great deal of insecurity as she looked to the future.

The women we spoke with did not plan to stay single. While prolonging marriage was appealing to some women when they first moved, it worried many in their late twenties and early thirties—but not so much that they would sacrifice other goals and aspirations. As we see with Amira, the degree of concern was linked to the kind of singlehood they could imagine—the life they could lead. In many respects, being single is the result of a set of choices women have made, but, as we see from the research in other contexts, even where cohabitation is possible and forming relationships or marriages is largely the purview of the individuals, women faced difficulty finding compatible partners and/or partners willing to have a family.[21] Being single, then, is not a predetermined choice, but the outcome of a set of other choices and preferences, and the reality of shifting preferences that come with age and experience.

As we heard from Jihan in chapter 4, committing to a career as a nurse far from her home at the age of eighteen had far-reaching implications for her and her family. Jihan took great pride in her professional accomplishments, as well as her ability to help educate her younger siblings and support her widowed mother. However, these decisions entailed sacrifices on her part, and as Jihan entered her thirties, she reflected on the decisions she had made and the prospects of starting her own family:

> Sometimes I do feel some regret about the choices I made, especially when I see my girlfriends who have families—kids and a life partner who shares their concerns and feels what they are feeling. The feeling of stability is a beautiful feeling. I do not think about it a lot, but people keep reminding you, "You're still not married!" I regret not being more open to the options around me. There were many who were suitable. But I held onto this one relationship that did not work out, and then I had all these family responsibilities. If I regret anything, it is that I was not attuned enough to the need to balance my responsibilities to them with my responsibilities to myself. There are many days I feel lonely. But I am also at ease knowing that I accomplished a lot and that I took care of my family.

Jihan had a relationship with a colleague that did not lead to marriage. In the end, the two families could not see eye to eye about the amount of dowry. This led to other disagreements the young couple could not overcome. At that point, according to Jihan, she had forfeited many opportunities. In 2016, Jihan was promoted to a job that brought her back to her hometown and enabled her to live at home for the first time in more than a decade. While she was home again, we corresponded, and I asked her if she had any regrets. Reflecting on this question, Jihan said she regretted not having her own home. At the same time, Jihan's regret was tempered by her sense that she had done right by her family. While Jihan at that time was pessimistic about ever being able to marry, within a few years of returning to her hometown she was engaged to be married to a medical professional from her province.

Conclusion

The internal labor migration of single women in Jordan has affected their marriage prospects in different ways. While migration provides many new opportunities—to meet people, to earn a salary and potentially gain financial independence, and to gain broader and more diverse social experiences—it also creates new responsibilities, challenges, and expectations. Clearly, being single in Jordan is still a challenging position—if not materially, socially. As Ibtisam reflected after she married, "People speak to you differently when you are married. They treat you differently." The challenges Ibtisam faced, however, went beyond being single and were colored by the significant biases she faced as a woman from the south living and working in the capital. Thus, her social status as a single woman cannot be divorced from issues of class and geography, and specific family dynamics. Nevertheless, Ibtisam was determined to pursue postgraduate education and to seek new professional opportunities. She was also resolute in her conviction to marry someone who respected her accomplishments, as she did nearly ten years after leaving home. Other women remained single and began to reckon with being single as a longer term reality. Salam, who had initially lamented her single status, reflected on this when we last met:

> Marriage is no longer a central thing for me. It is secondary. If I get married, I get married. If I don't, I don't. I have many accomplishments in my life. If marriage comes on its own, okay. I am not looking for it. I am working on my master's degree, my career, and other things. It is not something that preoccupies me.

These comments may reflect the acceptance of a reality that is unlikely to change—being single. But Salam has also made a nice life for herself and seems increasingly at peace with it. Her successful career and supportive family, of course, help in shaping her views on being single. Noor shared a similar perspective:

> Marriage is destiny [nasib]. Whether I am here [in Amman], or on the moon, or at my parents' home, if it is my destiny it will happen. But I am not going to marry just to marry, [only] if the right person comes along.

Noor captures for us, again, the interplay between what is possible, what is expected (what "ought" to happen), and what is destined. While the belief in a larger power at work in one's life is felt most strongly by those with greater faith, Noor being among them, the figurative acknowledgment of that power is ubiquitous in everyday speech. "Marriage is fate" is a common refrain. But Noor, like nearly all the women we spoke with, believed she had an important role to play in finding that fate.

Conclusion

By focusing closely on particular individuals and their changing relationships, one would necessarily subvert the most problematic connotations of culture: homogeneity, coherence, and timelessness. Individuals are confronted with choices, struggle with others, make conflicting statements, argue about points of view on the same events, undergo ups and downs in various relationships and changes in their circumstances and desires, face new pressures, and fail to predict what will happen to them or those around them.

LILA ABU-LUGHOD, "Writing against Culture"[1]

Men make their own history, but they do not make it as they please; they do not make it under self-selected circumstances, but under circumstances existing already, given and transmitted from the past.

KARL MARX[2]

In these pages, I have endeavored to capture some of the complexities of individual women's lives. I could never capture the full richness of their stories, but I have tried to provide greater nuance to issues of women's labor and mobility, family relationships, and the "alternatives that become visible" to them as they move through their world.[3] We might read the stories of women such as Noor, Maysoon, Amira, Hannan, Sameera, and many others as exceptional—as examples of particularly strong and motivated women uniquely able to overcome "traditional" gender roles. Indeed, in chapter 4, Hannan, the young woman who faced much opposition from her father to her move, said as much: "You feel at times that a girl in our rural communities almost has to be extraordinary, an overachiever, or very unique in order to overcome these obstacles." In many respects, they are extraordinary women who have overcome many obstacles—personal and structural—to create particular futures. At the same time, in pointing to their creative agency, it is not my intention to juxtapose them with other women, or to paint a picture of the lives of the majority of women as somehow homogeneous or, worse yet, unsuccessful or failed. Each of us makes our way forward in the world with "circumstances existing already."

The experience of each of these women is singular—in the way that all human experience is unique—but their lives are very much the product of socioeconomic developments that have unfolded gradually over the last few

decades, and the values and norms that have evolved to make sense of a rapidly changing social and cultural context. The lives of women profiled here
are also shaped by relationships, especially those with their parents and siblings who have been essential to their stories. Throughout this book, I have
highlighted the ways in which their individual stories are very much embedded in these familial relations and structural conditions.

These women have much to show us about the workings of class, gender,
and social change. Drawing on their experiences, I have argued that attention
to the everyday practices of women who migrate for work in Jordan helps
to illuminate the incremental ways in which social change unfolds. Reading
the dominant narratives about women in Jordan, it's hard to imagine that
these women even exist. But exist they do, and they hail from communities
all over the country—from villages to urban centers. They come to Amman
seeking jobs, social status, and particular futures: professional opportunities,
autonomy, better marriages, and respect.

Several factors have been key to the stories I have shared. Chief among
them is educational access and academic achievement of women. Those who
are at the center of this book hold their status as educated women in high
regard and frame their decision to move to Amman as closely linked to their
educational achievement. They aspire to a future they believe their education
makes possible, if not necessary. Uneven development and geographic disparities in economic opportunities are also a key factor in shaping migration
to Amman. Very few women who successfully made a life for themselves in
the capital imagined they could return to their provincial communities. Even
if jobs became available in their hometowns, most said they would not return
because they had come to appreciate the professional and social benefits of
being in a relatively large urban center—mobility, anonymity, and greater diversity. Wanting to stay in Amman did not negate the reality that they also
missed home and, especially when they first arrived, felt out of place. For
some women, this feeling of being out of place was tied to the preconceptions
others held about them as provincial women, particularly in the workplace.
It was also tied to their own insecurities about making their way in the city—
insecurities exacerbated by their youth and lack of experience in Amman. All
of this contributed to the feeling of *ghurba* that I discussed earlier in the book,
but still, with time, they have made the city their own.

The experiences of these women also serve to challenge hegemonic narratives about the provinces, provincial values, and politics. Ethnographic research on Jordan is sparse, and scholarship on the provinces is even more
rare.[4] Stereotypes about people who live in the provinces are ubiquitous and
function as a system of internal othering that must be reckoned with. This

book contributes to a more nuanced understanding of geographic difference, and the ways in which it intersects with class and gender. In this way, it takes us well beyond staid binary tropes for analyzing politics and socioeconomic hierarchies in the country. Much remains to be done here.

Finally, the economic conditions and attendant ideologies surrounding labor, productivity, and value are central to the experiences depicted in this text. While neoliberal economic policies are a powerful force today in shaping the labor market within Jordan and globally, a much longer history of defining women's nonwaged labor in all its varieties as nonproductive, even when it is critical to family survival, is central to how educated women today shape their aspirations for the future. Nevertheless, I have argued against any kind of determinism in thinking through the effects of such forces.

Development discourses tend to flatten or oversimplify the interplay of economic and cultural forces, and the actions that people take given these contexts. Women, in particular, are often depicted as victims of their circumstances, and their interests defined as separate from the interests of families and communities.[5] The aspirations of these women and their trajectories, while clearly shaped by economic forces—perceived opportunities, ideas about valuable labor, and ongoing economic crisis—cannot be reduced to them. The women we met relocated to Amman seeking professional opportunities and personal fulfillment in a trajectory that they argue is the logical outcome of their efforts—what *ought* to be. At the same time, they work to support their birth families, to build their own families, and to make a suitable future for themselves. Their path is not linear, and their projects not always predictable. Through it all they work, create, reflect, and aspire anew.

Creative Agency

One of the key arguments I have made here is that we should think about the actions of these women as "creative agency." I give strong credit to the late Saba Mahmood for significantly expanding my conceptualization of agency, power, and resistance.[6] I read her article on this topic in 2002 after a summer of conducting ethnographic field research in a small town in Jordan.[7] Her insistence that the analysis of gender and power must move beyond a resistance/subordination binary resonated personally, and also provided a powerful analytical framework for the ethnographic research I had just begun. In her 2005 monograph, she argues:

> If the ability to effect change in the world and in oneself is historically and culturally specific (both in terms of what constitutes "change" and the means by

which it is effected), then the meaning and sense of agency cannot be fixed in advance, but must emerge through an analysis of the particular concepts that enable specific modes of being, responsibility, and effectivity . . . In this sense, agentival capacity is entailed not only in those acts that resist norms but also in the multiple ways in which one inhabits norms.[8]

Mahmood, given her interest in women's piety circles, was particularly interested in how and why women might choose to inhabit norms that ostensibly served to suppress them. In doing so, she paved a path for us to think about the varied ways in which women (and men) exert their "agentival capacity" in the world. "Creativity" here does not mean making something out of nothing. As I have argued, women's agency is creative in the sense of working with the structures they have inherited, but not always settling for what those structures have produced in the past or typically produce. At the same time, they hold fiercely onto norms surrounding respect and care for one's parents, and the obligation to care for family. But they embrace this norm on different terms.

The women whose stories we share in this book faced many challenges along the way—economic, personal, professional. These challenges are never strictly about gender or cultural norms. They are as much about class, geography, inequality, and the global economic systems that limit and shape opportunities for young people in the Global South, as they are about gender. Furthermore, the trials the women face in seeking particular futures are in many respects faced by their brothers, too, who also struggle to care for parents and siblings, and build their own families in difficult economic circumstances.[9] While gender cannot completely encapsulate their struggles, they experience them in gendered ways. The young women whom we met persisted in pursuing a life in Amman despite the difficulties they faced, at times moderating their aspirations and at other times expanding them. Or perhaps more aptly, their aspirations shifted and evolved in the ways that the unfolding of life (and all its randomness) and the accumulation of experience does for most of us. They navigated life in Amman as single women and took pride in personal and professional growth. They also took pride in caring for their families.

Ideology, Practice, and Change

If the social is always past, in the sense that it is always formed, we have indeed to find other terms for the undeniable experience of the present: not only the temporal present, the realization of this and this instant, but the specificity of present being, the inalienably physical, within which we may indeed discern and acknowledge institutions, formations, positions, but not always as fixed products, defining products. And then if the social is the fixed and explicit—the known relationships, institutions, formations, positions—all that is present and moving, all that escapes or seems to escape from the fixed and the explicit and the known, is grasped and defined as the personal: this, here, now, alive, active, "subjective."

RAYMOND WILLIAMS, *Marxism and Literature*[10]

What has changed? Society has started seeing more examples that encourage them to allow their girls [to move for work]. Honestly, I feel like our society has to have an example to follow from someone they know, not just from a foreign or random person. If you were to publicize it on TV for years that girls should go and fulfill their future aspirations, it wouldn't be the same as if their neighbor Um Ahmad sent her daughter to live on her own and she was doing well . . . The showcase has expanded, and they see successful stories of girls who maintained their social standing and were able to reach great achievements. So, they say, why not, why not my daughter? . . . A long time ago I don't think that many people would have accepted it.

NOOR, twenty-eight-year-old engineer

People learn from each other's experiences. If I had left to work in Amman, let's say, in 2003, if I had heard of a girl going to work in Amman at that time, I would have found it strange. I would say, "Why did she go, what's forcing her?" Even if they gave me 1,000 dinars in Amman, I wouldn't go work there. That's what I would have said, but as these experiences have become more frequent, people influence one another. And not necessarily in a direct way. You hear of people you know, and you say, "Well, look at her, she's happy and nothing is wrong with her."

SALAM, teacher in her thirties

In this book, I have centered women's experiences and their own narratives about their move to Amman as a means of capturing the everyday practices that make structural change. The overwhelming forces of global capitalism, neoliberal forms of governance, and patriarchy shape the context for their action. While women recognize the power of these structures over them, they are also living a life that *feels* different compared to those of their peers or female relatives.[11] This difference is palpable to the women themselves and informs their aspirations and struggles. It is the "present" to which Raymond Williams alludes to in the epigraph above: "all that is present and moving, all that escapes or seems to escape from the fixed and the explicit." In this vein, Salam, in the epigraph, conveys that her mobility, and that of others like her, is new—something she says might not have been common or even acceptable in 2003. We know that women have relocated for work in the past, but something about contemporary migration is qualitatively different in a number of ways—in terms of motivations, urban living, and career aspirations, among other factors.

Structurally, while it is impossible to fully understand or articulate how these individual experiences contribute to change in their own right, I argue that they are integral to the incremental change that is always part of the unfolding of history—a relatively short history of mass education, intensified capitalism, and local economies and labor markets today almost entirely defined and measured by waged labor. Both Salam and Noor talk about the importance of role models in their own communities. Noor emphasizes this point, arguing that examples of women moving, migrating, or relocating for work need to be local to affect how mothers, fathers, uncles, and brothers think about women's mobility and living in the city on their own. In this sense, Noor and Salam do see the decisions they have made as important for change. While the women profiled here did not start out with the intention of creating alternate pathways, in many respects they are contributing to making new realities through example. This gradual reconfiguration of the everyday is central to understanding the changes that have been unleashed by socioeconomic forces. While gender ideologies are powerful and hegemonic in Jordan as everywhere, we have seen throughout this book how everyday practices challenge, complicate, and push at the boundaries of such ideologies.

Tempering too positive an assessment of their own experiences, Sumaya reminded me and the other women in a focus group discussion in 2014 that women still face many limits: "You don't want to paint a picture which is too great. There are still huge obstacles and double standards for women. They say they want their daughters to be the best, but then they limit them." The recognition that women faced specific limits in pursuing opportunities or fulfilling aspirations was a sentiment that all of the women we spoke with would agree with on some level, even though some faced fewer such limits in their own lives than others did. Of course, one of the strongest limits they faced was a lack of good jobs, largely a function of Jordan's place in a global economic system that has led to increased precarity for many. They worked actively to overcome such limits—limits that were gendered but never entirely about gender. In the process, they were contributing to incremental shifts in social life.

Epilogue

We are in a different era of research now. Because of social media, LinkedIn, and the internet more broadly, as well as the intimacy of ethnographic research, I am still in touch with some of the women profiled here. Several have become close acquaintances, and we reconnect each time I return to Jordan. I can also follow major life developments, especially the professional developments, of many others. Because I did not seek their permission to keep abreast of new developments in this way, I will only speak generally here. It is no surprise that their lives have unfolded in ways they may not have anticipated. Some have gone abroad to work or study. Others have married, even though they thought they never would. Most continue in their careers, some with professional mobility and success, while others continue to work at a level and in spaces not much changed.

Jordan continues to be a country with high levels of education but with an economy, or rather a place in the global economy, that is not able to produce the kinds of jobs many of its citizens have come to expect due to their education and aspirations for a decent quality of life. The economic challenges have only been exacerbated by the COVID-19 pandemic. The women profiled in this book are not the most vulnerable to the vagaries of the economy. The situation of refugees, the poor, and those with less education is more precarious, and the struggle to meet the basic needs of their families is constant. Yet, young people like the women we have met in this book still struggle to build a better life for themselves and their families. How they define a better life has been shaped by their education, their migration, and the aspirations that have been formed in the process.

Acknowledgments

As with all such projects, there are many, many people for me to thank. First and foremost, I thank the women in Jordan who were willing to share their stories with me. It takes a great deal of trust to share your story with someone, and I hope I have been worthy of this trust, and that I have represented your narratives fairly. The strength and determination of the women who are the focus of this book will always be an inspiration to me. The limits of this work are only my own.

At my academic institution, Georgetown University, I have been supported in producing this work by a team of the most talented research assistants, among them Leen Alfatafta, Shifaa Alsairafi, Matison Hearn-Desautels, Leena Khan, Menatalla Mohamed, Adam Shaham, Ahmad Sharawi, and Cimrun Srivastava. I would also like to thank Samar Saeed and Tariq Adely for their very insightful comments on an earlier version of this text and for their intellectual engagement with this work. Thanks also go to Adrieh Abou Shehadeh for hours of transcription.

The research for this book would not have been possible without my research collaborators in Jordan. Afaf Al-Khoshman was instrumental every step of the way in the research process, and in her very thoughtful feedback on the final version of the manuscript. I have learned a great deal from Afaf and owe her a debt of gratitude. Also in Jordan, Helen Ayoub was instrumental in capturing the stories of an older generation of women who moved for work. Thank you, Helen.

At Georgetown, I have benefited from the feedback and support of many. My colleagues at the Center for Contemporary Arab Studies (Mohammad Alahmad, Belkacem Baccouche, Killian Clarke, Marwa Daoudy, Rochelle

Davis, Noureddine Jebnoun, Joseph Sassoon, and Judith Tucker) are my family at Georgetown, and I thank them for always making me feel I have a home in Washington, DC. The CCAS staff have also been a key part of this family. Thanks to Dana Dairani, Susan Douglass, Alison Glick, Kelli Harris, Coco Tate, and Vicki Valosik.

I have also benefited from the camaraderie of many others at Georgetown. Special thanks to Lahra Smith, Shiloh Krupar, and Elliot Colla for their friendship over the past years. Particular thanks go to Rochelle Davis for a most productive writing group, for many pep talks, and for very careful readings of several versions of this work. The book benefited significantly from her input and encouragement. Thanks also to Anna Newman for ongoing support during the writing process. I also want to acknowledge the support and friendship of Betty Anderson and Louise Cainkar during different phases of this project. My thanks also to three anonymous reviewers who gave very helpful comments on the manuscript. The research for this book was funded by a National Endowment for the Humanities Fellowship from the American Center for Oriental Research, as well as a Summer Academic Grant and Senior Research Fellowship from Georgetown University.

As always, nothing I have done would have been possible without my family. My siblings Suzanne, Hannan, Kathy, Amal, Lena, and Tariq keep my life full and joyful. Even though I have left town, they continue to be my center. My mother Ibtisam holds this center together, and I owe her much for her support throughout my life. Her labor as the mother of seven, in our family bodega (the "store"), as the hairdresser of the family, and in the everyday ways she cares for neighbors, extended family, and the hundreds of friends that have come through our home for one of her delicious meals—always welcoming, always generous—is a model to which I continue to aspire. My partner in life, Aiman, makes everything easier, makes what feels daunting surmountable, makes me feel I can do anything. While "marriage is fate," choosing to spend my life with him was the best decision I have ever made. My daughters Samar and Laila were very young when this project began and put up with lots of absences from their mother while she was doing research. They are young women now, embarking on their own new journeys, and I so look forward to hearing about their adventures. Laila edited two versions of this manuscript with the eye of an experienced professional. She is a budding writer herself, and I look forward to reading more of her work. Samar always asks me how my day went and checks in regularly to share her news. Her presence and her love help keep me motivated.

In the course of writing this book, I lost my father Issa Salim Adely. I would not be where I am today without his many, many years of working multiple jobs. He toiled endlessly, but he also laughed and loved and had a knack for storytelling (shared with his mother, my grandmother Shaikha) to which I can only aspire. I miss his being in the world. It is to you, Baba, that I dedicate this book.

Notes

Introduction

1. See, for example, Eunsook Jee, "Unmarried Daughters as Family Caregivers: Evolving Family Relationships, Gender Order, and Singlehood in Japan," *Korean Anthropology Review* 5 (2021); Ariana Kaci and Helene Starks, "Caring for the Elderly in Algeria within the Discourse of Traditionalism and Modernism: Is There a Kabyle 'Woman Problem'?" *IJFAB: International Journal of Feminist Approaches to Bioethics* 6, no. 2 (2013): 163; Maya Rosenfeld, *Confronting the Occupation: Work, Education, and Political Activism of Palestinian Families in a Refugee Camp* (Stanford: Stanford University Press, 2004), 149–50, 183–85.

2. With the onset of the Syrian conflict and the influx of Syrian refugees, international aid organizations have proliferated in Jordanian communities where they had been largely absent in the past. One outcome has been to create good-paying jobs for young women in the provinces.

3. Lila Abu-Lughod, "Writing against Culture," in *Recapturing Anthropology: Working in the Present*, ed. Richard G. Fox (Sante Fe, NM: School of American Research, 1991); Lila Abu-Lughod, *Writing Women's Worlds: Bedouin Stories* (Berkeley: University of California Press, 1993).

4. Fida Adely, *Gendered Paradoxes: Educating Jordanian Women in Nation, Faith, and Progress* (Chicago: University of Chicago Press, 2012). "Gendered paradox" was a term used in a World Bank report about women and gender in Jordan in 2005, one that I took up in my book *Gendered Paradoxes*. The term continues to be used to label the ostensibly paradoxical nature of demographic trends in the region. For example, see Ragui Assaad, Rana Hendy, Moundir Lassassi, and Shaimaa Yassin, "Explaining the MENA Paradox: Rising Educational Attainment, Yet Stagnant Female Labor Force Participation," *Demographic Research* 43, no. 28 (2020).

5. Fida Adely, "Educating Women for Development: The Arab Human Development Report 2005 and the Problem with Women's Choices," *International Journal of Middle East Studies* 41, no. 1 (2009); Adely, *Gendered Paradoxes*.

6. Timothy Mitchell, "America's Egypt," *Middle East Report* 169 (March–April 1991).

7. Fida Adely, Ankushi Mitra, Menatalla Mohamed, and Adam Shaham, "Poor Education, Unemployment and the Promise of Skills: The Hegemony of the 'Skills Mismatch' Discourse," *International Journal of Educational Development* 82 (2021); Mayssoun Sukarieh, "On Class, Culture, and the Creation of the Neoliberal Subject: The Case of Jordan," *Anthropological Quarterly* 89, no. 4 (2016).

8. Seteney Shami, and Lucine Taminian, "Women's Participation in the Jordanian Labour Force: A Comparison of Rural and Urban Patterns," in *Women in Arab Society: Work Patterns and Gender Relations in Egypt, Jordan and Sudan*, ed. Seteney Shami et al. (Paris: Bergir UNESCO, 1990).

9. Mahmoud Ali Hailat, "Education of Jordanians: Outcomes in a Challenging Environment," in *The Jordanian Labor Market: Between Fragility and Resilience*, ed. Caroline Krafft and Ragui Assaad (New York: Oxford University Press, 2019), 221; ʿAbdallah al Kafaween, "Madaris Lam Yanjah fiha Ahid: Hal Yuhal al-Damj al-Mushkila?" [Schools in Which Nobody Passed: Will Merging Solve the Problem?], *7iber*, December 1, 2015. Much of the scholarship on educational inequality in Jordan also highlights the importance of family wealth and parents' education as strong determinants of educational outcomes. See Rana Hendy and Nejla Ben Mimoune, "Evolution of Inequality of Opportunity in Education in the Jordanian Case: From 2008 to 2017," Economic Research Forum, 2021; Reham Rizk and Ronia Hawash, "Education Gap and Youth: A Growing Challenge in the MENA Region," LIS Working Paper Series 790 (2020).

10. Fida Adely, Angela Haddad, Abdel Hakim Al-Husban, and Afaf Al-Khoshman, "Getting In and Getting Through: Navigating Higher Education in Jordan," *Comparative Education Review* 63, no. 1 (2019); Ahmad Yousef Tall, *al-Taʿlīm al-ʿālī fī al-Urdun* (Lajnat Tārīkh al-Urdun, 1998).

11. Ayman Al Sharafat, "Spatial Inequality in Jordan," *Journal of Economics & Management* 36 (2019); Racha Ramadan, *Determinants of Income Inequality in Jordan* (Cairo: Economic Research Forum, 2021).

12. Jordan is officially divided into twelve governorates and three regions (North, Central, and South) (Jordan Ministry of Interior, "Governorates and Sectors," https://moi.gov.jo/En/List /Governorates_and_Sectors). While one finds rural communities in all the governorates, some governorates are significantly more rural, and parts the country are sparsely populated. Throughout this book, I will use the term *governorate* and *province* interchangeably.

13. Jordan Department of Statistics (JDoS), Databank, 2021, https://jorinfo.dos.gov.jo/Data bank/pxweb/en/.

14. Janet Roitman, *Anti-crisis* (Durham, NC: Duke University Press, 2013).

15. Mayssoun Sukarieh, *A Global Idea: Youth, City Networks, and the Struggle for the Arab World* (Ithaca, NY: Cornell University Press, 2023).

16. André Elias Mazawi, "Naming the Imaginary: 'Building an Arab Knowledge Society' and the Contested Terrain of Educational Reforms for Development," in *Trajectories of Education in the Arab World: Legacies and Challenges*, ed. Osama Abi-Mershed (New York: Routledge, 2010).

17. Aihwa Ong, *Neoliberalism as Exception* (Durham, NC: Duke University Press, 2006).

18. Lois McNay, *Gender and Agency: Reconfiguring the Subject in Feminist and Social Theory* (Cambridge, UK: Polity Press, 2000), 22–23.

19. Sherry B. Ortner, *Making Gender: The Politics and Erotics of Culture* (Boston: Beacon Press, 1996), 19.

20. Lila Abu-Lughod, "The Romance of Resistance: Tracing Transformations of Power through Bedouin Women," *American Ethnologist* 17 (1990); Saba Mahmood, *Politics of Piety: The Islamic Revival and the Feminist Subject* (Princeton: Princeton University Press, 2011). This work is also part of a broader literature informed by theories of power, especially Michel Foucault, *The History of Sexuality: An Introduction* (New York: Vintage, 1990); and of gender and performance, especially Judith Butler, "Performative Acts and Gender Constitution: An Essay in Phenomenology and Feminist Theory," *Theatre Journal* 40, no. 4 (1988): 519–31.

21. Abu-Lughod, "Romance of Resistance," 48.

22. Lois McNay, "Agency, Anticipation and Indeterminacy in Feminist Theory," *Feminist Theory* 4, no. 2 (2003): 140–41.

23. Raymond Williams, *Marxism and Literature* (Oxford: Oxford Paperbacks, 1977); Farha Ghannam, *Live and Die like a Man: Gender Dynamics in Urban Egypt* (Stanford: Stanford University Press, 2013), 3.

24. Geoffrey F. Hughes, *Kinship, Islam, and the Politics of Marriage in Jordan: Affection and Mercy* (Bloomington: Indiana University Press, 2021). The language of crisis has varied iterations and a long history; see, for example, Hanan Kholoussy, *For Better, for Worse: The Marriage Crisis that Made Modern Egypt* (Stanford: Stanford University Press, 2010). In contemporary Jordan it references the inability of young people to get married and/or the delay of marriage due to economic reasons, and public anxieties about the moral implications of delayed marriage. See also Diane Singerman, "The Economic Imperatives of Marriage: Emerging Practices and Identities among Youth in the Middle East," Middle East Youth Initiative Working Paper 6 (Wolfensohn Centre for Development / Dubai School of Government, Dubai, September 2007).

25. Fida Adely, "The Emergence of a New Labor Movement in Jordan," *Middle East Report* 264 (2012).

26. Stephen Castles, "Understanding Global Migration: A Social Transformation Perspective," *Journal of Ethnic and Migration Studies* 36, no. 10 (2010): 1576.

27. Frances S. Hasso and Zakia Salime, eds., *Freedom without Permission: Bodies and Space in the Arab Revolutions* (Durham, NC: Duke University Press, 2016).

28. My research assistant and I did two interviews together, after which she interviewed thirty women on her own, sending the recordings to me. I also interviewed an additional thirteen women. We met women through our personal networks and by asking women we had already met to connect us with others. Seeking some geographical diversity, we also inquired with others about women who came from different parts of the country. Most of these initial interviews were conducted between 2012 and 2014. From 2014 to 2016, I conducted focus groups and multiple follow-up interviews, made informal visits to dormitories and apartments, and attended meetups in cafés and restaurants with a core group of women.

29. In order to protect the anonymity of those we interviewed, I do not name villages, towns, or provincial cities (with the exception of Irbid, which as the second-largest city is large enough to make it difficult to link any one person to it). Otherwise, I refer to region (north or south) and indicate the relative size of their home communities by designating their home as a village, town, or provincial city. If the women lived in a provincial capital, I refer to it as a provincial city.

30. My research assistant also gathered data about private dormitories and interviewed several dormitory supervisors.

31. Christians make up less than 5 percent of Jordan's population.

32. Laura M. Ahearn, *Invitations to Love: Literacy, Love Letters, and Social Change in Nepal* (Ann Arbor: University of Michigan Press, 2001).

33. In two of the ten oral history interviews, the stories were recorded with family members of the now deceased women (siblings and a daughter). The three who were not teachers were variously employed in the army as a physician, in a bank in Amman, and in UN organizations first in Amman and then abroad.

34. Suzanne Bergeron, "Economics, Performativity, and Social Reproduction in Global Development," *Globalizations* 8, no. 2 (April 2011).

35. Media stories about parents (or fathers) preventing their daughters from marrying so that they can keep taking the women's salaries may have fueled this perception. See Jordanian

National Commission for Women, "Awliya' Amur Yahrimun Binatihum al-Mawazifat min al-Zawaj Tam'a fi al-Ratib" [Parents Prevent Their Employed Daughters from Getting Married Out of Greed for Their Wages], November 14, 2011, https://women.jo/en/node/5763.

In 2015, a female-run news media site called Hono al-Zarqa' or "Here is Zarqa'" (http://honazarqa.com/) ran a feature about fathers or guardians preventing their daughters from marrying for different reasons, including wanting a daughter's salary. In the article, the author consults with a religious scholar about this phenomenon who labels this practice *a 'adil*, a pre-Islamic practice of preventing one's daughter from marrying. See Bin 'Abdalman'am al-Rifa'i, Khalid, "Mina' al-Ab Ibnatuhu min al-Zawaj" [A Father Prevents His Daughters from Getting Married] *Al-Aluka*, December 14, 2017, https://www.alukah.net/fatawa_counsels/0/123417/.

36. A similar discourse emerged about "working girls" in the United States in the early twentieth century. See Lynne Weiner, *From Working Girl to Working Mother: The Female Labor Force in the United States, 1820–1980* (Chapel Hill: University of North Carolina Press, 1985).

Interlude One

1. Interestingly, of the ten women we interviewed of this generation, one was a bank employee in Amman, reminding us that there are always exceptions to the assumed rules or more variety in practice than people tend to assume.

2. Full-length loose dress, similar to an *abaya* or *dishdash*.

Chapter One

1. Mary Christina Wilson, *King Abdullah, Britain and the Making of Jordan* (Cambridge: Cambridge University Press, 1990), 26–27. The terms of this agreement were articulated in the McMahon-Hussein Correspondence of 1915–16.

2. Benjamin C. Fortna, *Imperial Classroom: Islam, the State, and Education in the Late Ottoman Empire* (New York: Oxford University Press, 2002), 27.

3. The most significant state employer was the military in these early years of the state. See Richard T. Antoun, *Arab Village: A Social Structural Study of a Transjordanian Peasant Community* (Bloomington: Indiana University Press, 1972), 27–33; Anne Marie Baylouny, "Militarizing Welfare: Neo-liberalism and Jordanian Policy," *Middle East Journal* 62, no. 2 (Spring 2008): 285; Ian Seccombe, "Labour Migration and the Transformation of a Village Economy: A Case Study from North-West Jordan," in *The Middle Eastern Village: Changing Economic and Social Relations*, ed. Richard Lawless (Kent, UK: Croom Helm, 1987), 126–27.

4. Elias and Hoda came from Christian families in rural areas, and they attended Christian schools (Catholic and Orthodox) in their communities.

5. Like any such imposition on a native population, the claim to leadership of this new emirate did not go uncontested. Wilson, *Making of Jordan*; Jillian Schwedler, *Protesting Jordan: Geographies of Power and Dissent* (Stanford: Stanford University Press, 2022).

6. "Bedouin" is typically translated as "nomad" or "desert-dweller." As with any such labels or categories, the realities of how people placed in such categories live are more complex and fluid than implied by the category. Joseph Massad describes a process by which some tribes were designated "Bedouin" after Jordan's independence and treated as a different type of citizen, "anchored in a spatialized and temporalized essence," which the Jordanian government drew on after 1970 as representative of a unique Jordanian culture, albeit of the past (Joseph A. Massad,

Colonial Effects: The Making of National Identity in Jordan [New York: Columbia University Press, 2001], 50, 73–79). Nora Barakat's account of Ottoman state-formation projects, and the involvement of Bedouins in these processes, significantly problematizes static tropes that defined Bedouin communities, while also highlighting "the ways in which the nomadic tribe as an ideal type had specific historical effects in the administration of rights to property in the Ottoman context" (Nora Elizabeth Barakat. *Bedouin Bureaucrats: Mobility and Property in the Ottoman Empire* [Stanford: Stanford University Press, 2023], 13). In contemporary Jordan and the region more broadly, the image of the Bedouin is idealized as a noble and free nomad, while continuing to be associated with "traditionalism," an old and outdated way of life that is in contradiction with modernity or progress. "Bedouin" and "tribal" are sometimes used synonymously, even though some of the largest "tribes" are not and/or do not identify as Bedouin. The concept of tribe similarly functions as an ideal type in many respects.

7. Sara Ababneh, "The Time to Question, Rethink and Popularize the Notion of 'Women's Issues': Lessons from Jordan's Popular and Labor Movements from 2006 to Now," *Journal of International Women's Studies* 21, no. 1 (2020): 279; Jillian Schwedler. "Amman Cosmopolitan: Spaces and Practices of Aspiration and Consumption," *Comparative Studies of South Asia, Africa and the Middle East* 30, no. 3 (2010): 552. Even the current leader of Jordan, King Abdullah, was quoted in a long-form interview in *The Atlantic* as referring to the leaders of the National Current Party (a party which the author states has "the support of many East Bankers from the south") as "old dinosaurs." Jeffrey Goldberg, "The Modern King in the Arab Spring," *The Atlantic*, 2013.

8. Linda L. Layne, "'Tribalism': National Representations of Tribal Life in Jordan," *Urban Anthropology and Studies of Cultural Systems and World Economic Development* 16, no. 2 (1987); Linda L. Layne, "The Dialogics of Tribal Self-Representation in Jordan," *American Ethnologist* 16, no. 1 (1989); Massad, *Colonial Effects*.

9. Some exceptions can be found in the literature on the history of the Jordanian women's movement. For example, see Ibtesam Al-Atiyat, "Harvests of the Golden Decades: Contemporary Women's Activism in Jordan," in *Mapping Arab Women's Movements: A Century of Transformations from Within*, ed. Pernille Arenfeldt and Nawar Al-Hassan Golley (Cairo: American University Press, 2012), 133–70; Suhair Salti Al-Tal, *Tarikh al-haraka al-nisaʾiya al-urdunniya, 1944–2008* [A History of Women's Activism in Jordan: 1944–2008] (Amman: Dar Azmina li-l-nashr wa-l-tawziʿa, 2014).

10. Colin Powers, "How Neoliberalism Comes to Town: Policy Convergence, (Under) Development, and Jordanian Economics under King Abdullah," *Middle East Law and Governance* 12, no. 2 (2020).

11. While Iman says more teachers were needed in the West Bank, the need was more generally in rural areas; indeed, many of the teachers in Jordan came from cities in Palestine. Nevertheless, there were some teachers from the East Bank who taught in the West Bank when it was part of Jordan (1950–67).

12. Vartan Manoug Amadouny, "The British Role in the Development of an Infrastructure in TransJordan during the Mandate Period, 1921–1946," PhD diss., University of Southampton, 1993; Mohammad Salim al Tarawnah, *Tarikh Mantiqat al-Balqaʾ wa Maʿan wa al-Karak, 1281–1337H/1864–1918M* [The History of the Balqa, Maan and Karak Regions, 1864–1918] (Amman: Matabiʿ al-Dustour al-Tijariyyah, 1992); Eugene L. Rogan, *Frontiers of the State in the Late Ottoman Empire: Transjordan, 1850–1921* (Cambridge: Cambridge University Press, 1999), 154–57.

13. Amadouny, "British Role." This is corroborated by memoirs and educational histories documenting the travels of young men and, to a lesser degree, women to neighboring countries for additional education: Ahmad Abu Khalil, "Min al-Ta'sis wa-hata al-Istiqlal: Fasl min Sira al-Ta'lim fi al-Urdun" [From Founding to Independence: A Chapter of the Story of Education in Jordan], *7iber*, April 17, 2022; Betty S. Anderson, *Nationalist Voices in Jordan: The Street and the State* (Austin: University of Texas Press, 2005). See Massad, *Colonial Effects*, for a discussion of British military schools for Bedouin communities.

14. Lars Wählin, "Diffusion and Acceptance of Modern Schooling in Rural Jordan," in *The Middle Eastern Village: Changing Economic and Social Relations*, ed. Richard Lawless (Kent, UK: Croom Helm, 1987).

15. Wählin, "Diffusion and Acceptance of Modern Schooling in Rural Jordan," 147.

16. Wählin reports that in 1979, 49 percent of teachers in rural areas were male and Palestinian; 27 percent were men from the local community; 12 percent were female Palestinians; and 7 percent were local women (Wählin, "Diffusion and Acceptance of Modern Schooling in Rural Jordan," 163–64).

17. Hilary Falb Kalisman, "The Next Generation of Cultivators: Teaching Agriculture in Iraq, Palestine and Transjordan (1920–1960)," *Histoire de l'éducation* 148 (2017): 143–64; Sara Pursley. *Familiar Futures: Time, Selfhood, and Sovereignty in Iraq* (Stanford: Stanford University Press, 2019); Spencer Segalla, "'According to a Logic Befitting the Arab Soul': Cultural Policy and Popular Education in Morocco since 1912," in *Trajectories of Education in the Arab World*, ed. Osama Abi-Mershed (New York: Routledge, 2009), 100–124.

18. Kalisman, "Next Generation of Cultivators," 152–53.

19. Abla M. Amawi, "The Consolidation of the Merchant Class in Transjordan during the Second World War," in *Village, Steppe and State: The Social Origins of Modern Jordan*, ed. Eugene Rogan and Tareq Tell (London: British Academic Press, 1994), 162–86; Kalisman, "Next Generation of Cultivators," 143–64.

20. Rochelle Davis, *Palestinian Village Histories: Geographies of the Displaced* (Stanford: Stanford University Press, 2010); Walid Khalidi, Sharif S. Elmusa, and Muhammad Ali Khalidi, *All That Remains: The Palestinian Villages Occupied and Depopulated by Israel in 1948* (Washington, DC: Institution for Palestine Studies, 1992); Ilan Pappé, "An Indicative Archive: Salvaging Nakba Documents," *Journal of Palestine Studies* 49, no. 3 (2020); Fayez Sayegh, "Zionist Colonialism in Palestine (1965)," *Settler Colonial Studies* 2, no. 1 (2012).

21. Jalal Al Husseini, "Jordan and the Palestinians," in *Atlas of Jordan: History, Territories and Society*, ed. Myriam Ababsa (Beirut: Presses de l'Ifpo, 2013).

22. Al Husseini, "Jordan and the Palestinians"; Laurie A. Brand, "Palestinians and Jordanians: A Crisis of Identity," *Journal of Palestine Studies* 24, no. 4 (Summer 1995): 46–61.

23. There is some variation in reporting the numbers of Palestinian refugees who fled to Jordan in and around the 1967 war. Some sources cite a lower number of 350,000 refugees with 200,000 going to Jordan. See McGill University—Palestinian Refugee ResearchNet, "Palestinian Refugees: An Overview" (2010), http://prrn.mcgill.ca/background/; David McDowell, *Palestine and Israel: The Uprising and Beyond* (Berkeley: University of California Press, 1989); State of Palestine: Ministry of Foreign Affairs and Expatriates (PMFAE), "Refugees," 2022, http://www.mofa.pna.ps/en-us/fundamentalissues/refugees. However, Al Husseini's number is not limited to officially registered refugees, and therefore better reflects the scale of displacement. The overwhelming majority of Palestinians in Jordan are Jordanian citizens. One group that is a major exception is those Palestinians who were forcibly displaced from Gaza in the War of 1967 and

the resulting Israeli Occupation of the West Bank and Gaza, an illegal occupation that continues until this day (Al Husseini, "Jordan and the Palestinians," 19).

24. Musa Abboudeh Rabdah Samha, "Migration to Amman: Patterns of Movement and Population Structure," PhD diss., Durham University, 1979, 84.

25. Initially, the majority of Jordanian citizens who went to the Arab Gulf for work were from the West Bank.

26. Organisation for Economic Co-operation and Development (OECD), OECD Data, https://data.oecd.org.

27. Jordan Ministry of Education (MOE), *Statistical Report for Academic Year 2019-20* (Amman: Government of Jordan, 2020). Historically, UNRWA schools were considered to be of better quality because their teachers were paid better (or at least that was the prevailing belief) and received better on-the-job training. Abdul-Hamid and colleagues, citing higher scores on international standardized tests for students enrolled in UNRWA schools in Palestine and Jordan, point to teacher preparation and ongoing support, as well as school management, as important explanatory factors for better test scores. However, they emphasize that these factors do not sufficiently explain these differences. Based on field research, they argue that the shared experiences of teachers and students as refugees, and the sense of community that creates, are important factors. Husein Abdul-Hamid, Harry Patrinos, Joel Reyes, Jo Kelcey, and Andrea Diaz Varela, *Learning in the Face of Adversity: The UNRWA Education Program for Palestine Refugees* (Washington, DC: World Bank, 2015).

28. Colin Powers, "Producing Crisis/Surviving Crisis: Power, Capital, and the Social Structure of Accumulation in the Hashemite Kingdom of Jordan," PhD diss., Johns Hopkins University, 2020, 3, 29, 63.

29. Adely et al., "Getting In and Getting Through," 79–81; Jordan MOE, *Statistical Report for Academic Year 2020-21* (Amman: Government of Jordan, 2021); Jordan MOE, *Statistical Report for Academic Year 2011-12* (Amman: Government of Jordan, 2012). In academic year 2011–12, for example, 36.5 percent of K–12 students in Amman and 24 percent nationally were enrolled in private schools. In 2021, those figures had dropped to 31.5 percent in Amman and 20.4 percent nationally.

30. Linda L. Layne, "Education and Social Hierarchies in Rural Jordan," paper presented at the Annual Meeting of the American Anthropological Association, Chicago, November 1984.

31. Jordan MOE, *Statistical Report for Academic Year 2019-20*. I am unsure why these official statistics show a decrease, and whether they reflect an actual decrease in relative numbers of children enrolled in secondary school, or result from new ways of measuring or counting students. More recent data sets may reflect the large number of Syrians now residing in Jordan, and the fact that Syrians in Jordan are relatively less educated and have had their education interrupted by war.

32. Jordan MOE, *Statistical Report for Academic Year 2017-18* (Amman: Government of Jordan, 2018), https://moe.gov.jo/node/60145.

33. JDoS, Databank.

34. JDoS, Databank.

35. JDoS, Databank. From 2015 to 2020, at the higher education level, four out of twelve provinces show a higher rate of men enrolling and graduating more than women: Jarash, Ajlun, Tafiela, and Madaba. Over the same time span (2015–20), the majority of the provinces show women consistently enrolling and graduating at higher rates than men, and this is also true at the national level.

36. Jordan MOE, *Statistical Report for Academic Year 2019-20*; Jordan MOE, *Statistical Report for Academic Year 2017-18*. Far fewer girls are enrolled in the vocational track overall.

37. David Reilly, David L. Neumann, and Glenda Andrews, "Investigating Gender Differences in Mathematics and Science: Results from the 2011 Trends in Mathematics and Science Survey," *Research in Science Education* 49, no. 1 (2019).

38. Ahmad Tweissi et al., "Gender Gap in Student Achievement in Jordan Study Report," National Center for Human Resources Development (NCHRD) Publication Series: Monitoring & Evaluation Partnership (MEP) (2014); Natasha Ridge, *Education and the Reverse Gender Divide in the Gulf States: Embracing the Global, Ignoring the Local* (New York: Teachers College Press, 2014).

39. Lloyd et al., "The Impact of Educational Quality on School Exit in Egypt," *Comparative Education Review* 47, no. 4 (2003): 444–67; Ridge, *Education and the Reverse Gender Divide*.

40. Some villages or small towns lack the qualified math or science teachers to prepare students for this track or for success on the high school completion exams in these fields.

41. Adely, *Gendered Paradoxes*.

42. The more elite private schools prepare their students to take the exams of other systems based in the West, such as the British O-levels, SATs, and the International Baccalaureate, and do not take part in the same tracking system. Elite schools of this sort are found mainly in Amman, although some private education can be found in other cities or provincial towns. All of the women we spoke with attended public schools in the provinces.

43. ʿIzadīn al-Nātūr, "Talaba al-makārim yushakkalūn sabʿa wa ʿarbaʿīn min al-qabūl al-muwaḥḥad" [Makrama Students Make Up 47 Percent of Unified Admissions], *Amman Net*, October 23, 2014. http://ar.ammannet.net/news/238498; Suzanna Goussous, "Thabahtoona Criticises Higher Education Strategy," *Jordan Times*, June 27, 2015.

44. Jordan Ministry of Higher Education and Scientific Research, "Al-Siyasa al-ʿAma li-Qabul al Talba fi al-Jamaʿat al-Urduniyya li-Marhala al-Bakaluriyus li-l-ʿAm al-Jamaʿi 2021/2022" [Public Policy for Student Admission in Jordanian Universities for the Bachelor's Degree for the Academic Year 2021–22], June 18, 2021. In addition to quotas for civil and military employees of the state, a small number of seats are reserved for refugees (*makramat al mukhayamat*) and for the royal court (*al diwan al malakki*), which annually puts forth a list of students to be admitted into various faculties at different universities. Students and their families petition the royal court for such favors, either directly or through an intermediary. Patronage dispensed through the royal Hashemite court is not limited to university seats. A whole range of services can be accessed through this route, from medical care to jobs and scholarships.

45. "Al-Taʿlim al-ʿAli: Yuqar Taʿlimat Makrama Ibnaʾ al-ʿAshaʾir" [Higher Education Adopts Regulations of the Royal Grants for Tribal Students], ʿAmun, July 25, 2016, https://www.ammonnews.net/article/276370.

46. Jordan Ministry of Higher Education, "Admission in Jordanian Universities for 2021–22"; Ahmad Yousef Tall, *al-Taʿlīm al-ʿālī fī al-Urdun* (Lajnat Tārīkh al-Urdun, 1998).

47. Adely et al., "Getting In and Getting Through," 84–85. The parallel system was created to generate revenue for underresourced universities. Critics of this system maintain that it leads to overcrowding and to a decrease in quality as it allows students to enter with lower grades, and creates an undue advantage for those who can pay higher tuition rates: Nassar Massadeh, "Policies Governing Admission to Jordanian Public Universities," *Higher Education Policy* 25, no. 4 (December 2012): 535–50.

48. At times, more nuanced analysis can be found in the media: Ziyyad Al-Rifati, "Al-ʿAnf al-Jamaʿi: Al-Asbab al-Haqiqiyya wa-Hulul Muqtariha" [University Violence: The Real Reasons and Suggested Solutions], *Al-Ghad*, January 3, 2017. Jordanian scholars have taken up the question of reasons for violence on university campuses. One limitation of this research is that it

tends to rely on surveys of student perceptions about reasons for violence. For example, see Yazid Isa Alshoraty, "Reasons for University Students' Violence in Jordan," *International Education Studies* 8, no. 10 (2015). Nadhir Abu Na'ir surveyed faculty about violence at universities: see Abu Na'ir, "Zahira al-'Anf al-Jama'i wa-Dawr al-Jama'at fi al-Hud min Intishariha min Wajhat Nazr A'da' Hay'a al-Tadris fi al-Jama'at al-Urduniyya" [The Phenomenon of University Violence and the Role of Universities in Reducing the Spread from the Point of View of the Faculty Members in Jordanian Universities], *Dirasat fi al-'Alum al-Tarbawiyya* 43, no. 1 (2016). In two of the studies reviewed, students were asked about their participation in a continuum of aggressive acts and reasons for engaging in violence: Abdelhakeem M. Okour and Heba H. Hijazi, "Domestic Violence and Family Dysfunction as Risk Factor for Violent Behavior among University Students in North Jordan," *Journal of Family Violence* 24, no. 6 (2009); Lama M. Qaisy, "Aggressive Behavior among the University Students," *British Journal of Education, Society & Behavioural Science* 4, no. 9 (2014). Two additional studies delve into a range of disruptive behavior and correlations with poor academic performance: Husein F. Ramzoun, "Some Social Factors for Violence among University Students in Jordan: Case Study" (Amman: Zaytounah University, 2013); Qaisy, "Aggressive Behavior." These examples, though by no means a comprehensive list, provide some indication of the available research. More qualitative and ethnographic approaches are needed to better understand these phenomena.

49. For a more nuanced discussion of violence on university campuses see Daniele Cantini, *Youth and Education in the Middle East: Assessing the Performance and Practice of Urban Environments* (London: IB Tauris, 2016), 125–29.

50. Adely et al., "Getting In and Getting Through," 84–85; Massadeh, "Policies Governing Admission to Jordanian Public Universities."

51. Adely, *Gendered Paradoxes*; G. B. S. Mujahid, "Female Labour Force Participation in the Hashemite Kingdom of Jordan," ILO Working Papers 992175333402676, International Labour Organization, 1982; Samha, "Migration to Amman"; Seccombe, "Labour Migration." The research on this earlier period also paints a picture of remarkably stable contours of women's waged labor since the late 1970s, with single educated women most likely to be working, and their overwhelming concentration in professional fields.

52. Mona Amer, "School-to-Work Transition in Jordan, 2010–2016," and Ragui Assaad, Caroline Krafft, and Caitlyn Keo, "The Composition of Labor Supply," both in *The Jordanian Labor Market: Between Fragility and Resilience*, ed. Caroline Krafft and Ragui Assaad (New York: Oxford University Press, 2019).

53. For example, Hanna Rosin, "Who Wears the Pants in This Economy?" *New York Times*, August 30, 2012.

54. US Bureau of Labor Statistics (BLS), "Married Parents' Use of Time, 2003–06," US Department of Labor, May 8, 2008; US Bureau of Labor Statistics, "American Time Use Survey," US Department of Labor, July 22, 2021; Arlie Hochschild and Anne Machung, *The Second Shift: Working Families and the Revolution at Home* (New York: Penguin, 2012); Kim Parker and Wendy Wang, "Modern Parenthood," Pew Research Center's Social & Demographic Trends Project, 2013, https://www.pewresearch.org/social-trends/2013/03/14/modern-parenthood-roles-of -moms-and-dads-converge-as-they-balance-work-and-family/.

55. Arab Renaissance for Democracy and Development (ARDD), "Women's Informal Employment in Jordan: Challenges Facing Home-Based Businesses during COVID-19," *Women's Advocacy Issues Policy Brief* 3 (May 2021), Available at https://jordan.unwomen.org/en/digital -library/publications/2021/womens-informal-employment-in-jordan.

56. Ragui Assaad, *The Jordanian Labor Market in the New Millennium* (Oxford: Oxford University Press, 2014).

57. Jordanian activists have been at the forefront of demanding change in these arenas. For example, read about the work of Sadaqa: http://www.sadaqajo.org/aboutus.

58. Ragui Assaad and Colette Salemi, "The Structure of Employment," in *The Jordanian Labor Market: Between Fragility and Resilience*, ed. Caroline Krafft and Ragui Assaad (New York: Oxford University Press, 2019).

59. Dana Peebles, Nada Darwazeh, Hala Ghosheh, and Amal Sabbagh, *Factors Affecting Women's Participation in the Private Sector in Jordan* (Amman: Jordan National Centre for Human Development, 2007).

60. JDoS, Databank.

61. World Bank, *Hashemite Kingdom of Jordan—Understanding How Gender Norms in MNA Impact Female Employment Outcomes (English)* (Washington, DC: World Bank Group, 2018), 39.

62. Haya Al-Dajani, Sara Carter, and Colin Williams, "Women's Resourcefulness in the Informal Economy: Evidence from Jordan," in *Exploring Resources: Life-Balance and Well-Being of Women Who Work in a Global Context*, ed. Roxane L. Gervais and Prudence M. Millear (Cham, Switzerland: Springer, 2016).

63. Jordan Department of Financial Stability, *Taqrir al-Stiqrar al-Maly 2021* [Financial Stability Report 2021]; Human Rights Watch, *"We Lost Everything": Debt Imprisonment in Jordan* (March 16, 2021).

64. World Bank, *Hashemite Kingdom of Jordan—Understanding How Gender Norms in MNA Impact Female Employment Outcomes (English)*, 3.

65. The availability of on-site child care for public school teachers is one of the reasons why teaching is such an appealing profession for women.

66. Suzanne Bergeron, "The Post-Washington Consensus and Economic Representations of Women in Development at the World Bank," *International Feminist Journal of Politics* 5, no. 3 (2003): 397–419.

67. Adely et al., "'Skills Mismatch' Discourse"; Assaad and Salemi, "The Structure of Employment."

68. Women in the provinces, or "rural women," have been the object of much of the programming and policy concerned with the low rates of female labor participation in Jordan for decades. In the 1990s, for example, industrial zones, especially the Qualifying Industrial Zones (QIZs), were viewed as a way to create more female employment and address growing poverty rates: Kholoud Al-Khaldi, *Women Workers In the Textiles and Garments Industries in Jordan: A Research on the impact of Globalization* (Ministry of Labor, Jordan, and International Labor Organization, 2002); Ibrahim Saif, *The Socio-economic Implications of the Qualified Industrial Zones in Jordan* (Amman: Center for Strategic Studies, University of Jordan, 2006). Despite the hope that investment in manufacturing zones would lead to greater employment of Jordanian women, in 2019 less than 25 percent of workers in the garment industry were Jordanian, while most of the workers came from Bangladesh: International Labour Office, *Annual Report 2019: Better Work Jordan* (Geneva: International Labour Office; International Finance Corporation, 2019). Another major push to make women "economically active" is extensive microfinance, small business, and handicraft initiatives that have dominated the development and NGO scene since at least 2000: Shakir Jarrar and Omar Faris, "Al-Tamkin al-Mutawahish: Kif Anhakat al-Qurud al-Saghira Hayaat al-Nisa' wa-'A'ilatuhina" [Savage Empowerment: How Small Loans Stretched Thin the Livelihoods of Women and Their Families], *7iber*, July 2, 2019. On Egypt,

see Julia Elyachar, "Empowerment Money: The World Bank, Non-governmental Organizations, and the Value of Culture in Egypt," *Public Culture* 14, no. 3 (2002): 493–513.

69. Assaad, Krafft, and Keo, "Composition of Labor Supply," 11–41.

70. Rami Farouk Daher, "Discourses of Neoliberalism and Disparities in the City Landscape: Cranes, Craters, and an Exclusive Urbanity," and Daher, "Prelude: Understanding Cultural Change and Urban Transformations: Qualifying Amman: The City of Many Hats," both in *Cities, Urban Practices and Nation Building in Jordan*, ed. Myriam Ababsa and Rami Farouk Daher (Beirut: Presses de l'Ifpo, 2011); Seteney Shami, "Amman Is Not a City: Middle Eastern Cities in Question," in *Urban Imaginaries: Locating the Modern City*, ed. Alev Çinar and Thomas Bender (Minneapolis: University of Minnesota Press, 2007).

71. Arda Dargarabedian, "Armenian Women in Jordan," *Al-Raida Journal* 1 (2003): 24–26; Rochelle Davis, Grace Benton, Will Todman, and Emma Murphy, "Hosting Guests, Creating Citizens: Models of Refugee Administration in Jordan and Egypt," *Refugee Survey Quarterly* 36, no. 2 (2017): 1–32. Armenians were also displaced to Jordan after the 1948 Nakba and the 1967 Israeli occupation of the West Bank and Gaza.

72. Amawi, "Merchant Class in Transjordan"; Rogan, *Frontiers of the State in the Late Ottoman Empire*; Beshara Doumani, *Rediscovering Palestine: Merchants and Peasants in Jabal Nablus, 1700–1900* (Berkeley: University of California Press, 1995).

73. Anderson, *Nationalist Voices in Jordan*; Wilson, *Making of Jordan*.

74. Khalidi, Elmusa, and Khalidi, *All That Remains*; Pappé, "Salvaging Nakba Documents," 22–40; Sayegh, "Zionist Colonialism (1965)."

75. UNRWA, "Jordan: Where We Work," 2022, https://www.unrwa.org/where-we-work/jordan.

76. One significant exception are the Palestinians who came from Gaza, which was under Egyptian administration, in and around 1967. Today it is estimated that there are between 150,000 and 170,000 Palestinians from Gaza without citizenship residing in Jordan. Oroub El Abed, "Immobile Palestinians: Ongoing Plight of Gazans in Jordan," *Forced Migration Review* 26 (2006): 17–18; UNRWA, "Protection in Jordan," March 2018, https://www.unrwa.org/activity/protection-jordan.

77. Myriam Ababsa, "The Socio-economic Composition of the Population," in *Atlas of Jordan: History, Territories and Society*, ed. Myriam Ababsa (Beirut: Presses de l'Ifpo, 2013).

78. Rula Amin, "Jordan Issues Record Number of Work Permits to Syrian Refugees," UNHCR, January 25, 2022, https://www.unhcr.org/en-us/news/press/2022/1/61effaa54/jordan-issues-record-number-work-permits-syrian-refugees.

79. Christoph Wilcke, *Stateless Again: Palestinian-Origin Jordanians Deprived of Their Nationality* (New York: Human Rights Watch, 2010), https://www.hrw.org/report/2010/02/01/stateless-again/palestinian-origin-jordanians-deprived-their-nationality. Jordanian census data showed about 140,000 Iraqis resident in Jordan (JDoS, Databank). Of these about 67,000 are registered as refugees (UNHCR, "Jordan: Statistics for Registered Iraqi Refugees," January 2022, https://data.unhcr.org).

80. Ababsa, "The Socio-economic Composition of the Population," 344–53; Caroline Krafft and Ragui Assaad, eds., *The Jordanian Labor Market: Between Fragility and Resilience* (Oxford: Oxford University Press, 2019).

81. Ian J. Seccombe, "International Migration for Employment and Domestic Labour Market Development: The Jordanian Experience," PhD diss., Durham University, 1983.

82. "Qualifying Industrial Zones—Jordan," International Trade Administration, US Department of Commerce, https://www.trade.gov/qiz-jordan.

83. Alex Nasri, *Migrant Domestic and Garment Workers in Jordan: A Baseline Analysis of Trafficking in Persons and Related Laws and Policies* (Geneva: International Labour Office, 2017); Jordan Ministry of Labor, "Employment and Manpower-Employment and Unemployment," Open Government Data Platform, 2022, https://form.jordan.gov.jo/wps/portal/Home/OpenDataMain.

84. Seccombe, "Labour Migration," 116.

85. Anderson, *Nationalist Voices in Jordan*; Abu Khalil, "From Founding to Independence."

86. Rex Brynen, "Economic Crisis and Post-Rentier Democratization in the Arab World: The Case of Jordan," *Canadian Journal of Political Science / Revue Canadienne de Science Politique* 25, no. 1 (1992): 69–97.

87. Before the Gulf War, a significant share of the Jordanian economy was based on remittances from abroad; remittances peaked in 1984, when they accounted for one-quarter (24.9 percent) of Jordan's GDP. After the migration outflows of the Gulf War, the share of GDP from remittances dropped to only 10 percent. However, immediately following the Gulf War, the dollar value of remittances steadily increased for nearly twenty-five years, climbing from US$450 million in 1991 to more than US$6 billion in 2014. The share of GDP based on remittances recovered to around one-fifth of GDP by 2000 but has declined every year since (to about 8.9 percent today). Even as remittances from the increasing numbers of Jordanians living abroad climbed into the billions in the twenty-first century, as the Jordanian economy has grown and diversified, remittances have held a smaller share of the Jordanian economy. World Bank, *Personal Remittances, Received (% of GDP)—Jordan*, World Bank Open Data, 2022. The number of Jordanians abroad remained fairly constant from 1990 to 2005 at around 350,000 people. However, since the mid-2000s, there has been a rapid growth in the number of Jordanians living abroad, with more than 150,000 moving out every five years since 2005, to more than 744,000 in 2017 (UN DESA, *Demographic Yearbook 2020* [New York: UN DESA, 2020]).

88. In her book based on family history, *My Damascus* (Ithaca, NY: Olive Branch Press, 2021), Suad Amiry describes the migration of her two aunts to Jordan from Damascus to work as teachers in the late 1930s.

89. And women were mobile in other ways, going to markets to sell their wares, walking to wells and springs to gather water, sometimes traversing miles daily to meet the basic needs of their families.

90. ʿAbd Al-Hirut et al., *Awl Miʾa Muʿalim* [First One Hundred Teachers] (Amman: University of International Islamic Sciences Press, 2016); ʿAbd Al-Hirut, "Awl 11 Muʿalima fi Tarikh al-Urdun" [The First 11 Female Teachers in Jordan's History], *Al-Raʾi*, November 11, 2021.

91. Wählin, "Diffusion and Acceptance of Modern Schooling in Rural Jordan," 145–74.

92. Laurie A. Brand, *Jordan's Inter-Arab Relations: The Political Economy of Alliance-Making* (New York: Columbia University Press, 1995).

93. Nabil A. Badran, "The Means of Survival: Education and the Palestinian Community, 1948–1967," *Journal of Palestine Studies* 9, no. 4 (1980): 62–65; Shami and Taminian, "Women's Participation in the Jordanian Labour Force"; Rosenfeld, *Confronting the Occupation*.

94. Seccombe, "Labour Migration," 127.

95. Eleonore Kofman, "The Invisibility of Skilled Female Migrants and Gender Relations in Studies of Skilled Migration in Europe," *International Journal of Population Geography* 6, no. 1 (January–February 2000): 45–59; Pierrette Hondagneu-Sotelo and Cynthia Cranford, "Gender and Migration," in *Handbook of the Sociology of Gender* (Boston: Springer, 2006), 105–26.

96. Caroline B. Brettell, "Gender, Family, and Migration," in *Oxford Handbook of the Politics of International Migration*, ed. Marc R. Rosenblum and Daniel J. Tichenor (Oxford: Oxford University Press, 2012).

97. Rachel Silvey, "Power, Difference and Mobility: Feminist Advances in Migration Studies," *Progress in Human Geography* 28, no. 4 (August 2004).

98. Lauren Carruth and Lahra Smith, "Building One's Own House: Power and Escape for Ethiopian Women through International Migration," *Journal of Modern African Studies* 60, no. 1 (March 2022): 94; Caitlin Killian, Jennifer Olmsted, and Alexis Doyle, "Motivated Migrants: (Re)framing Arab Women's Experiences," *Women's Studies International Forum* 35, no. 6 (November–December 2012).

99. Priya Deshingkar and Sven Grimm, *Internal Migration and Development: A Global Perspective* (New York: United Nations, 2005).

100. See, for instance, Arianne M. Gaetano, *Out to Work: Migration, Gender, and the Changing Lives of Rural Women in Contemporary China* (Honolulu: University of Hawaii Press, 2015); Mary Beth Mills, *Thai Women in the Global Labor Force: Consuming Desires, Contested Selves* (New Brunswick, NJ: Rutgers University Press, 1999); Aihwa Ong, *Spirits of Resistance and Capitalist Discipline: Factory Women in Malaysia* (Albany: SUNY Press, 1987).

101. For example, see Bina Fernandez, Marina De Regt, and Gregory Currie, eds., *Migrant Domestic Workers in the Middle East: The Home and the World* (New York: Palgrave Macmillan, 2014); Ray Jureidini, "Trafficking and Contract Migrant Workers in the Middle East," *International Migration* 48, no. 4 (2010); Rhacel Salazar Parreñas, *Unfree: Migrant Domestic Work in Arab States* (Stanford: Stanford University Press, 2021).

102. Fatma Khafagy, "Women and Labor Migration: One Village in Egypt," *MERIP Reports* 124 (June 1984): 17–21; Valentine M. Moghadam, "Women's Economic Participation in the Middle East: What Difference Has the Neoliberal Policy Turn Made?" *Journal of Middle East Women's Studies* 1, no. 1 (2005): 115; Elizabeth Taylor, "Egyptian Migration and Peasant Wives," *MERIP Reports* 124 (June 1984): 3–10.

103. Françoise De Bel-Air, *Migration Profile: Jordan* (Florence: Migration Policy Centre—European University Institute, June 2016).

104. Killian, Olmsted, and Doyle, "Motivated Migrants."

105. Samuli Schielke, *Migrant Dreams: Egyptian Workers in the Gulf States* (Cairo: American University Press, 2020), 7.

106. Schielke, *Migrant Dreams.*

107. See Farha Ghannam's article on the ways in which families keep those in *al ghurba* connected despite their long physical absence while working in the Arab Gulf countries: Farha Ghannam, "Keeping Him Connected: Labor Migration and the Production of Locality in Cairo," *City & Society* 10, no. 1 (June 1998).

108. Castles, "Understanding Global Migration," 1567.

109. Castles, "Understanding Global Migration," 1567–68.

110. Suad Joseph, ed., *Gender and Citizenship in the Middle East* (Syracuse, NY: Syracuse University Press, 2000).

Chapter Two

1. Part of envisioning Amman in this way is a function of place (where they reside in the provinces) and time (as they are at the start of their adult lives). Amman might become a step to other destinations (for example, at least two of the women we interviewed pursued professional opportunities in Arab Gulf countries), but it is the first step in pursuing their aspirations.

2. McNay, "Agency, Anticipation and Indeterminacy," 141.

3. Margaret Frye, "Bright Futures in Malawi's New Dawn: Educational Aspirations as Assertions of Identity," *American Journal of Sociology* 117, no. 6 (May 2012); Leya Mathew and Ritty Lukose, "Pedagogies of Aspiration: Anthropological Perspectives on Education in Liberalising India," *South Asia: Journal of South Asian Studies* 43, no. 4 (July 2020).

4. Powers, "How Neoliberalism Comes to Town."

5. Adely et al., "'Skills Mismatch' Discourse"; Mayssoun Sukarieh, "The Hope Crusades: Culturalism and Reform in the Arab World," *PoLAR: Political and Legal Anthropology Review* 35, no. 1 (May 2012).

6. Sara Ababneh, "Do You Know Who Governs Us? The Damned Monetary Fund," *Middle East Report*, June 30, 2018; Schwedler, *Protesting Jordan*.

7. Ong, *Neoliberalism as Exception*, 9.

8. Joan DeJaeghere, *Educating Entrepreneurial Citizens: Neoliberalism and Youth Livelihoods in Tanzania* (New York: Taylor & Francis, 2017).

9. DeJaeghere, *Educating Entrepreneurial Citizens*; Joan DeJaeghere, "Girls' Educational Aspirations and Agency: Imagining Alternative Futures through Schooling in a Low-Resourced Tanzanian Community," *Critical Studies in Education* 59, no. 2 (2018).

10. Musa Al-Sakat, "Tamkin al-Mir'a . . . Iqtisadiyan" [Empowering Women . . . Economically], *Al-Ghad*, January 29, 2020.

11. Sara Ahmed, *What's the Use? On the Uses of Use* (Durham, NC: Duke University Press, 2019), 55.

12. Ahmed, *What's the Use?*, 98.

13. Davis, *Palestinian Village Histories*, 105–7.

14. Judith E. Tucker, *Women in Nineteenth-Century Egypt* (Cambridge: Cambridge University Press, 1985).

15. Brittany Cook, "The Problem with Empowerment: Social Reproduction and Women's Food Projects in Jordan," *Annals of the American Association of Geographers* 111, no. 1 (January 2021); Homa Hoodfar, *Between Marriage and the Market* (Berkeley: University of California Press, 1997); Jamie Winders and Barbara Ellen Smith, "Social Reproduction and Capitalist Production: A Genealogy of Dominant Imaginaries," *Progress in Human Geography* 43, no. 5 (2019).

16. Only about a third of the mothers of those interviewed worked outside the home.

17. Adam Hanieh, *Lineages of Revolt: Issues of Contemporary Capitalism in the Middle East* (Chicago: Haymarket Books, 2013); David Harvey, *A Brief History of Neoliberalism* (New York: Oxford University Press, 2007).

18. Adely et al., "'Skills Mismatch' Discourse"; Sukarieh, "On Class, Culture, and the Creation of the Neoliberal Subject."

19. Xavier Bonal, "Education, Poverty, and the 'Missing Link': The Limits of Human Capital Theory as a Paradigm for Poverty Reduction," in *The Handbook of Global Education Policy*, ed. Karen Mundy, Andy Green, Bob Lingard, and Antoni Verger (Chichester, UK: John Wiley & Sons, 2016); Karen Mundy and Antoni Verger, "The World Bank and the Global Governance of Education in a Changing World Order," *International Journal of Educational Development* 40 (January 2015).

20. World Bank, *Gender and Development in the Middle East and North Africa: Women in the Public Sphere* (Washington, DC: World Bank, 2004); World Bank, *Opening Doors: Gender Equality and Development in the Middle East and North Africa* (Washington, DC: World Bank, 2013).

21. Al-Sakat, "Empowering Women . . . Economically."

22. Al-Sakat, "Empowering Women . . . Economically"; "Khabra': Musharaka al-Mara'a Iqtisadiyan fi al-Urdun Da'ifa" [News: Women's Economic Participation in Jordan Is Weak], *Al-Ghad*, January 10, 2019; Dana Al-Emam, "Women's Economic Participation 'Key to Higher GDP'—Experts," *Jordan Times*, October 11, 2016; Kweill Ellingrud et al., *The Power of Parity: Advancing Women's Equality in the United States*, McKinsey & Co., April 7, 2016, 2, https://www.mckinsey.com/featured-insights/employment-and-growth/the-power-of-parity-advancing-womens-equality-in-the-united-states.

23. Ana Revenga and Sudhir Shetty, "Empowering Women Is Smart Economics," World Economic Forum, March 2012, https://www.weforum.org/agenda/2018/01/this-is-why-women-must-play-a-greater-role-in-the-global-economy/; David Abney and Arancha González Laya, "This Is Why Women Must Play a Greater Role in the Global Economy," World Economic Forum, January 24, 2018, https://www.weforum.org/agenda/2018/01/this-is-why-women-must-play-a-greater-role-in-the-global-economy/.

24. Joni Hersch, "Opting Out among Women with Elite Education," *Review of Economics of the Household* 11, no. 4 (2013).

25. Linda R. Hirshman, *Get to Work . . . and Get a Life, Before It's Too Late* (New York: Penguin, 2006).

26. Jordan Kisner, "The Lockdown Showed How the Economy Exploits Women. She Already Knew," *New York Times*, February 17, 2021.

27. Ahmed, *What's the Use?*, 223.

28. DeJaeghere, "Girls' Educational Aspirations," 3, 6.

29. Frances Vavrus, *Schooling as Uncertainty: An Ethnographic Memoir in Comparative Education* (London: Bloomsbury Publishing, 2021); Gowri Vijayakumar, "'I'll Be like Water': Gender, Class, and Flexible Aspirations at the Edge of India's Knowledge Economy," *Gender & Society* 27, no. 6 (2013).

30. Rebecca Bryant and Daniel M. Knight, *The Anthropology of the Future* (Cambridge: Cambridge University Press, 2019), 58–62.

31. Vijayakumar, "I'll Be like Water," 793.

32. Vijayakumar, "I'll Be like Water," 779.

33. Craig Jeffrey, "Timepass: Youth, Class, and Time among Unemployed Young Men in India," *American Ethnologist* 37, no. 3 (August 2010): 465–81; Singerman, "Economic Imperatives of Marriage." The 2020 volume edited by Marcia Inhorn and Nancy J. Smith-Hefner is a recent exception: Marcia Inhorn and Nancy J. Smith-Hefner, eds., *Waithood: Gender, Education, and Global Delays in Marriage and Childbearing* (New York: Berghahn Books, 2020).

34. After the education sector, the next category of most common public sector jobs was health and social work, followed by public administration and defense. JDoS, Databank.

35. The inefficiency of the public sector has been a central tenet of "liberal" economics and the Washington Consensus, and formed part of the ideological foundation of structural adjustment policies, as well as austerity policies in the Global North.

36. Assaad and Salemi, "Structure of Employment."

37. Assaad and Salemi, "Structure of Employment"; JDoS, Databank.

38. Assaad and Salemi, "Structure of Employment," 58.

39. Amer, "School-to-Work Transition in Jordan, 2010–2016"; Ragui Assaad, *The Jordanian Labor Market in the New Millennium* (Oxford: Oxford University Press, 2014); JDoS, Databank.

40. Hernan Winkler and Alvaro Gonzalez, *Jobs Diagnostic Jordan* (Washington, DC: World Bank Group, 2019).

41. United States Agency for International Development, "USAID Pre-Service Teacher Education in Jordan: National Survey on Public Perceptions of the Teaching Profession," 2021.

42. The public has also conveyed support for teachers in other ways. The exploitation of private school teachers has been of particular focus in the media and in campaigns for labor rights. Lina Ejeilat, "Al-Mudaris al-Khasa: Tamyiz did al-Ma'lumat wa-Ruwatib dun al-Had al-Adna" [Private Schools: Discrimination against Female Teachers and Salaries below Minimum Wage], *7iber*, March 9, 2015; Dalal Salameh, "Mawt Ruba: Kif Khudhilat Mu'limat al-Mudaris al-Khasa?" [Death of Ruba: How Female Teachers at Private Schools Were Failed?], *7iber*, June 17, 2022; Dalal Salameh, "Al-Intihakat al-'Amaliya fi al-Mudaris al-Khasa: al-Ajihiza al-Raqabiya 'Jazur Ma'zula'" [Labor Violations in Private Schools: Regulatory Bodies Are 'Isolated Islands'], *7iber*, July 12, 2017.

43. Statistics for Jordan show that about 40 percent of women in the labor force are in the education sector in recent years. JDoS, Databank.

44. World Economic Forum, *The Global Gender Gap Report 2014* (World Economic Forum, 2014).

45. While a few elite private schools in Amman are known to pay quite well, teaching jobs in private schools are among the lowest paying jobs and they have been largely unregulated: Ejeilat, "Al-Mudaris al-Khasa"; Salameh, "Mawt Ruba" and "Al-Intihakat al-'Amaliya."

46. Facilitating the appointment as a public school teacher in this case meant moving her name up on a civil service list. New graduates seeking teaching jobs typically must wait their turn until a position opens up. For those in the humanities, this wait could be years. For a science or math teacher, the wait was shorter but still a reality. Leen's uncle used his connections to help her move faster up that list, and to be offered an appointment closer to home. Yazan Doughan, "Corruption in the Middle East and the Limits of Conventional Approaches," *GIGA Focus* 5:1–10 (German Institute of Global and Area Studies, Hamburg, September 2017), https://nbn-resolving.org/urn:nbn:de:0168-ssoar-53438-8.

47. Public sector work has typically followed an 8:00 a.m. to 3:00 p.m. schedule, and the main family meal is taken midday. This is all shifting and concerns about "exploitation" in the private sector are sometimes framed as longer hours.

48. On the growth of this aid-dependent sector, see Sukarieh, *A Global Idea*. The United Nations Relief and Works Agency for Palestine Refugees in the Near East (UNRWA), is an aid-dependent UN agency that has been a major employer of Palestinian refugees in Jordan since 1950, most of them Jordanian citizens. See Randa Farah, "UNRWA: Through the Eyes of Its Refugee Employees in Jordan," *Refugee Survey Quarterly* 28, nos. 2–3 (2009): 401.

49. JDoS, Databank.

50. In 2016 one Jordanian dinar was the equivalent of US$1.40. Thus, Wijdan's salary increased from US$367 per month to US$1,128, and again to US$1,411. In 2016, the average monthly salary was 493 dinars (458 dinars for women and 507 for men). JDoS, Databank.

Chapter Three

1. Tim Cresswell, "Towards a Politics of Mobility," *Environment and Planning D: Society and Space* 28, no. 1 (February 2010): 19.

2. Cresswell, "Towards a Politics of Mobility," 21.

3. Cresswell, "Towards a Politics of Mobility," 20.

4. Farha Ghannam, "Mobility, Liminality, and Embodiment in Urban Egypt," *American Ethnologist* 38, no. 4 (November 2011); Amelie Le Renard, *A Society of Young Women: Opportunities of Place, Power, and Reform in Saudi Arabia* (Stanford: Stanford University Press, 2014); Anouk De Koning, "Gender, Public Space and Social Segregation in Cairo: Of Taxi Drivers, Prostitutes and Professional Women," *Antipode* 41, no. 3 (June 2009); Anne Meneley, *Tournaments of Value: Sociability and Hierarchy in a Yemeni Town* (Toronto: University of Toronto Press, 1996); Aseel Sawalha, "Gendered Space and Middle East Studies," *International Journal of Middle East Studies* 46, no. 1 (February 2014).

5. Silvey, "Power, Difference and Mobility."

6. Ghannam, "Embodiment in Urban Egypt," 790–800.

7. Ghannam, "Embodiment in Urban Egypt," 791.

8. De Koning, "Social Segregation in Cairo," 533–56.

9. Ababneh, "Time to Question," 279; Schwedler, "Amman Cosmopolitan," 552.

10. See, for example, Gaetano, *Out to Work*; Natalie K. Jensen, "Mobility within Constraints: Gender, Migration, and New Spaces for Palestinian Women," PhD diss., University of South Carolina, 2011; Alison Mackinnon, *Love and Freedom: Professional Women and the Reshaping of Personal Life* (Cambridge: Cambridge University Press, 1997); Mills, *Thai Women in the Global Labor Force*; Weiner, *From Working Girl*.

11. According to the Economist Intelligence Unit's 2018 global assessment of cost of living (which compares 150 items in 133 different cities), Amman is considered the most expensive city in the Arab world (coming in at twenty-eighth worldwide).

12. Melissa S. Fisher, *Wall Street Women* (Durham, NC: Duke University Press, 2012).

13. Doreen B. Massey, *Space, Place, and Gender* (Minneapolis: University of Minnesota Press, 1994); Silvey, "Power, Difference and Mobility."

14. Samuli Schielke, "Surfaces of Longing: Cosmopolitan Aspiration and Frustration in Egypt," *City & Society* 24, no. 1 (2012): 30.

15. Jamal Ahmad Alnsour, "Managing Urban Growth in the City of Amman, Jordan," *Cities* 50 (2016): 94.

16. Alnsour, "Managing Urban Growth in the City of Amman, Jordan," 94; Yahya Farhan and Sireen Al-Shawamreh, "Impact of Rapid Urbanization and Changing Housing Patterns on Urban Open Public Spaces of Amman, Jordan: A GIS and RS Perspective," *Journal of Environmental Protection* 10, no. 1 (2019): 66.

17. Marwan D. Hanania, "From Colony to Capital: A Socio-economic and Political History of Amman, 1878–1958," PhD diss., Stanford University, 2011, 270.

18. Jordan Department of Statistics, *Jordan in Figures 2008* (Amman: Jordan Department of Statistics, 2008); Jordan Department of Statistics, *Jordan in Figures 2019* (Amman: Jordan Department of Statistics, 2019).

19. Daher, "Discourses of Neoliberalism"; Christopher Parker, "Tunnel-Bypasses and Minarets of Capitalism: Amman as Neoliberal Assemblage," *Political Geography* 28, no. 2 (February 2009).

20. Myriam Ababsa, "Introduction: Citizenship and Urban Issues in Jordan," in *Cities, Urban Practices and Nation Building in Jordan*, ed. Myriam Ababsa and Rami Farouk Daher (Beirut: Presses de l'Ifpo, 2011); Daher, "Discourses of Neoliberalism."

21. Eliana Abu-Hamdi, "The Jordan Gate Towers of Amman: Surrendering Public Space to Build a Neoliberal Ruin," *International Journal of Islamic Architecture* 5, no. 1 (2016); Farhan and Al-Shawamreh, "Impact of Rapid Urbanization."

22. Much of this literature has focused on the most prominent and "shiny" urban develop-ments in Western parts of the city. However, with growth and migration, new restaurants, malls, and cafés have emerged all over the city, and there is significant variability in tier and cost.

23. Daher, "Discourses of Neoliberalism"; Schwedler, "Amman Cosmopolitan"; Fida Adely, "A Different Kind of Love: Compatibility (Insijam) and Marriage in Jordan," *Arab Studies Jour-nal* 24, no. 2 (2016): 104, 109.

24. I borrow the term "Amman Cosmopolitan" from Jillian Schwedler, who used it as the title of her 2010 article.

25. Hazem Zureiqat, "Nahu Injah Mashru' al-Bus al-Sari'" [Toward the Success of the Rapid Bus Project], *7iber*, June 28, 2016.

26. At the time of our field research, Uber and Careem, a local ride share company, were operating in Amman and had gained a customer base even though they were not yet licensed.

27. Women born and raised in Amman use public transportation all the time to go to school, university, medical appointments, shopping, and other needs. This experience is classed, with wealthier residents of Amman less likely to use public transportation. University students around the country are also among the most significant users of public transportation.

28. Women often spoke in terms of morality, traditions, or culture, but rarely framed their discussion explicitly in terms of religion. It is for this reason that I do not center religion in this analysis, even though religion is clearly tied up with these concepts, more centrally for some women than for others. For a study that focuses on religious identities and discussions about piety in Jordan, see Sarah Tobin, *Everyday Piety: Islam and Economy in Jordan* (Ithaca, NY: Cor-nell University Press, 2016).

29. Ghada Al-Shaykh, "Sakan al-Talibat fi al-Urdun: Sa'ubat al-Takif wa-Qaswa Ijtima'ya" [Female Student Dormitories in Jordan: Difficulties Adapting and Social Challenges] *Al-'Arabi*, January 1, 2015, https://www.alaraby.co.uk/سكن-الطالبات-في-الأردن-صعوبات-التكيف-وقسوة-اجتماعية. Safety was also a concern. Fires were sometimes reported in female student dormitories; a fire in 2015 led to a student's death: "Wafaa Taliba Bahrayniyya wa-Asaba 5 Akhriyat fi Hariq li-Sakan Tali-bat fi al-Urdun" [Death of a Female Bahraini Student and 5 Others in a Fire in a Women's Stu-dent Dormitory in Jordan], *Al-Watan*, January 15, 2015. In another widely reported incident, a woman was raped in her dormitory room: "Al-Jiniyat: Tahil li-l-Mahkama Shaban Ightasib Fitaa Tadrus al-Tib fi Jama'at Rasmiyya" [The Prosecution Refers Young Man to Court for Raping a Young Woman Studying Medicine at an Official University], *'Amun*, July 20, 2007; "Habs Mughtasib Talibat-al-Tib fi Irbid 22 'Aman" [Rapist of a Female Medical Student in Irbid Sen-tenced to 22 Years in Prison], *Al-Sawsana*, October 15, 2007.

30. Weiner, *From Working Girl*.

31. Public universities also have student dormitories, typically on campus. These dormito-ries have a reputation for being much stricter: Susan Zayida, "Al-Sakan al-Jama'i li-l-Talibat: Ta-diyyiq 'ala al-Nazilat bi-'Mubarika' min al-Ahl" [University Dormitories for Female Students: Restriction of their Residents with 'Blessings' from the Family], *'Amun*, August 24, 2008.

32. In 2013, the General Amman Municipality reported twenty-two licensed female dormi-tories in Amman, twelve of which were licensed after 2000 (personal communication). While the number of female student dormitories has increased, it is not possible to attribute this growth entirely to female labor migration.

33. This price range is based on self-reporting of interviewees in 2011–16.

34. Pierre Bourdieu, *Distinction: A Social Critique of the Judgement of Taste*, translated by Richard Nice (Cambridge, MA: Harvard University Press, 1984).

35. Even in the United States, high-fives and fist-bumps in the workplace can be associated with particular corporate cultures, especially male-dominated ones (although the COVID-19 pandemic has given fist-bumps a new function in taking the place of the handshake). At the same time, some see the export of "friendly" workplace culture as beneficial. Kim and colleagues argue that there are benefits to promoting "cheerful interpersonal touch, such as high-fives, which may contribute to propagating vibrant workplace culture," and they test the ability of a wrist monitor to promote such forms of touch in contexts where such interaction is not the norm in the workplace. Yuhwan Kim et al., "High5: Promoting Interpersonal Hand-to-Hand Touch for Vibrant Workplace with Electrodermal Sensor Watches," in *Proceedings of the 2014 ACM International Joint Conference on Pervasive and Ubiquitous Computing* (Singapore Management University, 2014), 15–16.

36. Adely, *Gendered Paradoxes*; Fida Adely, "'God Made Beautiful Things': Proper Faith and Religious Authority in a Jordanian High School," *American Ethnologist* 39, no. 2 (May 2012).

37. Susan MacDougall, "Felt Unfreedom: Reflecting on Ethics and Gender in Jordan," *Ethnos* 86, no. 3 (2021): 514.

38. Hailat, "Education of Jordanians"; Hendy and Mimoune, "Evolution of Inequality"; Jordan MOE, *Statistical Report for Academic Year 2019–20*; World Bank, *Hashemite Kingdom of Jordan Education Sector Public Expenditure Review* (Washington, DC: World Bank Publications, 2016); Djavad Salehi-Isfahani, Nadia Belhaj Hassine, and Ragui Assaad, "Equality of Opportunity in Educational Achievement in the Middle East and North Africa," *Journal of Economic Inequality* 12, no. 4 (2014): 489–515. Research on inequality, as measured by school completion, *tawjihi* scores, and international standardized tests, points to disparities among governorates and within governorates along rural/urban lines, as well as type of school attended. Family background (wealth and education level of parents) is also a primary factor that intersects with geography to compound disadvantage.

39. Even when employers are subsidized to hire new graduates as trainees, researchers have found that this does not necessarily lead to long-term employment: Matthew Groh, Nandini Krishnan, David McKenzie, and Tara Vishwanath, "Do Wage Subsidies Provide a Stepping-stone to Employment for Recent College Graduates? Evidence from a Randomized Experiment in Jordan," *Review of Economics and Statistics* 98, no. 3 (2016).

40. While Khuzama's story highlights new and higher end places, not all malls are the same, and some cater to a more working-class or lower-middle-class clientele. Also, many people in high-end malls go to hang out and don't necessarily shop there. Groups of young men do not always have access to such spaces, as security guards at times turn them away. Groups of women are considered "family" or family-friendly, while young men can be viewed as a threat to the respectability of a place. This is also classed: based on their clothing and comportment, young men of lower classes face more policing in such spaces.

41. See Lara Deeb and Mona Harb's discussion of young Shiite youth in Lebanon and the ways in which they navigate spaces of leisure and consumption using flexible "moral rubrics." Lara Deeb and Mona Harb, *Leisurely Islam* (Princeton: Princeton University Press, 2013), 18–24.

42. Ghannam, "Embodiment in Urban Egypt"; Carla Freeman, *High Tech and High Heels in the Global Economy: Women, Work, and Pink-Collar Identities in the Caribbean* (Durham, NC: Duke University Press, 2000); Jensen, "Mobility within Constraints."

43. Here Maysoon is referencing the ways in which national origins are mapped onto geography and geographical biases. Most Jordanians in the governorates are of "East Bank" descent.

44. Dabouq is a relatively new upper-class neighborhood.

45. As a researcher in Jordan, I found that elites in Amman at times felt comfortable making disparaging remarks to me about women who veil. For example, one person told me that the problem with public education was that all the public school teachers veiled and were closed-minded. On anti-hijab bias in Lebanon, see Lara Deeb, *An Enchanted Modern: Gender and Public Piety in Shi'i Lebanon* (Princeton: Princeton University Press, 2006); Ali Kassem, "Anti-Muslim Hate on the Eastern Shores of the Mediterranean: Lebanon, the Hijab, and Modernity/Coloniality," *Ethnic and Racial Studies* 44, no. 12 (2021): 2213–33.

46. Spaces for women to gather in some provincial cities are expanding as these cities grow and further urbanize.

47. Deeb and Harb, *Leisurely Islam*, 15, 18–19.

48. Shami, "Amman Is Not a City," 207.

49. Shami, "Amman Is Not a City," 230.

50. One force these women did not have to contend with was nationalism and border-crossing. Relative to migrant laborers from other countries, these women had a great degree of liberty as citizens.

51. Deeb and Harb, *Leisurely Islam*.

Interlude Four

1. Hannan wears hijab as well, but unlike her sister, her way of dressing was not an issue in her professional life.

Chapter Four

1. Rosenfeld, *Confronting the Occupation*.

2. Naila Kabeer, *Reversed Realities: Gender Hierarchies in Development Thought* (New York: Verso, 1994); Naila Kabeer, "Women, Wages and Intra-household Power Relations in Urban Bangladesh," *Development and Change* 28, no. 2 (April 1997): 261–302.

3. Mary Kawar, "Gender, Employment and the Life Course: The Case of Working Daughters in Amman, Jordan," PhD diss., London School of Economics and Political Science, 1997; Mary Kawar, "Transitions and Boundaries: Research into the Impact of Paid Work on Young Women's Lives in Jordan," *Gender & Development* 8, no. 2 (July 2000): 56–65.

4. Kawar, "Working Daughters in Amman," 145.

5. Adely, "A Different Kind of Love"; Schwedler, "Amman Cosmopolitan."

6. Weiner, *From Working Girl*. Writing about female labor force participation in the United States from 1820 to 1980, Lynn Weiner talks about the ideological lag that ignored the reality of single women entering the waged labor force in significant numbers and framed their migration to the big city as a crisis. Weiner argues that race informed the narrative of crisis: "Although poor, black and immigrant women had long labored in the marketplace for subsistence wages, they had excited little public controversy because they had not been considered subject to middle-class expectations of domesticity" (4).

7. Hoodfar, *Between Marriage and the Market*; Jennifer C. Olmsted, "Is Paid Work the (Only) Answer? Neoliberalism, Arab Women's Well-Being, and the Social Contract," *Journal of Middle East Women's Studies* 1, no. 2 (Spring 2005); Kawar, "Working Daughters in Amman"; Kabeer, "Women, Wages and Intra-household Power."

8. Among single, university-educated Jordanians, women outnumbered men three to one in the "International Organizations" sector between 2017 and 2021. Among those married and university educated, men outnumbered women with men constituting 56 percent of those working in this sector. JDoS, Databank.

9. Maha Abdelrahman, "NGOs and the Dynamics of the Egyptian Labour Market," *Development in Practice* 17, no. 1 (February 2007); Ayah Al-Oballi, "Our Silenced Voices: What We Lose While Working with International 'Humanitarian' Organizations," *7iber*, January 5, 2020; Kathleen O'Reilly, "Women Fieldworkers and the Politics of Participation," *Signs: Journal of Women in Culture and Society* 31, no. 4 (Summer 2006).

10. Reem Farah, "Expat, Local, and Refugee: 'Studying Up' the Global Division of Labor and Mobility in the Humanitarian Industry in Jordan," *Migration and Society* 3, no. 1 (2020).

11. Al-Oballi, "Our Silenced Voices."

12. Janine A. Clark and Wacheke M. Michuki, "Women and NGO Professionalisation: A Case Study of Jordan," *Development in Practice* 19, no. 3 (2009): 336–37.

13. Clark and Michuki, "Women and NGO Professionalisation," 335.

14. Clark and Michuki, "Women and NGO Professionalisation," 336; Zachary Gallin, "Applications of Biopower to NGO-Donor Partnerships for HIV Prevention in Jordan," *Journal for Undergraduate Ethnography* 11, no. 3 (2021).

15. While both of her jobs were in Amman, limiting herself to one public sector job would make commuting more feasible because of predictable and shorter hours. With multiple jobs and an irregular schedule, she needed to be in Amman.

16. On the role of brothers in in the lives of their sisters and brother-sister relations, see Soraya Altorki, "Sisterhood and Stewardship in Sister-Brother Relations," in *The New Arab Family*, ed. Nicholas S. Hopkins (Cairo: American University Press, 2003); Suad Joseph, "Brother/Sister Relationships: Connectivity, Love, and Power in the Reproduction of Patriarchy in Lebanon," *American Ethnologist* 21, no. 1 (February 1994).

17. Deniz Kandiyoti, "Bargaining with Patriarchy," *Gender & Society* 2, no. 3 (1988): 274–90.

18. Williams, *Marxism and Literature.*

19. Anthony Giddens, *Central Problems in Social Theory: Action, Structure, Contradiction in Social Analysis* (Berkeley: University of California Press, 1979), 5.

20. Like people in many other societies, Jordanians participate in informal savings groups (*jami'at*) as a means of saving money without interest.

21. Kawar, "Working Daughters in Amman," 151. See also Suad Joseph, "Gender and Relationality among Arab Families in Lebanon," *Feminist Studies* 19, no. 3 (Autumn 1993).

22. Rosenfeld, *Confronting the Occupation*, 171.

23. Rosenfeld, *Confronting the Occupation*, 179.

24. Rosenfeld, *Confronting the Occupation*, 179–85.

25. Rosenfeld, *Confronting the Occupation*, 185.

26. Ghannam, "Embodiment in Urban Egypt."

27. Katharina Lenner, "Poverty and Poverty Reduction Policies in Jordan," in *Atlas of Jordan: History, Territories and Society*, ed. Myriam Ababsa (Beirut: Presses de l'Ifpo, 2013); Jameel Aljaloudi, "Increase in the State of Poverty in Jordan during the Period 2010–2017," *SocioEconomic Challenges* 4, no. 4 (January 2020): 39–47.

28. In 2016, 38 percent of men working in the public sector were in "protective services" of some kind. Assaad and Salemi, "Structure of Employment," 59, 74.

29. Assaad and Salemi, "Structure of Employment," 74.

30. Olmsted, "Is Paid Work the (Only) Answer?"

31. Rosenfeld, *Confronting the Occupation*, 185–90.

32. Sadaf Hasan and Cristina Pianca, *Invisible Women: The Working and Living Conditions of Irregular Migrant Domestic Workers in Jordan* (Amman: Tamkeen Fields for Aid, 2015), 16.

33. I am indebted to an anonymous reviewer for this insight.

34. Rhacel Salazar Parreñas, "Migrant Filipina Domestic Workers and the International Division of Reproductive Labor," *Gender & Society* 14, no. 4 (August 2000); Sylvia Federici, "Reproduction and the Feminist Struggle in the New International Division of Labor," in *Women, Development, and Labor of Reproduction: Struggles and Movements*, ed. Mariarosa Dalla Costa and Giovanna Franca Dalla Costa (Trenton, NJ: Africa World Press, 1999).

35. Myriam Ababsa, ed., *Atlas of Jordan: History, Territories and Society* (Beirut: Presses de l'Ifpo, 2013).

36. Penny Johnson, "Palestinian Single Women: Agency, Choice, Responsibility," *Review of Women's Studies* 4 (2007): 51.

37. Williams, *Marxism and Literature*.

Interlude Five

1. Sameera's comment here about Karak signals the ways in which residents of the provinces also have stereotypes about each other in some cases based on region.

Chapter Five

1. Maysoon implies that a husband who is less educated is more likely to be violent toward his wife, which is a stereotype.

2. Bryant and Knight, *Anthropology of the Future*.

3. Christine Sargent, "Kinship, Connective Care, and Disability in Jordan," *Medical Anthropology* 40, no. 2 (February–March 2021): 117.

4. Moral concerns emerge because sexual relations outside of marriage are not condoned culturally or religiously.

5. Hughes, *Politics of Marriage*.

6. Hughes, *Politics of Marriage*; Sandra Nasser El-Dine, "Love, Materiality, and Masculinity in Jordan: 'Doing' Romance with Limited Resources," *Men and Masculinities* 21, no. 3 (2018).

7. Rania Salem, "Trends and Differentials in Jordanian Marriage Behavior: Marriage Timing, Spousal Characteristics, Household Structure and Matrimonial Expenditures," in *The Jordanian Labor Market in the New Millennium*, ed. Ragui Assaad (Oxford: Oxford University Press, 2014).

8. Frances Hasso, *Consuming Desires: Family Crisis and the State in the Middle East* (Stanford: Stanford University Press, 2010); Hughes, *Politics of Marriage*.

9. Jordan Department of Statistics and ICF, *Jordan Population and Family Health Survey 2017–18* (Rockville, MD: Jordan Department of Statistics, 2019).

10. JDoS, *Family Health Survey 2017–18*, 64. In 1990, 35 percent of women aged twenty-five to forty-nine married before the age of eighteen, while in 2017–18 only 15 percent in this age group had married before age eighteen.

11. JDoS, Databank.

12. Peter Stein found similar issues for singles in the United States in the 1970s. Stein, *Single* (Englewood Cliffs, NJ: Prentice-Hall, 1976).

13. Here again, moral concern is in large part about relationships with men and the prevailing norm of female virginity before marriage. However, it could also encapsulate other norms as well.

14. JDoS, *Family Health Survey 2017–18*, 63.

15. Adely, "A Different Kind of Love."

16. Laura Pearl Kaya, "Dating in a Sexually Segregated Society: Embodied Practices of Online Romance in Irbid, Jordan," *Anthropological Quarterly* 82, no. 1 (Winter 2009).

17. Penny Johnson, "Unmarried in Palestine: Embodiment and (Dis)Empowerment in the Lives of Single Palestinian Women," *IDS Bulletin* 41, no. 2 (March 2010): 113.

18. Johnson, "Palestinian Single Women"; Hoda Rashad, "The Tempo and Intensity of Marriage in the Arab Region: Key Challenges and Their Implications," *DIFI Family Research and Proceedings* 25, no. 1 (2015); Hanan Halabi, "Profile of Single Women in Palestine," *Review of Women's Studies* 4 (January 2007).

19. Kawar, "Working Daughters in Amman"; Kawar, "Transitions and Boundaries"; Rosenfeld, *Confronting the Occupation*; Shami and Taminian, "Women's Participation in the Jordanian Labour Force"; Yusuf M. Sidani and Zeina T. Al Hakim, "Work–Family Conflicts and Job Attitudes of Single Women: A Developing Country Perspective," *International Journal of Human Resource Management* 23, no. 7 (2012).

20. Andrew Shryrock, "The New Jordanian Hospitality: House, Host, and Guest in the Culture of Public Display," *Comparative Studies in Society and History* 46, no. 1 (January 2004): 36.

21. Inhorn and Smith-Hefner, *Waithood*; Manon Vialle, "Blamed for Delay," in *Waithood: Gender, Education, and Global Delays in Marriage and Childbearing*, ed. Marcia Inhorn and Nancy J. Smith-Hefner (New York: Berghahn Books, 2020), 324–25.

Conclusion

1. Abu-Lughod, "Writing against Culture," 154.

2. Karl Marx, *The Eighteenth Brumaire of Louis Bonaparte* (International Publishers, 1937).

3. Ortner, *Making Gender*, 200–201.

4. An early exception is the work of Richard Antoun, *Arab Village: A Social Structural Study of a Transjordanian Peasant Community* (Bloomington: Indiana University Press, 1972). See also Hughes, *Politics of Marriage*.

5. Ababneh, "Time to Question."

6. And thanks go to Lila Abu-Lughod, who first assigned this reading in a course called "Genealogies of Feminism" at Columbia University.

7. Saba Mahmood, "Feminist Theory, Embodiment, and the Docile Agent: Some Reflections on the Egyptian Islamic Revival," *Cultural Anthropology* 16, no. 2 (May 2001): 202–36.

8. Mahmood, *Politics of Piety*, 14–15.

9. El-Dine, "Love, Materiality, and Masculinity"; Roozbeh Shirazi, "Being Late, Going with the Flow, Always Doing More: The Cruel Optimism of Higher Education in Jordan," *International Journal of Qualitative Studies in Education* 33, no. 3 (2020).

10. Williams, *Marxism and Literature*, 128.

11. Williams, *Marxism and Literature*.

Bibliography

Ababneh, Sara. "Do You Know Who Governs Us? The Damned Monetary Fund." *Middle East Report*, June 30, 2018.

———. "The Time to Question, Rethink and Popularize the Notion of 'Women's Issues': Lessons from Jordan's Popular and Labor Movements from 2006 to Now." *Journal of International Women's Studies* 21, no. 1 (2020): 271–88.

———. "Troubling the Political: Women in the Jordanian Day-waged Labor Movement." *International Journal of Middle East Studies* 48, no. 01 (February 2016): 87–112.

Ababsa, Myriam, ed. *Atlas of Jordan: History, Territories and Society*. Beirut: Presses de l'Ifpo, 2013.

———. "The Evolution of Upgrading Policies in Amman." *Sustainable Architecture and Urban Development* (July 2010): 1–17.

———. "Introduction: Citizenship and Urban Issues in Jordan." In *Cities, Urban Practices and Nation Building in Jordan*, edited by Myriam Ababsa and Rami Farouk Daher, 39–64. Beirut: Presses de l'Ifpo, 2011.

———. "The Socio-Economic Composition of the Population." In *Atlas of Jordan: History, Territories and Society*, edited by Myriam Ababsa, 344–53. Beirut: Presses de l'Ifpo, 2013.

Abdelrahman, Maha. "NGOs and the Dynamics of the Egyptian Labour Market." *Development in Practice* 17, no. 1 (February 2007): 78–84.

Abdul-Hamid, Husein, Harry Patrinos, Joel Reyes, Jo Kelcey, and Andrea Diaz Varela. *Learning in the Face of Adversity: The UNRWA Education Program for Palestine Refugees*. Washington, DC: World Bank, 2015.

Abney, David, and Arancha González Laya. "This Is Why Women Must Play a Greater Role in the Global Economy." World Economic Forum, January 24, 2018. https://www.weforum.org/agenda/2018/01/this-is-why-women-must-play-a-greater-role-in-the-global-economy/.

Abu-Dayyeh, Nabil I. "Persisting Vision: Plans for a Modern Arab Capital, Amman, 1955–2002." *Planning Perspectives* 19, no. 1 (2004): 79–110.

Abu-Hamdi, Eliana. "The Jordan Gate Towers of Amman: Surrendering Public Space to Build a Neoliberal Ruin." *International Journal of Islamic Architecture* 5, no. 1 (March 2016): 73–101.

Abu Khalil, Ahmad. "Min al-Ta'sis wa-hata al-Istiqlal: Fasl min Sira al-Ta'lim fi al-Urdun" [From Founding to Independence: A Chapter of the Story of Education in Jordan]. *7iber,* April 17, 2022.

Abu-Lughod, Lila. "The Romance of Resistance: Tracing Transformations of Power through Bedouin Women." *American Ethnologist* 17, no. 1 (February 1990): 41–55.

———. "Seductions of the 'Honor Crime.'" *Differences* 22, no. 1 (2011): 17–63.

———. "Writing against Culture." In *Recapturing Anthropology: Working in the Present,* edited by Richard G. Fox, 137–62. Sante Fe, NM: School of American Research, 1991.

———. *Writing Women's Worlds: Bedouin Stories.* Berkeley: University of California Press, 1993.

Abu Na'ir, Nadhir Sihan. "Zahira al-'Anf al-Jama'i wa-Dawr al-Jama'at fi al-Hud min Intishariha min Wajhat Nazr A'da' Hay'a al-Tadris fi al-Jama'at al-Urduniyya" [The Phenomenon of University Violence and the Role of Universities in Reducing the Spread from the Point of View of the Faculty Members in Jordanian Universities]. *Dirasat fi al-'Alum al-Tarbawiyya* 43, no. 1 (2016): 213–33.

Adely, Fida. "A Different Kind of Love: Compatibility (Insijam) and Marriage in Jordan." *Arab Studies Journal* 24, no. 2 (Fall 2016): 102–27.

———. "Educating Women for Development: The Arab Human Development Report 2005 and the Problem with Women's Choices." *International Journal of Middle East Studies* 41, no. 01 (February 2009): 105–22.

———. "The Emergence of a New Labor Movement in Jordan." *Middle East Report* 264 (Fall 2012): 34–37.

———. *Gendered Paradoxes: Educating Jordanian Women in Nation, Faith, and Progress.* Chicago: University of Chicago Press, 2012.

———. "'God Made Beautiful Things': Proper Faith and Religious Authority in a Jordanian High School." *American Ethnologist* 39, no. 2 (May 2012): 297–312.

Adely, Fida, Angela Haddad, Abdel Hakim Al-Husban, and Afaf Al-Khoshman. "Getting In and Getting Through: Navigating Higher Education in Jordan." *Comparative Education Review* 63, no. 1 (February 2019): 79–97.

Adely, Fida, Ankushi Mitra, Menatalla Mohamed, and Adam Shaham. "Poor Education, Unemployment and the Promise of Skills: The Hegemony of the 'Skills Mismatch' Discourse." *International Journal of Educational Development* 82 (April 2021): 102381.

Ahearn, Laura M. *Invitations to Love: Literacy, Love Letters, and Social Change in Nepal.* Ann Arbor: University of Michigan Press, 2001.

Ahmed, Sara. *What's the Use? On the Uses of Use.* Durham, NC: Duke University Press, 2019.

Al-Atiyat, Ibtesam. "Harvests of the Golden Decades: Contemporary Women's Activism in Jordan." In *Mapping Arab Women's Movements: A Century of Transformations from Within,* edited by Pernille Arenfeldt and Nawar Al-Hassan Golley, 133–70. Cairo: American University Press, 2012.

Al-Dajani, Haya, Sara Carter, and Colin Williams. "Women's Resourcefulness in the Informal Economy: Evidence from Jordan." In *Exploring Resources: Life-Balance and Well-Being of Women Who Work in a Global Context,* edited by Roxane L. Gervais and Prudence M. Millear, 35–54. Cham, Switzerland: Springer, 2016.

Al-Emam, Dana. "Women's Economic Participation 'Key to Higher GDP'—Experts." *Jordan Times,* October 11, 2016.

Al-Hirut, 'Abd al-Halim. "Awl 11 Mu'alima fi Tarikh al-Urdun" [The First 11 Female Teachers in Jordan's History]. *Al-Ra'i,* November 11, 2021. https://alrai.com/article/10709633.

Al-Hirut, 'Abd al-Halim Husayn, Muhamad Filah al-Khawalda, Murad 'Abd al-Hamid al-Shiyab, Ahmad Ibrahim al-'Alawana. *Awl Mi'a Mu'alim* [First One Hundred Teachers]. Amman: University of International Islamic Sciences Press, 2016.

Al Husseini, Jalal. "Jordan and the Palestinians." In *Atlas of Jordan: History, Territories and Society*, edited by Myriam Ababsa, 230–45. Beirut: Presses de l'Ifpo, 2013.

Aljaloudi, Jameel. "Increase [in] the State of Poverty in Jordan during the Period 2010–2017." *SocioEconomic Challenges* 4, no. 4 (January 2020): 39–47.

"Al-Jiniyat: Tahil li-l-Mahkama Shaban Ightasib Fitaa Tadrus al-Tib fi Jama'at Rasmiyya" [The Prosecution Refers Young Man to Court for Raping a Young Woman Studying Medicine at an Official University]. *'Amun*, July 20, 2007.

Al Kafaween, 'Abdallah. "Madaris Lam Yanjah fiha Ahid: Hal Yuhal al-Damj al-Mushkila?" [Schools in Which Nobody Passed: Will Merging Solve the Problem?]. *7iber*, December 1, 2015.

Al-Khaldi, Kholoud. *Women Workers in the Textiles and Garments Industries in Jordan: A Research on the Impact of Globalization*. Ministry of Labor, Jordan, and International Labor Organization, 2002.

Al-Nātūr, 'Izadīn. "Talaba al-makārim yushakkalūn sab'a wa 'arba'īn min al-qabūl al-muwaḥḥad" [Makrama Students Make Up 47 Percent of Unified Admissions]. *Amman Net*, October 23, 2014. http://ar.ammannet.net/news/238498.

Alnsour, Jamal Ahmad. "Managing Urban Growth in the City of Amman, Jordan." *Cities* 50 (February 2016): 93–99.

Al-Oballi, Ayah. "Our Silenced Voices: What We Lose While Working with International 'Humanitarian' Organizations." *7iber*, January 5, 2020.

Al-Rifati, Ziyyad. "Al-'Anf al-Jama'i: Al-Asbab al-Haqiqiyya wa-Hulul Muqtariha" [University Violence: The Real Reasons and Suggested Solutions]. *Al-Ghad*, January 3, 2017.

Al-Sakat, Musa. "Tamkin al-Mir'a . . . Iqtisadiyan" [Empowering Women . . . Economically]. *Al-Ghad*, January 29, 2020.

Al Sharafat, Ayman. "Spatial Inequality in Jordan." *Journal of Economics & Management* 36 (2019): 71–83.

Al-Shaykh, Ghada. "Sakan al-Talibat fi al-Urdun: Sa'ubat al-Takif wa-Qaswa Ijtima'ya" [Female Student Dormitories in Jordan: Difficulties Adapting and Social Challenges]. *Al-'Arabi*, January 1, 2015. https://www.alaraby.co.uk/-التكيف-صعوبات-الأردن-في-الطالبات-اجتماعيةسكن-وقسوة.

Alshoraty, Yazid Isa. "Reasons for University Students' Violence in Jordan." *International Education Studies* 8, no. 10 (2015): 150–57.

Alsuwaigh, Siham A. "Women in Transition: The Case of Saudi Arabia." *Journal of Comparative Family Studies* 20, no. 1 (Spring 1989): 67–78.

Al-Tal, Suhair Salti. *Tarikh al-haraka al-nisa'iya al-urdunniya, 1944–2008* [A History of Women's Activism in Jordan: 1944–2008]. Amman: Dar Azmina li-l-nashr wa-l-tawzi'a, 2014.

"Al-Ta'lim al-'Ali: Yuqar Ta'limat Makrama Ibna' al-'Asha'ir" [Higher Education Adopts Regulations of the Royal Grants for Tribal Students]. *'Amun*, July 25, 2016. https://www.ammon news.net/article/276370.

Al Tarawnah, Mohammad Salim. *Tarikh Mantiqat al-Balqa' wa Ma'an wa al-Karak, 1281–1337H/1864–1918M* [The History of the Balqa, Maan, and Karak Regions, 1864–1918]. Amman: Matabi' al-Dustour al-Tijariyyah, 1992.

Altorki, Soraya. "Sisterhood and Stewardship in Sister-Brother Relations." In *The New Arab Family*, edited by Nicholas S. Hopkins, 181–200. Cairo: American University Press, 2003.

Amadouny, Vartan Manoug. "The British Role in the Development of an Infrastructure in Trans-Jordan during the Mandate Period, 1921–1946." PhD diss., University of Southampton, 1993.

Amawi, Abla M. "The Consolidation of the Merchant Class in Transjordan during the Second World War." In *Village, Steppe and State: The Social Origins of Modern Jordan*, edited by Eugene Rogan and Tareq Tell, 162–86. London: British Academic Press, 1994.

Amer, Mona. "School-to-Work Transition in Jordan, 2010–2016." In *The Jordanian Labor Market: Between Fragility and Resilience*, edited by Caroline Krafft and Ragui Assaad, 225–58. New York: Oxford University Press, 2019.

Amin, Rula. "Jordan Issues Record Number of Work Permits to Syrian Refugees." United Nations High Commission for Refugees, January 25, 2022. https://www.unhcr.org/en-us/news /press/2022/1/61effaa54/jordan-issues-record-number-work-permits-syrian-refugees.

Amin, Sajeda, and Nagah H. Al-Bassusi. "Education, Wage Work, and Marriage: Perspectives of Egyptian Working Women." *Journal of Marriage and Family* 66, no. 5 (December 2004): 1287–99.

Amiry, Suad. *My Damascus*. Ithaca, NY: Olive Branch Press, 2021.

Anderson, Betty S. *Nationalist Voices in Jordan: The Street and the State*. Austin: University of Texas Press, 2005.

Antoun, Richard T. *Arab Village: A Social Structural Study of a Transjordanian Peasant Community*. Bloomington: Indiana University Press, 1972.

Arab Renaissance for Democracy and Development (ARDD). "Women's Informal Employment in Jordan: Challenges Facing Home-Based Businesses during COVID-19." *Women's Advocacy Issues Policy Brief* 3 (May 2021). Available at https://jordan.unwomen.org/en/digital -library/publications/2021/womens-informal-employment-in-jordan.

Assaad, Ragui. *The Jordanian Labor Market in the New Millennium*. Oxford: Oxford University Press, 2014.

Assaad, Ragui, Rana Hendy, Moundir Lassassi, and Shaimaa Yassin. "Explaining the MENA Paradox: Rising Educational Attainment, Yet Stagnant Female Labor Force Participation." *Demographic Research* 43, no. 28 (2020): 817–50.

Assaad, Ragui, Rana Hendy, and Chaimaa Yassine. "Gender and the Jordanian Labor Market." In *The Jordanian Labor Market in the New Millennium*, edited by Ragui Assaad, 105–43. Oxford: Oxford University Press, 2014.

Assaad, Ragui, Caroline Krafft, and Caitlyn Keo. "The Composition of Labor Supply." In *The Jordanian Labor Market: Between Fragility and Resilience*, edited by Caroline Krafft and Ragui Assaad, 11–41. New York: Oxford University Press, 2019.

Assaad, Ragui, Caroline Krafft, and Djavad Salehi-Isfahani. "Does the Type of Higher Education Affect Labor Market Outcomes? Evidence from Egypt and Jordan." *Higher Education* 75, no. 6 (2018): 945–95.

Assaad, Ragui, and Colette Salemi. "The Structure of Employment." In *The Jordanian Labor Market: Between Fragility and Resilience*, edited by Caroline Krafft and Ragui Assaad, 43–78. New York: Oxford University Press, 2019.

Aswad, Barbara C. "Visiting Patterns among Women of the Elite in a Small Turkish City." *Anthropological Quarterly* 47, no. 1 (January 1974): 9–27.

Badran, Nabil A. "The Means of Survival: Education and the Palestinian Community, 1948–1967." *Journal of Palestine Studies* 9, no. 4 (1980): 44–74.

Barakat, Nora Elizabeth. "An Empty Land? Nomads and Property Administration in Hamidian Syria." PhD diss., University of California Berkeley, 2015.

Bartlett, Lesley, and Frances Vavrus. "Comparative Case Studies: An Innovative Approach." *Nordic Journal of Comparative and International Education (NJCIE)* 1, no. 1 (2017).

Baylouny, Anne Marie. "Militarizing Welfare: Neo-liberalism and Jordanian Policy." *Middle East Journal* 62, no. 2 (Spring 2008): 277–303.

Bergeron, Suzanne. "Economics, Performativity, and Social Reproduction in Global Development." *Globalizations* 8, no. 2 (April 2011): 151–61.

———. "The Post-Washington Consensus and Economic Representations of Women in Development at the World Bank." *International Feminist Journal of Politics* 5, no. 3 (2003): 397–419.

Bin ʿAbdalmanʿam al-Rifaʿi, Khalid. "Minaʿ al-Ab Ibnatuhu min al-Zawaj" [A Father Prevents His Daughters from Getting Married]. *Al-Aluka*, December 14, 2017. https://www.alukah .net/fatawa_counsels/0/123417/.

Bonal, Xavier. "Education, Poverty, and the 'Missing Link': The Limits of Human Capital Theory as a Paradigm for Poverty Reduction." In *The Handbook of Global Education Policy*, edited by Karen Mundy, Andy Green, Bob Lingard, and Antoni Verger, 97–110. Chichester, UK: John Wiley & Sons, 2016.

Bourdieu, Pierre. *Distinction: A Social Critique of the Judgement of Taste*. Translated by Richard Nice. Cambridge, MA: Harvard University Press, 1984.

Brand, Laurie A. *Jordan's Inter-Arab Relations: The Political Economy of Alliance-Making*. New York: Columbia University Press, 1995.

———. "Palestinians and Jordanians: A Crisis of Identity." *Journal of Palestine Studies* 24, no. 4 (Summer 1995): 46–61.

Brettell, Caroline B. "Gender, Family, and Migration." In *Oxford Handbook of the Politics of International Migration*, edited by Marc R. Rosenblum and Daniel J. Tichenor. Oxford: Oxford University Press, 2012.

Bryant, Rebecca, and Daniel M. Knight. *The Anthropology of the Future*. Cambridge: Cambridge University Press, 2019.

Brynen, Rex. "Economic Crisis and Post-Rentier Democratization in the Arab World: The Case of Jordan." *Canadian Journal of Political Science / Revue Canadienne de Science Politique* 25, no. 1 (March 1992): 69–97.

Butler, Judith. "Performative Acts and Gender Constitution: An Essay in Phenomenology and Feminist Theory." *Theatre Journal* 40, no. 4 (December 1988): 519–31.

Cantini, Daniele. *Youth and Education in the Middle East: Assessing the Performance and Practice of Urban Environments*. London: I. B. Tauris, 2016.

Carapico, Sheila. *Political Aid and Arab Activism: Democracy Promotion, Justice, and Representation*. Cambridge: Cambridge University Press, 2013.

Carruth, Lauren, and Lahra Smith. "Building One's Own House: Power and Escape for Ethiopian Women through International Migration." *Journal of Modern African Studies* 60, no. 1 (March 2022): 85–109.

Castles, Stephen. "Understanding Global Migration: A Social Transformation Perspective." *Journal of Ethnic and Migration Studies* 36, no. 10 (2010): 1565–86.

Clark, Janine A., and Wacheke M. Michuki. "Women and NGO Professionalisation: A Case Study of Jordan." *Development in Practice* 19, no. 3 (May 2009): 329–39.

Cook, Brittany. "The Problem with Empowerment: Social Reproduction and Women's Food Projects in Jordan." *Annals of the American Association of Geographers* 111, no. 1 (January 2021): 52–67.

Cresswell, Tim. "Towards a Politics of Mobility." *Environment and Planning D: Society and Space* 28, no. 1 (February 2010): 17–31.

Daher, Rami Farouk. "Discourses of Neoliberalism and Disparities in the City Landscape: Cranes, Craters, and an Exclusive Urbanity." In *Cities, Urban Practices and Nation Building in Jordan*, edited by Myriam Ababsa and Rami Farouk Daher, 273–95. Beirut: Presses de l'Ifpo, 2011.

———. "Prelude: Understanding Cultural Change and Urban Transformations: Qualifying Amman: The City of Many Hats." In *Cities, Urban Practices and Nation Building in Jordan*, edited by Myriam Ababsa and Rami Farouk Daher, 65–89. Beirut: Presses de l'Ifpo, 2011.

Dargarabedian, Arda. "Armenian Women in Jordan." *Al-Raida Journal*, nos. 101–2 (2003): 24–26.

Davis, Rochelle. *Palestinian Village Histories: Geographies of the Displaced*. Stanford: Stanford University Press, 2010.

Davis, Rochelle, Grace Benton, Will Todman, and Emma Murphy. "Hosting Guests, Creating Citizens: Models of Refugee Administration in Jordan and Egypt." *Refugee Survey Quarterly* 36, no. 2 (2017): 1–32.

De Bel-Air, Françoise, *Migration Profile: Jordan*. Florence: Migration Policy Centre—European University Institute, June 2016.

Deeb, Lara. *An Enchanted Modern: Gender and Public Piety in Shi'i Lebanon*. Princeton: Princeton University Press, 2006.

Deeb, Lara, and Mona Harb. *Leisurely Islam*. Princeton: Princeton University Press, 2013.

DeJaeghere, Joan. *Educating Entrepreneurial Citizens: Neoliberalism and Youth Livelihoods in Tanzania*. New York: Taylor & Francis, 2017.

———. "Girls' Educational Aspirations and Agency: Imagining Alternative Futures through Schooling in a Low-Resourced Tanzanian Community." *Critical Studies in Education* 59, no. 2 (2018): 237–55.

De Koning, Anouk. "Gender, Public Space and Social Segregation in Cairo: Of Taxi Drivers, Prostitutes and Professional Women." *Antipode* 41, no. 3 (June 2009): 533–56.

Deshingkar, Priya, and Sven Grimm. *Internal Migration and Development: A Global Perspective*. New York: United Nations, 2005.

Doughan, Yazan. "Corruption in the Middle East and the Limits of Conventional Approaches." *GIGA Focus* 5 (September 2017): 1–10. German Institute of Global and Area Studies, Hamburg. https://nbn-resolving.org/urn:nbn:de:0168-ssoar-53438-8.

Doumani, Beshara. *Rediscovering Palestine: Merchants and Peasants in Jabal Nablus, 1700–1900*. Berkeley: University of California Press, 1995.

Economist Intelligence Unit. *Worldwide Cost of Living Index 2018*. London: The Economist, 2018.

Ejeilat, Lina. "Al-Mudaris al-Khasa: Tamyiz did al-Ma'lumat wa-Ruwatib dun al-Had al-Adna" [Private Schools: Discrimination against Female Teachers and Salaries below Minimum Wage]. *7iber*, March 9, 2015.

El Abed, Oroub. "Immobile Palestinians: Ongoing Plight of Gazans in Jordan." *Forced Migration Review* 26 (August 2006): 17–18.

Elder, Sara. "What Does NEETs Mean and Why Is the Concept So Easily Misinterpreted?" Technical Brief No. 1. International Labour Office, January 2015.

Ellingrud, Kweill, Anu Madgavkar, James Manyika, Jonathan Woetzel, Vivian Riefberg, Mekala Krishnan, and Mili Seoni. *The Power of Parity: Advancing Women's Equality in the United States*. McKinsey & Co., April 7, 2016. https://www.mckinsey.com/featured-insights/employment-and-growth/the-power-of-parity-advancing-womens-equality-in-the-united-states.

Elyachar, Julia. "Empowerment Money: The World Bank, Non-governmental Organizations, and the Value of Culture in Egypt." *Public Culture* 14, no. 3 (Fall 2002): 493–513.

Farah, Randa. "UNRWA: Through the Eyes of Its Refugee Employees in Jordan." *Refugee Survey Quarterly* 28, nos. 2–3 (2009): 389–411.

Farah, Reem. "Expat, Local, and Refugee: 'Studying Up' the Global Division of Labor and Mobility in the Humanitarian Industry in Jordan." *Migration and Society* 3, no. 1 (2020): 130–44.

Farhan, Yahya, and Sireen Al-Shawamreh. "Impact of Rapid Urbanization and Changing Housing Patterns on Urban Open Public Spaces of Amman, Jordan: A GIS and RS Perspective." *Journal of Environmental Protection* 10, no. 1 (2019): 57–79.

Federici, Silvia. "Reproduction and the Feminist Struggle in the New International Division of Labor." In *Women, Development, and Labor of Reproduction: Struggles and Movements*, edited by Mariarosa Dalla Costa, and Giovanna Franca Dalla Costa, 47–82. Trenton, NJ: Africa World Press, 1999.

Ferguson, James. "The Uses of Neoliberalism." *Antipode* 41, no. S1 (January 2010): 166–84.

Fernandez, Bina, Marina De Regt, and Gregory Currie, eds. *Migrant Domestic Workers in the Middle East: The Home and the World*. New York: Palgrave Macmillan, 2014.

Fisher, Melissa S. *Wall Street Women*. Durham, NC: Duke University Press, 2012.

Fortna, Benjamin C. *Imperial Classroom: Islam, the State, and Education in the Late Ottoman Empire*. New York: Oxford University Press, 2002.

Foucault, Michel. *The History of Sexuality: An Introduction*. New York: Vintage, 1990.

Freeman, Carla. *High Tech and High Heels in the Global Economy: Women, Work, and Pink-Collar Identities in the Caribbean*. Durham, NC: Duke University Press, 2000.

Frye, Margaret. "Bright Futures in Malawi's New Dawn: Educational Aspirations as Assertions of Identity." *American Journal of Sociology* 117, no. 6 (May 2012): 1565–1624.

Gaetano, Arianne M. *Out to Work: Migration, Gender, and the Changing Lives of Rural Women in Contemporary China*. Honolulu: University of Hawaii Press, 2015.

Gallin, Zachary. "Applications of Biopower to NGO-Donor Partnerships for HIV Prevention in Jordan." *Journal for Undergraduate Ethnography* 11, no. 3 (2021): 84–101.

Ghannam, Farha. "Keeping Him Connected: Labor Migration and the Production of Locality in Cairo." *City & Society* 10, no. 1 (June 1998): 65–82.

———. *Live and Die like a Man: Gender Dynamics in Urban Egypt*. Stanford: Stanford University Press, 2013.

———. "Mobility, Liminality, and Embodiment in Urban Egypt." *American Ethnologist* 38, no. 4 (November 2011): 790–800.

Goldberg, Jeffrey. "The Modern King in the Arab Spring." *The Atlantic*, 2013.

Gordon, Wendy M. *Mill Girls and Strangers: Single Women's Independent Migration in England, Scotland, and the United States, 1850–1881*. Albany: SUNY Press, 2012.

Goussous, Suzanna. "Thabahtoona Criticises Higher Education Strategy." *Jordan Times*, June 27, 2015.

Groh, Matthew, Nandini Krishnan, David McKenzie, and Tara Vishwanath. "Do Wage Subsidies Provide a Stepping-stone to Employment for Recent College Graduates? Evidence from a Randomized Experiment in Jordan." *Review of Economics and Statistics* 98, no. 3 (2016): 488–502.

Guégnard, Christine, Xavier Matheu, and Mūsá Shutaywī. *Unemployment in Jordan*. Luxembourg: Office for Official Publications of the European Communities, 2005.

"Habs Mughtasib Talibat al-Tib fi Irbid 22 ʿAman" [Rapist of a Female Medical Student in Irbid Sentenced to 22 Years in Prison]. *Al-Sawsana*, October 15, 2007.

Hailat, Mahmoud Ali. "Education of Jordanians: Outcomes in a Challenging Environment." In *The Jordanian Labor Market: Between Fragility and Resilience*, edited by Caroline Krafft and Ragui Assaad, 203–23. New York: Oxford University Press, 2019.

Halabi, Hanan. "Profile of Single Women in Palestine." *Review of Women's Studies* 4 (January 2007): 27–46.

Hanania, Marwan D. "From Colony to Capital: A Socio-economic and Political History of Amman, 1878–1958." PhD diss., Stanford University, 2011.

Hanieh, Adam. *Lineages of Revolt: Issues of Contemporary Capitalism in the Middle East*. Chicago: Haymarket Books, 2013.

Harvey, David. *A Brief History of Neoliberalism*. New York: Oxford University Press, 2007.

Hasan, Sadaf, and Cristina Pianca. *Invisible Women: The Working and Living Conditions of Irregular Migrant Domestic Workers in Jordan*. Amman: Tamkeen Fields for Aid, 2015.

Hasso, Frances. *Consuming Desires: Family Crisis and the State in the Middle East*. Stanford: Stanford University Press, 2010.

Hasso, Frances S., and Zakia Salime, eds. *Freedom without Permission: Bodies and Space in the Arab Revolutions*. Durham, NC: Duke University Press, 2016.

Hendy, Rana, and Nejla Ben Mimoune. "Evolution of Inequality of Opportunity in Education in the Jordanian Case: From 2008 to 2017." Economic Research Forum (ERF), 2021.

Hersch, Joni. "Opting Out among Women with Elite Education." *Review of Economics of the Household* 11, no. 4 (2013): 469–506.

Hirshman, Linda R. *Get to Work . . . and Get a Life, Before It's Too Late*. New York: Penguin, 2006.

Hochschild, Arlie, and Anne Machung. *The Second Shift: Working Families and the Revolution at Home*. New York: Penguin, 2012.

Hondagneu-Sotelo, Pierrette, and Cynthia Cranford. "Gender and Migration." In *Handbook of the Sociology of Gender*, 105–26. Boston: Springer, 2006.

Hoodfar, Homa. *Between Marriage and the Market*. Berkeley: University of California Press, 1997.

Hughes, Geoffrey F. "The Chastity Society: Disciplining Muslim Men." *Journal of the Royal Anthropological Institute* 23, no. 2 (June 2017): 267–84.

——. *Kinship, Islam, and the Politics of Marriage in Jordan: Affection and Mercy*. Bloomington: Indiana University Press, 2021.

Human Rights Watch. *"We Lost Everything": Debt Imprisonment in Jordan*. Human Rights Watch, March 16, 2021.

Inhorn, Marcia C., and Nancy J. Smith-Hefner, eds. *Waithood: Gender, Education, and Global Delays in Marriage and Childbearing*. New York: Berghahn Books, 2020.

International Labour Office. *Annual Report 2019: Better Work Jordan*. Geneva: International Labour Office; International Finance Corporation, 2019.

Jad, Islah. "NGOs: Between Buzzwords and Social Movements." *Development in Practice* 17, nos. 4–5 (August 2007): 622–29.

Jaludi, Aliyaan, and Muḥammad ʿAdnan Bakhit. *Qaḍāʾ ʿAjlūn fī ʿaṣr al-tanẓīmāt al-ʿUthmānīyah: 1281–1337H/1864–1918M*. Amman: al-Lajnah al-ʿAlīyān li-Kitābat Tārīkh al-Urdun, 1992.

Jarrar, Shakir, and Omar Faris. "Al-Tamkin al-Mutawahish: Kif Anhakat al-Qurud al-Saghira Hayaat al-Nisaʾ wa-ʾAʾilatuhina" [Savage Empowerment: How Small Loans Stretched Thin the Livelihoods of Women and Their Families]. *7iber*, July 2, 2019.

Jee, Eunsook. "Unmarried Daughters as Family Caregivers: Evolving Family Relationships, Gender Order, and Singlehood in Japan." *Korean Anthropology Review* 5 (February 2021): 85–116.

Jeffrey, Craig. "Timepass: Youth, Class, and Time among Unemployed Young Men in India." *American Ethnologist* 37, no. 3 (August 2010): 465–81.

Jensen, Natalie K. "Mobility within Constraints: Gender, Migration, and New Spaces for Palestinian Women." PhD diss., University of South Carolina, 2011.

Johnson, Penny. "Palestinian Single Women: Agency, Choice, Responsibility." *Review of Women's Studies* 4 (2007): 47–64.

———. "Unmarried in Palestine: Embodiment and (Dis)Empowerment in the Lives of Single Palestinian Women." *IDS Bulletin* 41, no. 2 (March 2010): 106–15.

Jordan Department of Financial Stability, *Taqrir al-Stiqrar al-Maly 2021* [Financial Stability Report 2021].

Jordan Department of Statistics (JDoS). Databank. Amman: Jordan Department of Statistics, 2021. https://jorinfo.dos.gov.jo/Databank/pxweb/en/.

———. *Jordan in Figures 2008*. Amman: Jordan Department of Statistics, 2008.

———. *Jordan in Figures 2019*. Amman: Jordan Department of Statistics, 2019.

Jordan Department of Statistics and ICF. *Jordan Population and Family Health Survey 2017–18*. Rockville, MD: Jordan Department of Statistics, 2019.

Jordanian National Commission for Women. "'Awliya' Amur Yahrimun Binatihum al-Mawazifat min al-Zawaj Tam'a fi al-Ratib" [Parents Prevent Their Employed Daughters from Getting Married Out of Greed for Their Wages]. November 14, 2011. https://women.jo/en/node/5763.

Jordan Ministry of Education (MOE). *Statistical Report for Academic Year 2011–12*. Amman: Government of Jordan, 2012.

———. *Statistical Report for Academic Year 2016–17*. Amman: Jordan Ministry of Education, 2018.

———. *Statistical Report for Academic Year 2017–18*. Amman: Government of Jordan, 2018. https://moe.gov.jo/node/60145.

———. *Statistical Report for Academic Year 2019–20*. Amman: Government of Jordan, 2020.

———. *Statistical Report for Academic Year 2020–21*. Amman: Government of Jordan, 2021.

Jordan Ministry of Higher Education and Scientific Research. "Al-Siyasa al-'Ama li-Qabul al Talba fi al-Jama'at al-Urduniyya li-Marhala al-Bakaluriyus li-l-'Am al-Jama'i 2021/2022" [Public Policy for Student Admission in Jordanian Universities for the Bachelor's Degree for the Academic Year 2021–22]. June 18, 2021.

Jordan Ministry of Labor. "Employment and Manpower-Employment and Unemployment." Open Government Data Platform. 2022. https://form.jordan.gov.jo/wps/portal/Home/Open DataMain.

Jordan Office of the Prime Minister. *Jordan 2025: A National Vision and Strategy*. Amman: Government of Jordan, 2015.

Joseph, Suad. "Brother/Sister Relationships: Connectivity, Love, and Power in the Reproduction of Patriarchy in Lebanon." *American Ethnologist* 21, no. 1 (February 1994): 50–73.

———, ed. *Gender and Citizenship in the Middle East*. Syracuse, NY: Syracuse University Press, 2000.

———. "Gender and Relationality among Arab families in Lebanon." *Feminist Studies* 19, no. 3 (Autumn 1993): 465–86.

Jureidini, Ray. "Trafficking and Contract Migrant Workers in the Middle East." *International Migration* 48, no. 4 (2010): 142–63.

Kabeer, Naila. *Reversed Realities: Gender Hierarchies in Development Thought*. New York: Verso, 1994.

———. "Women, Wages and Intra-household Power Relations in Urban Bangladesh." *Development and Change* 28, no. 2 (April 1997): 261–302.

Kaci, Ariana, and Helene Starks. "Caring for the Elderly in Algeria within the Discourse of Traditionalism and Modernism: Is There a Kabyle 'Woman Problem'?" *IJFAB: International Journal of Feminist Approaches to Bioethics* 6, no. 2 (Fall 2013): 160–78.

Kalisman, Hilary Falb. "The Next Generation of Cultivators: Teaching Agriculture in Iraq, Palestine and Transjordan (1920–1960)." *Histoire de l'éducation* 148 (2017): 143–64.

Kandiyoti, Deniz. "Bargaining with Patriarchy." *Gender & Society* 2, no. 3 (1988): 274–90.

Kasoolu, Semiray, Timothy O'Brien, Ricardo Hausmann, and Miguel Santos. "Female Labor in Jordan: A Systematic Approach to the Exclusion Puzzle." Center for International Development Working Paper Series 365. Cambridge, MA: Harvard University, 2019.

Kassem, Ali. "Anti-Muslim Hate on the Eastern Shores of the Mediterranean: Lebanon, the Hijab, and Modernity/Coloniality." *Ethnic and Racial Studies* 44, no. 12 (2021): 2213–33.

Kawar, Mary. "Gender, Employment and the Life Course: The Case of Working Daughters in Amman, Jordan." PhD diss., London School of Economics and Political Science, 1997.

———. "Transitions and Boundaries: Research into the Impact of Paid Work on Young Women's Lives in Jordan." *Gender & Development* 8, no. 2 (July 2000): 56–65.

Kaya, Laura Pearl. "Dating in a Sexually Segregated Society: Embodied Practices of Online Romance in Irbid, Jordan." *Anthropological Quarterly* 82, no. 1 (Winter 2009): 251–78.

Kenney, Jeffrey T. "Selling Success, Nurturing the Self: Self-Help Literature, Capitalist Values, and the Sacralization of Subjective Life in Egypt." *International Journal of Middle East Studies* 47, no. 4 (November 2015): 663–80.

"Khabra': Musharaka al-Mara'a Iqtisadiyan fi al-Urdun Da'ifa" [News: Women's Economic Participation in Jordan Is Weak]. *Al-Ghad*, January 10, 2019.

Khafagy, Fatma. "Women and Labor Migration: One Village in Egypt." *MERIP Reports* 124 (June 1984): 17–21. https://doi.org/10.2307/3011613.

Khalidi, Walid, Sharif S. Elmusa, and Muhammad Ali Khalidi. *All That Remains: The Palestinian Villages Occupied and Depopulated by Israel in 1948*. Washington, DC: Institution for Palestine Studies, 1992.

Kholoussy, Hanan. *For Better, for Worse: The Marriage Crisis That Made Modern Egypt*. Stanford: Stanford University Press, 2010.

Killian, Caitlin, Jennifer Olmsted, and Alexis Doyle. "Motivated Migrants: (Re)framing Arab Women's Experiences." *Women's Studies International Forum* 35, no. 6 (November–December 2012): 432–46.

Kim, Yuhwan, Seungchul Lee, Inseok Hwang, Hyunho Ro, Youngki Lee, Miri Moon, and Junehwa Song. "High5: Promoting Interpersonal Hand-to-Hand Touch for Vibrant Workplace with Electrodermal Sensor Watches." In *Proceedings of the 2014 ACM International Joint Conference on Pervasive and Ubiquitous Computing*, 15–19. Singapore Management University, 2014.

Kisner, Jordan. "The Lockdown Showed How the Economy Exploits Women. She Already Knew." *New York Times*, February 17, 2021.

Kofman, Eleonore. "The Invisibility of Skilled Female Migrants and Gender Relations in Sudies of Skilled Migration in Europe." *International Journal of Population Geography* 6, no. 1 (January–February 2000): 45–59.

Krafft, Caroline, and Ragui Assaad, eds. *The Jordanian Labor Market: Between Fragility and Resilience*. Oxford: Oxford University Press, 2019.

Layne, Linda L. "The Dialogics of Tribal Self-Representation in Jordan." *American Ethnologist* 16, no. 1 (February 1989): 24–39.

———. "Education and Social Hierarchies in Rural Jordan." Paper presented at the Annual Meeting of the American Anthropological Association, Chicago, November 1984.

———. " 'Tribalism': National Representations of Tribal Life in Jordan." *Urban Anthropology and Studies of Cultural Systems and World Economic Development* 16, no. 2 (1987): 183–203.

Lenner, Katharina. "Poverty and Poverty Reduction Policies in Jordan." In *Atlas of Jordan: History, Territories and Society*, edited by Myriam Ababsa, 335–40. Beirut: Presses de l'Ifpo, 2013.

Lenner, Katharina, and Lewis Turner. "Learning from the Jordan Compact." *Forced Migration Review* 57 (2018): 48–51.

Le Renard, Amelie. *A Society of Young Women: Opportunities of Place, Power, and Reform in Saudi Arabia*. Stanford: Stanford University Press, 2014.

Lloyd, Cynthia B., Sahar El Tawila, Wesley H. Clark, and Barbara S. Mensch. "The Impact of Educational Quality on School Exit in Egypt." *Comparative Education Review* 47, no. 4 (November 2003): 444–67.

MacDougall, Susan. "Felt Unfreedom: Reflecting on Ethics and Gender in Jordan." *Ethnos* 86, no. 3 (2021): 510–29.

Mackinnon, Alison. *Love and Freedom: Professional Women and the Reshaping of Personal Life*. Cambridge: Cambridge University Press, 1997.

Mahmood, Saba. "Feminist Theory, Embodiment, and the Docile Agent: Some Reflections on the Egyptian Islamic Revival." *Cultural Anthropology* 16, no. 2 (May 2001): 202–36.

———. *Politics of Piety: The Islamic Revival and the Feminist Subject*. Princeton: Princeton University Press, 2011.

Marx, Karl. *The Eighteenth Brumaire of Louis Bonaparte*. Moscow: Progress Publishers, 1937.

Massad, Joseph A. *Colonial Effects: The Making of National Identity in Jordan*. New York: Columbia University Press, 2001.

Massadeh, Nassar. "Policies Governing Admission to Jordanian Public Universities." *Higher Education Policy* 25, no. 4 (December 2012): 535–50.

Massey, Doreen B. *Space, Place, and Gender*. Minneapolis: University of Minnesota Press, 1994.

Mathew, Leya, and Ritty Lukose. "Pedagogies of Aspiration: Anthropological Perspectives on Education in Liberalising India." *South Asia: Journal of South Asian Studies* 43, no. 4 (July 2020): 691–704.

Mazawi, André Elias. "Naming the Imaginary: 'Building an Arab Knowledge Society' and the Contested Terrain of Educational Reforms for Development." In *Trajectories of Education in the Arab World: Legacies and Challenges*, edited by Osama Abi-Mershed, 201–25. New York: Routledge, 2010.

McDowall, David. *Palestine and Israel: The Uprising and Beyond*. Berkeley: University of California Press, 1989.

McGill University—Palestinian Refugee ResearchNet. "Palestinian Refugees: An Overview." 2010. http://prrn.mcgill.ca/background/.

McNay, Lois. "Agency, Anticipation and Indeterminacy in Feminist Theory." *Feminist Theory* 4, no. 2 (2003): 139–48.

———. *Gender and Agency: Reconfiguring the Subject in Feminist and Social Theory*. Cambridge: Polity Press, 2000.

Meneley, Anne. *Tournaments of Value: Sociability and Hierarchy in a Yemeni Town*. Toronto: University of Toronto Press, 1996.

Mills, Mary Beth. *Thai Women in the Global Labor Force: Consuming Desires, Contested Selves.* New Brunswick, NJ: Rutgers University Press, 1999.

Milovanovitch, Mihaylo. "Increasing Female Participation in Employment through Vocational Education and Training in Jordan." PRIME Issues Paper. Turin: European Training Foundation, 2016.

Mitchell, Timothy. "America's Egypt." *Middle East Report* 169 (March–April 1991).

Moghadam, Valentine M. "Women's Economic Participation in the Middle East: What Difference Has the Neoliberal Policy Turn Made?" *Journal of Middle East Women's Studies* 1, no. 1 (Winter 2005): 110–46.

Mujahid, G. B. S. "Female Labour Force Participation in the Hashemite Kingdom of Jordan." ILO Working Papers 992175333402676. International Labour Organization, 1982.

Mundy, Karen, and Antoni Verger. "The World Bank and the Global Governance of Education in a Changing World Order." *International Journal of Educational Development* 40 (January 2015): 9–18.

Nasri, Alex. *Migrant Domestic and Garment Workers in Jordan: A Baseline Analysis of Trafficking in Persons and Related Laws and Policies.* Geneva: International Labour Office, 2017.

Nasser El-Dine, Sandra. "Love, Materiality, and Masculinity in Jordan: 'Doing' Romance with Limited Resources." *Men and Masculinities* 21, no. 3 (2018): 423–42.

Nelson, Richard R., and Sidney G. Winter. "Toward an Evolutionary Theory of Economic Capabilities." *American Economic Review* 63, no. 2 (May 1973): 440–49.

Okour, Abdelhakeem M., and Heba H. Hijazi. "Domestic Violence and Family Dysfunction as Risk Factor for Violent Behavior among University Students in North Jordan." *Journal of Family Violence* 24, no. 6 (August 2009): 361–66.

Olmsted, Jennifer C. "Is Paid Work the (Only) Answer? Neoliberalism, Arab Women's Well-Being, and the Social Contract." *Journal of Middle East Women's Studies* 1, no. 2 (Spring 2005): 112–39.

Ong, Aihwa. "Neoliberalism as a Mobile Technology." *Transactions of the Institute of British Geographers* 32, no. 1 (January 2007): 3–8.

———. *Neoliberalism as Exception.* Durham, NC: Duke University Press, 2006.

———. *Spirits of Resistance and Capitalist Discipline: Factory Women in Malaysia.* Albany: SUNY Press, 1987.

O'Reilly, Kathleen. "Women Fieldworkers and the Politics of Participation." *Signs: Journal of Women in Culture and Society* 31, no. 4 (Summer 2006): 1075–98.

Organization for Economic Co-operation and Development (OECD). OECD Data. https://data.oecd.org.

Ortner, Sherry B. *Making Gender: The Politics and Erotics of Culture.* Boston: Beacon Press, 1996.

Pappé, Ilan. "An Indicative Archive: Salvaging Nakba Documents." *Journal of Palestine Studies* 49, no. 3 (2020): 22–40.

Parker, Christopher. "Tunnel-Bypasses and Minarets of Capitalism: Amman as Neoliberal Assemblage." *Political Geography* 28, no. 2 (February 2009): 110–20.

Parker, Kim, and Wendy Wang. "Modern Parenthood." Pew Research Center, Social & Demographic Trends Project, 2013. https://www.pewresearch.org/social-trends/2013/03/14/modern-parenthood-roles-of-moms-and-dads-converge-as-they-balance-work-and-family/.

Parreñas, Rhacel Salazar. "Migrant Filipina Domestic Workers and the International Division of Reproductive Labor." *Gender & Society* 14, no. 4 (August 2000): 560–80.

———. *Unfree: Migrant Domestic Work in Arab States*. Stanford: Stanford University Press, 2021.

Peebles, Dana, Nada Darwazeh, Hala Ghosheh, and Amal Sabbagh. *Factors Affecting Women's Participation in the Private Sector in Jordan*. Amman: Jordan National Centre for Human Development, 2007.

Powers, Colin. "How Neoliberalism Comes to Town: Policy Convergence, (Under) Development, and Jordanian Economics under King Abdullah." *Middle East Law and Governance* 12, no. 2 (2020): 167–97.

———. "Producing Crisis/Surviving Crisis: Power, Capital, and the Social Structure of Accumulation in the Hashemite Kingdom of Jordan." PhD diss., Johns Hopkins University, 2020.

Pursley, Sara. *Familiar Futures: Time, Selfhood, and Sovereignty in Iraq*. Stanford: Stanford University Press, 2019.

Qaisy, Lama. M. "Aggressive Behavior among the University Students." *British Journal of Education, Society & Behavioural Science* 4, no. 9 (January 2014): 1221–33.

"Qualifying Industrial Zones—Jordan." International Trade Administration, US Department of Commerce. https://www.trade.gov/qiz-jordan.

Ramadan, Racha. *Determinants of Income Inequality in Jordan*. Cairo: Economic Research Forum (ERF), 2021.

Ramzoun, Husein F. "Some Social Factor[s] for Violence among University Students in Jordan: Case Study." Amman: Zaytounah University, 2013.

Rashad, Hoda. "The Tempo and Intensity of Marriage in the Arab Region: Key Challenges and Their Implications." *DIFI Family Research and Proceedings* 25, no. 1 (2015): 2.

Reilly, David, David L. Neumann, and Glenda Andrews. "Investigating Gender Differences in Mathematics and Science: Results from the 2011 Trends in Mathematics and Science Survey." *Research in Science Education* 49, no. 1 (2019): 25–50.

Reiter, Yitzhak. "Higher Education and Sociopolitical Transformation in Jordan." *British Journal of Middle Eastern Studies* 29, no. 2 (November 2002): 137–64.

Revenga, Ana, and Sudhir Shetty. "Empowering Women Is Smart Economics." World Economic Forum, March 2012. https://www.weforum.org/agenda/2018/01/this-is-why-women-must-play-a-greater-role-in-the-global-economy/.

Ridge, Natasha. *Education and the Reverse Gender Divide in the Gulf States: Embracing the Global, Ignoring the Local*. New York: Teachers College Press, 2014.

Rignall, Karen E. "Is Rurality a Form of Gender-based Violence in Morocco?" *Journal of Applied Language and Culture Studies* 2 (2019): 15–33.

Rizk, Reham, and Ronia Hawash. "Education Gap and Youth: A Growing Challenge in the MENA Region." LIS Working Paper Series 790. Luxembourg: Luxembourg Income Study (LIS), 2020.

Rogan, Eugene L. *Frontiers of the State in the Late Ottoman Empire: Transjordan, 1850–1921*. Cambridge: Cambridge University Press, 1999.

Rogan, Eugene L., and Tariq Tell, eds. *Village, Steppe and State: The Social Origins of Modern Jordan*. London: British Academic Press, 1994.

Roitman, Janet. *Anti-crisis*. Durham, NC: Duke University Press, 2013.

Rosenfeld, Maya. *Confronting the Occupation: Work, Education, and Political Activism of Palestinian Families in a Refugee Camp*. Stanford: Stanford University Press, 2004.

Rosin, Hanna. "Who Wears the Pants in This Economy?" *New York Times*. August 30, 2012.

Saif, Ibrahim. *The Socio-economic Implications of the Qualified Industrial Zones in Jordan*. Amman: Center for Strategic Studies, University of Jordan, 2006.

Salameh, Dalal. "Al-Intihakat al-ʿAmaliya fi al-Mudaris al-Khasa: al-Ajihiza al-Raqabiya 'Jazur Maʿzula'" [Labor Violations in Private Schools: Regulatory Bodies Are 'Isolated Islands']. 7iber, July 12, 2017.

———. "Mawt Ruba: Kif Khudhilat Muʿlimat al-Mudaris al-Khasa?" [Death of Ruba: How Female Teachers at Private Schools Were Failed?]. 7iber, June 17, 2022.

Salehi-Isfahani, Djavad, Nadia Belhaj Hassine, and Ragui Assaad. "Equality of Opportunity in Educational Achievement in the Middle East and North Africa." Journal of Economic Inequality 12, no. 4 (2014): 489–515.

Salem, Rania. "Trends and Differentials in Jordanian Marriage Behavior: Marriage Timing, Spousal Characteristics, Household Structure and Matrimonial Expenditures." In The Jordanian Labor Market in the New Millennium, edited by Ragui Assaad, 189–217. Oxford: Oxford University Press, 2014.

Samha, Musa Abboudeh Rabdah. "Migration to Amman: Patterns of Movement and Population Structure." PhD diss., Durham University, 1979.

Sargent, Christine. "Kinship, Connective Care, and Disability in Jordan." Medical Anthropology 40, no. 2 (February–March 2021): 116–28.

Sawalha, Aseel. "Gendered Space and Middle East Studies." International Journal of Middle East Studies 46, no. 1 (February 2014): 166–68.

Sayegh, Fayez. "Zionist Colonialism in Palestine (1965)." Settler Colonial Studies 2, no. 1 (2012): 206–25.

Schank, Hana, and Elizabeth Wallace. "When Women Choose Children over a Career." The Atlantic, December 19, 2016.

Schielke, Samuli. Migrant Dreams: Egyptian Workers in the Gulf States. Cairo: American University Press, 2020.

———. "Surfaces of Longing: Cosmopolitan Aspiration and Frustration in Egypt." City & Society 24, no. 1 (April 2012): 29–37.

Schwedler, Jillian. "Amman Cosmopolitan: Spaces and Practices of Aspiration and Consumption." Comparative Studies of South Asia, Africa and the Middle East 30, no. 3 (2010): 547–62.

———. Protesting Jordan: Geographies of Power and Dissent. Stanford: Stanford University Press, 2022.

Seccombe, Ian J. "International Migration for Employment and Domestic Labour Market Development: The Jordanian Experience." PhD diss., Durham University, 1983.

———. "Labour Migration and the Transformation of a Village Economy: A Case Study from North-West Jordan." In The Middle Eastern Village: Changing Economic and Social Relations, edited by Richard Lawless, 115–44. Kent, UK: Croom Helm, 1987.

Segalla, Spencer. "'According to a Logic Befitting the Arab Soul': Cultural Policy and Popular Education in Morocco since 1912." In Trajectories of Education in the Arab World, edited by Osama Abi-Mershed, 100–124. New York: Routledge, 2009.

Shami, Seteney. "Amman Is Not a City: Middle Eastern Cities in Question." In Urban Imaginaries: Locating the Modern City, edited by Alev Çinar and Thomas Bender, 208–35. Minneapolis: University of Minnesota Press, 2007.

Shami, Seteney, and Lucine Taminian. "Women's Participation in the Jordanian Labour Force: A Comparison of Rural and Urban Patterns." In Women in Arab Society: Work Patterns and Gender Relations in Egypt, Jordan and Sudan, edited by Seteney Shami, Lucine Taminian, Soheir Morsy, Zeinab El Bakri, and El Wathig Kameir, 1–86. Paris: Bergir UNESCO, 1990.

Shirazi, Roozbeh. "Being Late, Going with the Flow, Always Doing More: The Cruel Optimism of Higher Education in Jordan." *International Journal of Qualitative Studies in Education* 33, no. 3 (2020): 293–310.

Shryock, Andrew. "The New Jordanian Hospitality: House, Host, and Guest in the Culture of Public Display." *Comparative Studies in Society and History* 46, no. 1 (January 2004): 35–62.

Sidani, Yusuf M., and Zeina T. Al Hakim. "Work–Family Conflicts and Job Attitudes of Single Women: A Developing Country Perspective." *International Journal of Human Resource Management* 23, no. 7 (2012): 1376–93.

Silvey, Rachel. "Power, Difference and Mobility: Feminist Advances in Migration Studies." *Progress in Human Geography* 28, no. 4 (August 2004): 490–506.

Singerman, Diane. "The Economic Imperatives of Marriage: Emerging Practices and Identities among Youth in the Middle East." Middle East Youth Initiative Working Paper 6. Wolfensohn Centre for Development / Dubai School of Government, Dubai. September 2007.

State of Palestine: Ministry of Foreign Affairs and Expatriates (PMFAE). "Refugees." 2022. http://www.mofa.pna.ps/en-us/fundamentalissues/refugees.

Stein, Peter. *Single*. Englewood Cliffs, NJ: Prentice-Hall, 1976.

Sukarieh, Mayssoun. *A Global Idea: Youth, City Networks, and the Struggle for the Arab World.* Ithaca, NY: Cornell University Press, 2023.

———. "The Hope Crusades: Culturalism and Reform in the Arab World." *PoLAR: Political and Legal Anthropology Review* 35, no. 1 (May 2012): 115–34.

———. "On Class, Culture, and the Creation of the Neoliberal Subject: The Case of Jordan." *Anthropological Quarterly* 89, no. 4 (Fall 2016): 1201–25.

Sweidan, Manal. "Migration in Jordan, a Statistical Portrait from a Gender Perspective." Tokyo: United Nations Statistics Division, 2018. https://unstats.un.org/unsd/demographic-social/meetings/2018/tokyo-globalforum-genderstat/.

Tall, Ahmad Yousef. *al-Taʿlīm al-ʿālī fī al-Urdun.* Lajnat Tārīkh al-Urdun, 1998.

Taylor, Elizabeth. "Egyptian Migration and Peasant Wives." *MERIP Reports* 124 (June 1984): 3–10. https://doi.org/10.2307/3011611.

Tobin, Sarah A. *Everyday Piety: Islam and Economy in Jordan*. Ithaca, NY: Cornell University Press, 2016.

Tucker, Judith E. *Women in Nineteenth-Century Egypt*. Cambridge: Cambridge University Press, 1985.

Tweissi, Ahmad, Imad Ababneh, Khattab Abu Lebdih, and Sheren Hamed. "Gender Gap in Student Achievement in Jordan Study Report." National Center for Human Resources Development (NCHRD) Publication Series: Monitoring & Evaluation Partnership (MEP) Project, 2014.

United Nations Department of Economic and Social Affairs (UN DESA)—Statistics Department. *Demographic Yearbook 2020*. New York: UN DESA, 2020.

United Nations High Commission for Refugees (UNHCR). "Jordan: Statistics for Registered Iraqi Refugees." January 2022. https://data.unhcr.org.

United Nations Relief and Works Agency for Palestine Refugees (UNRWA). "Jordan: Where We Work." 2022. https://www.unrwa.org/where-we-work/jordan.

———. "Protection in Jordan," March 2018. https://www.unrwa.org/activity/protection-jordan.

United States Agency for International Development. "USAID Pre-Service Teacher Education in Jordan: National Survey on Public Perceptions of the Teaching Profession." 2021.

United States Bureau of Labor Statistics (BLS). "American Time Use Survey." United States Department of Labor, July 22, 2021.

————. "Married Parents' Use of Time, 2003–06." United States Department of Labor, May 8, 2008.

Vavrus, Frances. *Schooling as Uncertainty: An Ethnographic Memoir in Comparative Education*. London: Bloomsbury, 2021.

Vialle, Manon. "Blamed for Delay." In *Waithood: Gender, Education, and Global Delays in Marriage and Childbearing*, edited by Marcia Inhorn and Nancy J. Smith-Hefner, 317–38. New York: Berghahn Books, 2020.

Vijayakumar, Gowri. "'I'll Be like Water': Gender, Class, and Flexible Aspirations at the Edge of India's Knowledge Economy." *Gender & Society* 27, no. 6 (2013): 777–98.

"Wafaa Taliba Bahrayniyya wa-Asaba 5 Akhriyat fi Hariq li-Sakan Talibat fi al-Urdun" [Death of a Female Bahraini Student and 5 Others in a Fire in a Women's Student Dormitory in Jordan]. *Al-Watan*, January 15, 2015.

Wählin, Lars. "Diffusion and Acceptance of Modern Schooling in Rural Jordan." In *The Middle Eastern Village: Changing Economic and Social Relations*, edited by Richard Lawless, 145–74. Kent, UK: Croom Helm, 1987.

Ward, Patricia. "Capitalising on 'Local Knowledge': The Labour Practices behind Successful Aid Projects: The Case of Jordan." *Current Sociology* 69, no. 5 (September 2021): 705–22.

Weiner, Lynne. *From Working Girl to Working Mother: The Female Labor Force in the United States, 1820–1980*. Chapel Hill: University of North Carolina Press, 1985.

Wilcke, Christoph. *Stateless Again: Palestinian-Origin Jordanians Deprived of Their Nationality*. New York: Human Rights Watch, 2010. https://www.hrw.org/report/2010/02/01/stateless-again/palestinian-origin-jordanians-deprived-their-nationality.

Williams, Raymond. *Marxism and Literature*. Oxford: Oxford University Press, 1977.

Wilson, Mary Christina. *King Abdullah, Britain and the Making of Jordan*. Cambridge: Cambridge University Press, 1990.

Winders, Jamie, and Barbara Ellen Smith. "Social Reproduction and Capitalist Production: A Genealogy of Dominant Imaginaries." *Progress in Human Geography* 43, no. 5 (2019): 871–89.

Winkler, Hernan, and Alvaro Gonzalez. *Jobs Diagnostic Jordan*. Washington, DC: World Bank Group, 2019.

World Bank. *Gender and Development in the Middle East and North Africa: Women in the Public Sphere*. MENA Development Report. Washington, DC: World Bank, 2004.

————. *Hashemite Kingdom of Jordan Education Sector Public Expenditure Review*. Washington, DC: World Bank Publications, 2016.

————. *Hashemite Kingdom of Jordan—Understanding How Gender Norms in MNA Impact Female Employment Outcomes (English)*. Washington, DC: World Bank, 2018.

————. *Opening Doors: Gender Equality and Development in the Middle East and North Africa*. MENA Development Report. Washington, DC: World Bank, 2013.

————. *Personal Remittances, Received (% of GDP)—Jordan*. Washington, DC: World Bank Data, 2022. https://data.worldbank.org.

————. *Population: Jordan, 2004–2015*. Washington, DC: World Bank Data, 2022. https://data.worldbank.org.

World Economic Forum. *The Global Gender Gap Report 2014*. World Economic Forum, 2014.

Zayida, Susan. "Al-Sakan al-Jama'ili-l-Talibat: Tadiyyiq 'ala al-Nazilat bi-'Mubarika' min al-Ahl" [University Dormitories for Female Students: Restriction of Their Residents with "Blessings" from the Family]. *'Amun*, August 24, 2008.

Zureiqat, Hazem. "Nahu Injah Mashru' al-Bus al-Sari'" [Toward the Success of the Rapid Bus Project]. *7iber*, June 28, 2016.

Index

Abdul-Hamid, Husein, 163n27
Abdullah, Emir, 23–24
Abdullah, King, 27, 161n7
Abu-Lughod, Lila, 9–10, 146
Africa, 35, 37
agency, 4, 10, 14, 148; aspirations, link with, 52–53; creative nature of, 9; family relations and, 114. *See also* creative agency; female agency
Ahmed, Sara, 49–50, 52
Ajlun (Jordan), 36
al bint al gawiyyeh (tough girl), 70
Algeria, 38
al ghurba, 102
Al-Khoshman, Afaf, 13
Al-Oballi, Ayah, 106
Amiry, Suad, 168n88
Amman (Jordan), 1–7, 9, 11–16, 22, 26, 29–30, 32, 35–36, 41, 43–45, 47–49, 52–53, 56, 63–66, 75–76, 90–93, 96–97, 99, 105–7, 113–14, 120–21, 124, 128, 135, 139, 143, 147, 150, 163n29, 176n45; advantages of, 81; "anything goes" attitude in, 80; class in, 87, 132; as cosmopolitan, 71, 77; cultural diversity, 72, 77–78, 88; culture shock in, 79; dormitories, 73–74, 83, 95, 101–4, 109, 126–27, 140–41, 174n32; economic inequality in, 71; elite private schools, 164n42; English-language skills in, 82; as expensive city, 69–70, 86, 127, 173n11; female anonymity in, 136; financial difficulties in, 84–87; as "foreign country," 41; freedoms in, 18; as function of place and time, 169n1; further education in, 57; growth of, 28, 71, 102; leisure space, 69–70; marriage prospects, effect on, 127, 129–32, 141; men and women in, norms surrounding interaction between, 80, 95; migration of

young women, opportunities for, 19, 57–58; mobility, opportunities for, 17; movement of women in, as struggle, 67; move to, as escape, 46; multiple mobilities in, 89; negotiating of space in, 89; openness of, 79; opportunities in, 133; potential marriage partners and, 136–37; private schools, 172n45; private sector jobs, 61–62, 125–26; professional mobility in, seeking of, 68; professional opportunities in, seeking of, 148; professional women, 13, 73; provincial girls in, stereotype of, 83, 88; public sector jobs, 59, 117; public space, reshaping of, 71; public transportation system, 71–72, 89, 174n27; ride share companies, 174n26; single women in, 14, 18, 69, 73, 94, 111, 131, 137, 141, 144–45, 149; structural barriers and biases, 81–82; trainees in, 84; upward mobility in, possibility of, 55, 58; urban development projects, 71, 174n22; urbanization in, 102; women on their own in, moral stature of, 60; women's movements in, as dangerous, 18–19; workplace culture, 78–80, 87, 175n35. *See also* female migrants
Anderson, Betty, "educational pilgrimages," 37
Arab Gulf countries, 2, 28, 37, 56, 121, 169n1; single women in, 39–40, 142; teachers in, 38–39
Arab nationalism, 24
Arab Spring, 12
Armenian genocide, 36
Asia, 35–36, 39
Ayoub, Helen, 15

banat al sakanat (dormitory girls), stereotypes about, 73
Barakat, Nora, 160–61n6
bayt (home), 142–43. *See also* home